Heidrun S̶   ̶aiman,

Talent D   nce

Talentförderung Expertiseentwicklung Leistungsexzellenz

herausgegeben von

Prof. Dr. Kurt A. Heller
(Universität München)
und
Prof. Dr. Albert Ziegler
(Universität Erlangen-Nürnberg)

Band 11

LIT

Talent Development
and Excellence

edited by

Heidrun Stoeger
Abdullah Aljughaiman
Bettina Harder

LIT

Bibliographic information published by the Deutsche Nationalbibliothek
The Deutsche Nationalbibliothek lists this publication in the Deutsche
Nationalbibliografie; detailed bibliographic data are available in the Internet at
http://dnb.d-nb.de.

ISBN 978-3-643-90230-6

A catalogue record for this book is available from the British Library

©LIT VERLAG GmbH & Co. KG Wien,
Zweigniederlassung Zürich 2012
Klosbachstr. 107
CH-8032 Zürich
Tel. +41 (0) 44-251 75 05
Fax +41 (0) 44-251 75 06
e-Mail: zuerich@lit-verlag.ch
http://www.lit-verlag.ch

LIT VERLAG Dr. W. Hopf
Berlin 2012
Fresnostr. 2
D-48159 Münster
Tel. +49 (0) 2 51-620 320
Fax +49 (0) 2 51-23 19 72
e-Mail: lit@lit-verlag.de
http://www.lit-verlag.de

Distribution:
In Germany: LIT Verlag Fresnostr. 2, D-48159 Münster
Tel. +49 (0) 2 51-620 32 22, Fax +49 (0) 2 51-922 60 99, e-mail: vertrieb@lit-verlag.de

In Austria: Medienlogistik Pichler-ÖBZ, e-mail: mlo@medien-logistik.at

In Switzerland: B + M Buch- und Medienvertrieb, e-mail: order@buch-medien.ch

In the UK: Global Book Marketing, e-mail: mo@centralbooks.com

Talent development and excellence

Heidrun Stoeger, Abdullah Aljughaiman, & Bettina Harder

The field of educational sciences has three primary objectives when it comes to talent development and excellence. First, it seeks to develop and articulate adequate theories of talent development and excellence. Second, researchers, practitioners, and institutions draw on this theoretical basis to develop ways of promoting individuals who are working their way towards excellent achievements. Third, the field studies and evaluates the effectiveness of these measures and uses these results to further improve both the theory and practices of talent development and excellence. These three objectives accordingly comprise the overarching perspectives of this book. *Talent Development and Excellence* describes new theoretical approaches, discusses their implementation into practice, and reports on evaluation studies. The volume's contributions draw a picture of current advances in research and practical work and their interplay. This bird's-eye view will, it is our hope, help readers to develop their understanding of the topic and, by highlighting new insights and ideas, to draw beneficial conclusions on how to fruitfully integrate scientific knowledge into practical implementation.

The book consists of four thematically delineated parts. With its focus on the systemic theory of giftedness, Part One explores a relatively new theoretical approach to giftedness research and gifted education. In an introductory chapter, *Bettina Harder* reviews the theoretical advances made with models of giftedness developed over the last decades and describes in more detail the emergence of a systemic theory of giftedness. Her chapter then takes a closer look at one specific systemic theory, Ziegler's actiotope model of giftedness (2005). The actiotope model lays the groundwork for the following chapters in Part One. In the second chapter, *Bettina Harder* describes an empirical validation of the actiotope model's construct validity and predictive validity for students in post-secondary education. *Xiaoju Duan* and *Anjulie Arora* then present an actiotope-based investigation of gender and cross-cultural differences in the domains of sciences, technology, engineering, and mathematics. *Magdalena Kist* relates the results of an investigation of secondary-level EFL students. Kist bases her study on the actiotope model and places a special focus on the students' surrounding environment and the influence of this environment on their language-learning progress. In her contribution, *Katharina Schurr* focuses on the practical implementation of the actiotope model of giftedness in the field of counseling. She describes a systemic counseling strategy based on the actiotope model and exemplifies the strategy with a case study. *Shane Phillipson* draws together the various actiontope-based lines of inquiry pursued throughout Part One with his concluding discussion of the aforementioned chapters and the actiotope model as a systemic model of giftedness from a meta-theoretical perspective.

Part Two focuses on developmental aspects of giftedness and early fostering. In her exploration of how gifted elementary school students understand the social context of learning, *Marion Porath* identifies a clear age-related progression in the way children explain social behavior: the youngest respondents tend to incorporate action-based rationales; older respondents begin to consider intentions; and the most mature responses include references to personality variables. *Wilma Vialle* also examines processes of social understanding in gifted children. Her case studies from investigations with preschoolers illustrate the complex interplay of social understanding, emotional maturity, and intellectual precocity in young children and the consequences for educational policies. *Philipp Martzog, Wei Chen, Heidrun Stoeger, Jian-Nong Shi, and Albert Ziegler* then present an empirical study which specifies the relationship between fine motor skills and cognitive abilities. Their cross-cultural study demonstrates the relevance of fine motor skills for the cognitive development of preschoolers. *Marianne Nolte* explores the early development of mathematical giftedness by investigating mathematically gifted preschoolers and their parents. *Dagmar Bergs-Winkels, Doren Prinz,* and *Peter Winkels* report on measures to individually support preschoolers in developing self-regulated learning skills. They consider conditions of the preschoolers' environment as well as educators' qualifications and attitudes.

The two chapters which make up Part Three shed light upon students' characteristics. *Christine Sontag, Bettina Harder, Heidrun Stoeger,* and *Albert Ziegler* investigate the relationship between students' intelligence and their preference for self-regulated learning. Although practitioners and researchers often suppose that gifted (and here especially highly intelligent) students show more self-regulated learning, evidence did not support this assumption. Quite to the contrary, receiving training in self-regulation skills seems to be just as important for highly intelligent learners as it is for learners of average intelligence. *Mei Tan, Catalina Mourues, Abdullah Aljughaiman, Alaan Ayoub, Samuel Mandelman, Dimitris Zbainos,* and *Elena Grigorenko* report on an empirical study of methods of assessing aspects of practical intelligence. They introduce the Toy Shadows subtest of the Aurora Battery and describe a validation study.

The book's last section, Part Four, looks at teachers' characteristics and attitudes as they relate to talent development and excellence. *Martina Endephols-Ulpe* reports on attitudes of German secondary school teachers towards students' early placement at university. In general, teachers look upon the measure favorably but at the same time they fear organizational and social problems for the students as well as additional work for themselves. *Afonso Galvao* and *Catia Perfeito* provide information on the characteristics of expert primary school teachers as nominated by their peer-teachers. The features which made the nominated teachers stand out from other teachers were their extraordinary technical skills along with special attitudes and high involvement in their work.

The chapters of this book comprise many interesting topics, describe promising research methods, and suggest numerous practical implications. We hope each reader will find inspiring insights and useful suggestions within the broad array of contents brought together within this volume.

References

Ziegler, A. (2005). The Actiotope model of giftedness. In R. J. Sternberg & J. E. Davidson (Eds.), *Conceptions of giftedness* (2nd ed., pp. 411-436). New York, NY: Cambridge University Press.

III. Students' Characteristics and Gifted Education at School

IV. Teachers' Characteristics and Attitudes

I. A Systemic Theory of Giftedness

Bettina Harder

Towards a Systemic Theory of Giftedness

Abstract

This chapter gives an introduction to current theories in giftedness and excellence research. After an overview on the development of models of giftedness in the course of the last century I focus on the recent paradigm shift towards systemic theories of giftedness. I outline characteristics of the systemic approach and the advances in systemic theories over the last years to conclude with a description of the probably most comprehensive systemic model to date – the actiotope model of giftedness. This introduction serves as the basis for the following chapters on empirical investigations and implementations of the actiotope model of giftedness.

Today, the research on giftedness and excellent performance includes many different conceptual models and their accompanying operationalizations in both education and counseling. In the research literature it is common to encounter many familiar names such as Spearman, Thurstone, Cattell, Jaeger, Renzulli, Mönks, Tannenbaum, Sternberg, Ericsson, Heller, Gagné, or Perleth, to name only a few. The theories of the aforementioned authors derive from different traditions or perspectives on the subject of giftedness and excellence which has undergone fundamental changes in the last about 100 years. Recently, however, Ziegler (2005) has argued that many of these models are over reliant on traits such as intelligence and creativity. In contrast, a systemic approach focuses on the interactions between the individual and their environment and is thus able to account for the complex processes necessary for the emergence of excellence (cf. Ziegler & Phillipson, in press).

In this chapter I briefly describe the development of the major theories of giftedness by classifying them into five approaches and outline their shortcomings. I then focus on the development of systemic theories of giftedness, concluding with the probably most comprehensive and detailed theory of its type – the actiotope model of giftedness (Ziegler, 2005). This chapter provides the theoretical basis for the following four chapters describing several empirical investigations of and the implementation of the actiotope model of giftedness.

1   A Conceptual Overview of Theories of Giftedness

1.1   General Elements of Theories of Giftedness

Theories of giftedness try to explain the genesis of extraordinary performances in various domains. Stripped to the core they consist of three main statements: theories of giftedness describe some sort of *potential* which undergoes a process of *transformation* to result in excellent *performance*. Differences between specific theories can be traced back to differences in the understanding of these three core concepts and the weight they are assigned for the emergence of excellence (ranging from non-consideration to centrality). To point out possible differences between theories the three concepts should be explained in more detail.

- *Potential*

Theories of giftedness show the largest differences in their conceptualization of potential. Giftedness is a term widely used in this context with very different connotations. Until today there exists neither a uniform definition nor is the ontological status of gifts commonly agreed on (Howe, Davidson, & Sloboda, 1998) due to the lacking connection to a psychological entity. Giftedness is a hypothetical construct or as Borland put it, "an invention, not a discovery" (Borland, 2005, p. 6). The chances for integrating definitions of giftedness into one commonly accepted version is thwarted by the synonymous use of different terms (e.g., gifted, talented, precocious, highly intelligent) as well as the use of the same term for different traits and the mixing with lay-terms. Main differences between conceptions of potential lie in the assumed relevant components making up the necessary potential for excellence (e.g., cognitive and non-cognitive personal characteristics, certain environmental conditions), in the interaction of these components, and in their assumed origin (genetic vs. environmental determination).

▪ *Transformation*

The process of transformation is a relatively new element in theories of giftedness. Static approaches can be distinguished from dynamic theories whereby only the latter explicitly refer to a transformation. This developmental process is theorized to be lengthy and complex as it is influenced by multiple internal and external factors and is most often described as learning and practicing. Static models on the contrary suggest a stable potential which is expressed by means of performance.

▪ *Performance*

The differentiation between potential and performance is not self-evident. Early models of giftedness treated intelligence (synonym for giftedness) and performance as one and the same, thereby jeopardizing opportunities to clearly describe the emergence of excellent performance. Modern models have begun to differentiate between the two concepts: Gagné, for example, redefined the terms "gifts" and "talents" in the sense of potential and performance (Gagné, 2005). Performances can be differentiated further by distinguishing reproducible superior performances and single creative performances (cf. Ericsson, Roring, & Nandagopal, 2007). While the former can be investigated under controlled experimental conditions the latter pose some serious methodological problems to researchers. The Measurement of creative performances is hard to objectify and therefore a rather rare topic in current publications.

1.2 Developments in Theories of Giftedness and Achievement Excellence

A closer look at existing theories of giftedness and achievement excellence with these three concepts in mind makes five different approaches become evident (see also Table 1). Partly following the four-group classification suggested by Mönks and Katzko (2005) the approaches can be characterized as psychometric, multi-component, performance based, moderator and systemic models.

The beginning of giftedness research was marked by the upcoming of *psychometric models*. They conceptualize giftedness as a stable personality trait (potential) which is deemed independent of other variables like environmental or historical context. The main issue of the approach was the description and measurement of this trait, using instruments such as intelligence tests. In academic domains giftedness is synonymous with intelligence (e.g., Spearman, 1904; Cattell, 1963), sometimes also with creativity which was held as particularly relevant for domains such as music, art, or handcrafts (e.g., Winner & Martino, 1993). The possibilities of dichotomous classifications in gifted vs. non-gifted persons soon proved to be insufficient to describe the observed spectrum of academic gifts. This lead to the creation of subcategories of gifted persons like "schoolhouse activists" and "problem solving innovators" (cf. Callahan & Miller, 2005; Gallagher & Courtright, 1986; Renzulli, 1986; Winner, 1997) but giftedness is still viewed as domain-independent. Psychometric models do not differentiate between potential and performance, nor is a transformation specified. Potential or high intelligence automatically becomes evident in extraordinary performance. The underlying process is fundamentally autocatalytic, meaning that the transformation from potential to exceptional achievement depends on the natural development of self.

Due to the very restricted perspective of psychometric theories narrowed on intelligence *multi-component models* were brought up. They take an analytic approach to cognitive processes of information processing identifying different relevant components (e.g., Sternberg, 1985, 2005) and/or consider other (non-cognitive) components of potential aside of intelligence. Examples for additional components are creativity or task commitment (e.g. Renzulli, 1986, 2005; Mönks & Katzko, 2005). To define giftedness all of the hypothesized components must emerge mutually as they are all assumed to be necessary contributions to giftedness of equal importance (potential). Their interaction is not made explicit and also the transformation into performance is not specified. Subsequently potential and performance still cannot be clearly distinguished.

These shortcomings are remedied by performance based models. *Performance based models* are dynamic in nature and explicitly describe the transformation process. Thus they hold the key to possible interventions to foster the transformation of potential in general or to take up remedial measures if problems occur, for example underachievement. Significantly, Stern (1916) had realized the necessity of a transformative process, concluding that giftedness is only a potential for extraordinary achievement. However, psychometric and multi-component models dominated the field for decades before expertise research attracted attention and influenced models of giftedness. Performance based models (e.g., Ericsson, Krampe, & Tesch-Römer, 1993) are highly dynamic and focus on the learning process thereby urging personality traits into the background. Potential is rather defined by the momentary competence level in a specific domain which has been acquired through previous learning and builds the basis for future knowledge acquisition.

This process oriented perspective made way for the investigation of moderating influences on the transformation. The result of this extension of perspective was a further development of multi-component models into *moderator models*. While different components were treated as equally important in the former models, moderator models distinguish them by their role in the transformation process. Moderator models assume that domain specific gifts (basic skills) are transformed via learning into more and more differentiated performances in that

Table 1: Characteristics of the Five Different Approaches to Giftedness and Excellent Achievements

Approach	Assumptions concerning		
	Potential	Transformation	Performance
Psychometric models (e.g., Spearman, 1904; Cattell, 1963;)	Single, domain independent trait (e.g., intelligence, creativity)	Not specified, autocatalytic	General, domain independent
Multi-component models (e.g., Renzulli, 2005; Mönks & Katzko, 2005)	Multiple components of equal importance (e.g., cognitive processing components, traits) No interaction between components	Not specified, autocatalytic	General, domain independent Sometimes domain specific
Performance-based models (e.g., Ericsson, Krampe, & Tesch-Römer, 1993)	Current competence level and possibilities for learning	Center of the theory Lengthy and effortful process of learning	Domain specific, depending on acquired competences
Moderator models (e.g., Heller, Perleth, & Lim, 2005; Gagné, 2005, 2009)	Multiple components in hierarchy Focus on gifts as personal traits (domain specific basic skills) Additional factors as moderators Interaction of components	Transformation of gifts into performance via learning processes Moderation by personal and environmental influences	Domain specific, depending on initial gifts and acquired competences (supported by moderators)
Systemic models (e.g., Ziegler, 2005)	System's property, potential lies in the interaction of all system parts	Complex evolution of the complete system to enhance performance capacities	Domain specific, depending on system's orientation

domain. This process is moderated by various personal and environmental factors which imply their secondary role in the development of excellence (e.g., Heller, Perleth, & Lim, 2005; Gagné, 2005, 2009). In a nutshell, the differences lie in the implementation of the transformation process including the accompanying differentiation between potential and performance and in the application of a hierarchy to the causal factors. The latter interact with each other to different extents depending on the specific theory and together build the potential for excellent achievements.

The fifth and last approach represents a further extension of the interaction idea towards a *systemic perspective* which no longer perceives potential as a person's characteristic or sum of characteristics but as a property of the system the person is part of (e.g., Ziegler, 2005). Thereafter performance cannot be explained analytically by means of single components but must be viewed from a holistic perspective. Performance is the result of complex interactions between the person and their environment which leads to an equally complex transformation process. The complete system with its current performance capacities (domain-specific system's potential) must evolve towards a more effective or more competent structure which enables the person to demonstrate performances on a higher level in this very domain.

2   Systemic Theories of Giftedness

2.1   System Properties

In the course of developing moderator models two important insights were made. First, context variables are important and second, they heavily interact with the complete development of a person's competences. For example Cronbach and Snow (1977) considered interactivity in their theory of aptitude-treatment-interaction but did not focus enough on context conditions which led to poor replication results (Rheinberg, Bromme, Minsel, Winteler, & Weidenmann, 2001; Trautwein, 2010). Moderator models took into account all context conditions as they are open to all personal and environmental moderator variables but somehow failed to mo-del interactions adequately as can be seen when tracing the model developments over the years – the most recent model by Perleth (1997, 2001) assumes full interaction between gifts, personal and environmental factors whereas Gagné (1985, 1995, 2000, 2005, 2009) and Heller (1992, 2001; Heller, Perleth, & Lim, 2005) rely on single unidirectional influences. Plucker and Barab (2005) criticize current models for viewing person and environment as separated factors instead of focusing on their interaction as the crucial element of theories. This stands in line with systemic thinking and adds up to the current change of perspective from an analytic-mechanic view to a holistic systemic one (Ziegler & Stöger, 2009) with the latter profiting from the analytic investigations of single factors that now can be integrated into a systemic context. According to Ziegler and Stöger systems have the following six key properties:

- Equifinality. In a system many different starting configurations can lead to the same result like achievement excellence (cf. Shavinina, 2004). There exist various possibilities for compensation which places single characteristics as intelligence or motivation in the background. More important is the comprehensive system which determines developmental options.

- Context dependency. A person's behavior always depends on the specific situation. This is why the same task may be solved very differently in another environment. Michel (1971) found that IQ-test scores assessed by different test administrators varied from 15 to 40 IQ-points. From the point of context dependency it seems quite absurd to identify a general measure of any person's characteristic as it will vary across situations.

- Interdependence. Within a system no event remains isolated but affects other system elements which on their part cause secondary reactions and also feedback to the original event. Single events in a system do not exist.

- Interconnectedness. This principle follows interdependence: The reactions in the system to one event do not happen accidentally but in a typical, ordered way. The system is a network that acts on its inherent rules which explains for example accumulations of excellence in a system like the three Pólgar sisters reaching chess expertise (Pólgar & Farkas, 1989).

- Excellence is based on different system levels. For the emergence of expertise many system parts must fulfill minimum demands, some parts must even reach extraordinary quality. If only one component of the system works on an excellent level (e.g., high intelligence) the output quality is by no means guaranteed, on the contrary, it is likey to be insufficient.

- Phase transition. Analytic-mechanic metaphors suggest that changes follow linear processes. However systems react abruptly. One event can completely change thinking, competences, feelings and so on. Sudden phase transitions are very common e.g., if one thinks about the choice between two similarly attractive alternatives. New information on one alternative will abruptly change the attractiveness and maybe make the decision, it is not a linear increase that slightly exceeds the attractiveness of the other alternative and thereby leads to the decision.

For the development of a system that includes achievement excellence as one outcome these properties imply that interventions must aim at the co-evolution of all system parts to ensure a smooth development. For a child to develop high level competences in mathematics for instance, parents can provide their child with encouraging and informative feedback, help him or her to find challenging and interesting learning materials and build up a supportive network of qualified teachers, other interested students, maybe professionals in the field of mathematics that engage as mentors. If the whole system is geared towards increasing competences in a domain, different contexts encourage the development and the reactions of parents, teachers, and peers can interact positively.

As it is contradictory to many ideas of an optimally running system I want to point out that the envisioned state of a system for talent development cannot be homeostatic (Ziegler & Stöger, 2009). To support the developmental process and to preserve any current state a system must constantly be supplied with energy for controlling chaotic influences (i.e., allostasis). Aside of the impossibility of homeostasis, it is not even a desirable state as expertise development would stagnate. A system needs some basic stability but at the same time must be open for developmental changes.

2.2   Advances in Systemic Theories of Giftedness

Currently only few systemic models for the description of performance development exist. This is probably due to the difficulties of modeling complex system interactivity as mentioned before. Some authors simply take a basic systemic perspective when interpreting empirical results (Avery & VanTassel-Baska, 2001; Jeltova & Grigorenko, 2005; Mooij, 2008; Moore, Ford, & Milner, 2005; Moran & Gardner, 2006; Subotnik & Rickoff, 2010). Others focus on single systemic aspects like the gene-environment-interaction in the context of talent development (Simonton, 2005). Plucker and Barab (2005) criticize the lack of systemic understanding in current models of giftedness. They bring up that theories should consider person and environment in their interaction instead of independent of each other to create gifted transactions, i.e. effective learning possibilities. However concrete specifications in theoretical or practical means are left to others.

A concrete systemic theory is formulated by Csikszentmihalyi and Wolfe (2002). He explains creative performances – a part of excellent achievements – according to evolutionary principles. In nature something new is "created" by means of a genetic variation in the existing gene pool. This variation is tested by the environmental conditions and if it is beneficial or functional for the species it will be included in the gene pool and be supplied to future generations by selection processes. For creative achievements Csikszentmihalyi and Wolfe provide an analogous explanation: the existing information in a domain is varied by an individual who generates a new product. The domain specific environment evaluates this product. If it is approved of the new information is added to the domains information pool and available for future use. However, this very functional description only applies to extraordinary creative products which normally are not found within children's and adolescents' performances but are achieved later in life after reaching an expert status in the domain (Ericsson et al., 2007).

Dai and Renzulli (2008) propose a systemic theory of giftedness which describes general principles for the acquisition of expertise based on a literature review. They use the metaphor of snowflakes for a person in their systemic context. In snowflakes, the water molecules spontaneously form complex structures on their way to the ground. In the same way persons live in open, self-organizing, adaptive systems. A person's competence development is conceptualized as a continuous adaptation to new environmental conditions driven by the person's intentions, genetic disposition and environmentally induced learning experiences. The person is cognitively flexible and creative which all leads to spontaneous adaption processes and calls for a balance between stability – to ensure the system's functioning – and instability – to enable further adaptations. Within these general processes Dai and Renzulli identified three facets of transformation processes which alternate in cycles. *Selective affinity* describes an early manifestation of talents due to biological dispositions which increase the affinity for certain stimuli and thereby a domain. With *maximal grip* they entitle phases of deliberate practice geared to reaching higher levels of competence. During such phases aspirations, feedback, social comparisons, self evaluations and decisions lead to domain specific adaptations of the system. The third phase, *at the edge of chaos*, describes phases in which the incorporation of domain specific knowledge results in a critical strained state demanding a leap into the unknown. According to the person's willingness to take risks they can choose a more conventional way to proceed e.g., a further integration of existing information, or a more innovative way of redefining matters, taking up new directions of thinking and thereby risking conflicts and chaos.

Aside of this sheer descriptive approach which cannot explain the process necessary for the development of expertise in detail one functional systemic model was developed by Ziegler (2005). His model differs from the aforementioned theories in at least two points. First the actiotope model is a general theory of action which can be applied to all levels of competence and all domains. Second it explains competence development with functionally defined constructs instead of descriptive reductionist constructs. This surmounts the problems of older models of giftedness and also Dai and Renzulli's (2008) theory to name all the psychological instances involved in the process. The actiotope model of giftedness and recent extensions of the core theory will be outlined in the following.

3   The Actiotope Model of Giftedness

The actiotope model focuses on actions as they represent the core of expertise – the ability to perform on an excellent level in a domain. Subsequently, the goal of the transformation process is to build up such action competences. The developmental process is assumed to follow a successive sequential principle: each learning step is based on the previous one using the acquired abilities and knowledge to proceed to the next higher level (Ziegler & Stöger, 2009). Within this context giftedness is viewed as the current probability for the person with their abilities and their environment to reach achievement excellence. The person is called *talented* if excellence is possible, *highly gifted* if it is probable, and *excellent* if it is already achieved.

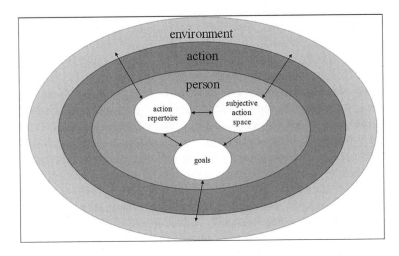

Figure 1: The actiotope model of giftedness (adapted from Ziegler, 2005)

A person's action competence in a certain domain is his or her domain-specific actiotope, i.e. his or her action space (cf. biotope, sociotope). This action space is determined by the interplay of the domain-specific environment and the person and consists of four functionally defined components: three interacting components within the person of which each also interacts with the fourth component, the environment (cf. Figure 1). The personal components consist of (1) a regulating executive function, (2) a store of action options comparable to a database, and (3) goals which the actiotope should develop towards (e.g., achievement aspirations). The action repertoire represents all actions that currently can be carried out from an objective point of view e.g., actions possible through domain-specific skills or self-regulatory competences. Goals on the other hand determine the desired system state and thereby are relevant for the choice between different action options, for energizing actions and for directing regulative processes before and during actions. Finally, the executive component or „subjective action space": Within the subjective action space person and environment are represented which results in all the actions that the person deems suitable in a given environment to reach a goal. This decision is influenced by subjective evaluations e.g., of one's own capabilities, as well as by expectations of the situation or others' reactions to the behavior in question. Therefore the subjective action space normally is smaller than the action repertoire. The subjective action space selects actions from the action repertoire and controls it during its execution.

The interdependence and interaction of the three components is best illustrated with an example. Imagine a twelve year-old girl who is interested in physics. She pursues the goal to learn more about mechanics than the knowledge provided in school lessons. She picks that *goal* in dependence of her current action repertoire: She already gained a deeper understanding of related matters and the mathematical skills to now proceed with mechanics as a next step towards extended knowledge of physics. Her decision also depends on her finding it appropriate to enter the domain of physics because her parents always encourage her to follow her interests and trust her abilities to master her goals if she puts in enough effort. Of course, her *action repertoire* in physics depends on her former goals and self-evaluations (subjective action space) which led her to learn and build up competences she now has at her disposal. Furthermore, her *subjective action space* is shaped according to the competences she sees in herself and her goals constitute an important part of her self-representation which is considered when selecting an action. All of these three personal components interact with the environment. To continue the example: The actions and reactions of her environment strongly influence that girl's subjective action space (role models of women in physics, encouragement, support in dealing with failure) as well as the setting of goals. To build up the action repertoire she benefits from the feedback of teachers and others. But on the reverse she also seeks and forms her learning environment by acting according to her goals, subjective action space and action repertoire displaying her interests.

The environment consists of agents interacting with her, of resources implemented in situations which are more or less helpful to develop skills. Ziegler (2010) classified the environment into different sociotopes according to two distinctive aspects: First the objective action space, that is the possibility for actions in the talent domain (positive vs. negative), and second the normative action space which can be either reinforcing, neutral or hindering for actions in the talent domain. From the combinations of objective and normative action space result 2 x 3 sociotopes which are described in Table 2.

Table 2: Description of Sociotopes (cf. Ziegler, 2010)

Sociotope	Objective action space	Normative action space	Description
Learning sociotope	+	+	Learning is possible and supported e.g., school lessons, museum, enrichment classes
Infrastructural sociotope	+	0	Learning is not actively intended but it is possible to engage in domain specific activities e.g., libraries, a sports complex
Avoiding sociotope	+	−	Learning would be possible but has negative consequences e.g., girls in STEM (science, technology, engineering, mathematics) subjects where good performance is estimated unfeminine, a concert of a professional musician (who already should have mastered the piece he/she presents)
Thematic sociotope	−	+	Learning actions cannot be performed but domain-specific activities are reinforced e.g., talking about the talent domain during dinner (football, piano music)
Competing sociotope	−	0	Learning is impossible and would have neutral consequences e.g., leisure time activities competing with the preparation for a biology test
Antagonistic sociotope	−	−	Learning is impossible and punished e.g., practicing the trumpet during mathematics lessons

Learning sociotopes are indispensable for reaching excellent levels of performance. Furthermore infrastructural and thematic sociotopes are supposed to have positive effects on expertise development whereas avoiding, competing and antagonistic sociotopes should hinder the development. Only professional sociotopes, a special case of avoiding sociotopes, can influence the learning process in a positive way by posing an incentive to pursue a systematic skill development in that domain. The analysis of sociotopes allow a raw estimation of fostering conditions in the environment in the sense of the existence and amount of time spent in favorable sociotopes. However only little can be said about the quality of fostering in the sociotopes. Learning sociotopes can differ greatly in effectiveness or instruction quality to name only one example. To determine their quality more closely Ziegler and Stöger (2011) use the concept of available resources or capitals to support the development. This will be outlined in more detail in the context of the developmental process below.

The developmental process of the whole system is revealed from a dynamic perspective. Ziegler (2005, 2009) specifies five mechanisms which are assumed to cause the development. The learner (1) must recognize learning possibilities and use them, he/she must (2) be able to distinguish efficient from inefficient actions in certain situations and (3) be able to generate new action variations for a further extension of the action repertoire. Besides the system must (4) anticipate and prepare itself for future challenges and (5) make available effective feedback and feedforward loops.

These mechanisms or the regulation of the system in the course of expertise acquisition requires resources. Ziegler and Stöger (2011) differentiate endogenous and exogenous resources. While the first can only be regulated by the person him/herself and the environment has indirect influences at maximum, the latter are provided by the environment. Instead of resources Ziegler and Stöger use the term capital as it can also take on negative values (e.g., debts), sorts of capitals can be transformed into one another (with limitations) and the term capital implies that it must be created and can grow. Educational capital (exogenous resources that can be used for education and the support of learning) comprises economic, cultural, social, infrastructural and didactic capital. Endogenous capital of the person is entitled learning capital and consists of organismic, actional, telic, episodic and attentive learning capital. The quantity of available educational and learning capital determines the developmental process decisively.

Besides the perspective on actiotope components and the dynamic view the theory also considers the state of the complete system. For the progression of the system towards expertise some stability is necessary, i.e. the system must be able to sustain the basic functioning while changes in different areas jeopardize the traditional interplay of system parts. On the other hand the system must be flexible or modifiable to allow changes and thereby the further development of competences. This also means that a system has to be oriented towards change and development in an active way – contrary to traditional beliefs of an auto-catalytic development of gifts into competences and high achievement. To change a system also implies the necessity of co-evolution of all system parts. To ensure stability all sub-systems must evolve in the same direction e.g., the actiotope of the talent domain and the actiotopes for social competences or behaviors to stay healthy. Expertise in a talent domain (academic, sport, music, art) is only attainable if the actiotopes necessary for every day life also are cultivated in a reasonable manner or other persons like parents, partners or managers adopt responsibility for this caretaking to relieve the learner and make available more resources for the learning process. Still, such compensating constellations must evolve, too, in a symbiotic interplay with the other system parts.

The actiotope model is the first and so far only model to describe and explain the interaction of (all) the relevant components in the achieving system. Other systemic models miss this specificity. The validity of the model is currently researched in various ways, also by practical implementations to foster expertise development. The following chapters present current explorations of the actiotope model of giftedness. Three studies examine the prescriptions of the model while the fourth chapter illustrates how the model can be put into practice: First Harder investigated the content and construct validity of the actiotope model in its core formulation. Second Duan and Arora elucidate gender and cross-cultural differences in actiotopes concerning the domains of science, technology, engineering and mathematics (STEM). Third Kist researched the importance of sociotopes in addition to actiotopes for learning English as a foreign language at school. These empirical reports are followed by Schurr's description of the actiotope theory's practical implementation in a counseling philosophy for advising gifted children and their parents. Finally Phillipson discusses the previous chapters and draws some conclusions for future research.

References

Avery, L. D., & VanTassel-Baska, J. (2001). Investigating the impact of gifted education evaluation at state and local levels: Problems with traction. *Journal for the Education of the Gifted, 25*(2), 153-176.

Borland, J. H. (2005). Gifted education without gifted children. In R. J. Sternberg & J. E. Davidson (Eds.), *Conceptions of giftedness* (2nd ed., pp. 1-19). New York, NY: Cambridge University Press.

Callahan, C. M., & Miller, E. M. (2005). A child-responsive model of giftedness. In R. J. Sternberg & J. E. Davidson (Eds.), *Conceptions of giftedness* (2nd ed., pp. 38-51). New York, NY: Cambridge University Press.

Cattell, R. B. (1963). Theory of fluid and crystallized intelligence: A critical experiment. *Journal of Educational Psychology, 54*, 1-22.

Cronbach, L. J., & Snow, R. E. (1977). *Aptitudes and instructional methods: A handbook for research on interactions*. New York, NY: Irvington.

Csikszentmihalyi, M., & Wolfe, R. (2002). New conceptions and research approaches to creativity: Implications of a systems perspective for creativity in education. In K. A. Heller, F. J. Mönks, R. J. Sternberg & R. F. Subotnik (Eds.), *International handbook of giftedness and talent* (pp. 81-94). Oxford: Elsevier.

Dai, D. Y., & Renzulli, J. S. (2008). Snowflakes, living systems, and the mystery of giftedness. *Gifted Child Quarterly, 52*(2), 114.

Ericsson, K. A., Krampe, R. T., & Tesch-Römer, C. (1993). The role of deliberate practice in the acquisition of expert performance. *Psychologial Review, 100*(3), 363-406.

Ericsson, K. A., Roring, R. W., & Nandagopal, K. (2007). Giftedness and evidence for reproducibly superior performance: An account based on the expert performance framework. *High Ability Studies, 18*(1), 3-56.

Gagné, F. (1985). Giftedness and talent: Reexamining a reexamination of the definitions. *Gifted Child Quarterly, 29,* 103-112.

Gagné, F. (1995). From giftedness to talent: A developmental model and its impact on the language of the field. *Roeper Review, 18*(103-111).

Gagné, F. (2000). Understanding the complex choreography of talent development through DMGT-based analysis. In K. A. Heller, F. J. Mönks, & A. H. Passow (Eds.), *International handbook of giftedness and talent* (2nd ed.). Oxford: Pergamon.

Gagné, F. (2005). From gifts to talents: The DMGT as a developmental model. In R. J. Sternberg & J. E. Davidson (Eds.), *Conceptions of giftedness* (2nd ed., pp. 98-119). New York, NY: Cambridge University Press.

Gagné, F. (2009). Building gifts into talents: Detailed overview of the DMGT 2.0. In B. MacFarlane & T. Stambaugh (Eds.), *Leading change in gifted education: The festschrift of Dr. Joyce VanTassel-Baska* (pp. 61-80). Waco, TX: Prufrock Press.

Gallagher, J. J., & Courtright, R. D. (1986). The educational definition of giftedness and its policy implications. In R. J. Sternberg & J. E. Davidson (Eds.), *Conceptions of giftedness* (1st ed., pp. 93-111). Cambridge: Cambridge University Press.

Heller, K. A. (1992). Projektziele, Untersuchungsergebnisse und praktische Konsequenzen [Project goals, research results, and practical implications]. In K. A. Heller (Ed.), *Hochbegabung im Kindes- und Jugendalter [Giftedness in childhood and adolescence]* (2nd ed., pp. 18-36). Göttingen: Hogrefe.

Heller, K. A. (2001). Projektziele, Untersuchungsergebnisse und praktische Konsequenzen [Project goals, research results, and practical implications]. In K. A. Heller (Ed.), *Hochbegabung im Kindes- und Jugendalter [Giftedness in childhood and adolescence]* (2nd ed., pp. 22-41). Göttingen: Hogrefe.

Heller, K. A., Perleth, C., & Lim, T. K. (2005). The Munich model of giftedness designed to identify and promote gifted students. In R. J. Sternberg & J. E. Davidson (Eds.), *Conceptions of giftedness* (2nd ed., pp. 147-170). New York, NY: Cambridge University Press.

Howe, M. J. A., Davidson, J. W., & Sloboda, J. A. (1998). Innate talents: Reality or myth? *Behavioral and Brain Sciences, 21,* 399-442.

Jeltova, I., & Grigorenko, E. L. (2005). Systemic approaches to giftedness: Contributions of Russian psychology. In R. J. Sternberg & J. E. Davidson (Eds.), *Conceptions of giftedness* (2nd ed., pp. 171-186). New York, NY: Cambridge University Press.

Michel, L. (1971). *Allgemeine Grundlagen psychometrischer Tests. Handbuch der Psycholgie. Band 6 [Basic knowledge on psychometric tests. Handbook of psychology, Vol. 6].* Göttingen: Hogrefe.

Mönks, F. J., & Katzko, M. W. (2005). Giftedness and gifted education. In R. J. Sternberg & J. E. Davidson (Eds.), *Conceptions of giftedness* (2nd ed., pp. 187-200). New York, NY: Cambridge University Press.

Mooij, T. (2008). Education and self-regulation of learning for gifted pupils: Systemic design and development. *Research Papers in Education, 23*(1), 1-19.

Moore, J. L., Ford, D. Y., & Milner, H. R. (2005). Underachievement among gifted students of color: Implications for educators. *Theory into Practice, 44*(2), 167-177.

Moran, S., & Gardner, H. (2006). Extraordinary achievements: A developmental and systems analysis. In D. Kuhn & R. S. Siegler (Eds.), *Handbook of child psychology: Cognition, perception, and language* (6th ed., Vol. 2, pp. 905-949). New York, NY: Wiley.

Perleth, C. (1997). *Zur Rolle von Begabung und Erfahrung bei der Leistungsgenese. Ein Brückenschlag zwischen Begabungs- und Expertiseforschung [The role of gifts and experiences in the genesis of performance. Bridging the gap between giftedness and expertise research].* München: LMU.

Perleth, C. (2001). Follow-up-Untersuchungen zur Münchner Hochbegabungsstudie [Follow-up studies of the Munich longitudinal study of giftedness]. In K. A. Heller (Ed.), *Hochbegabung im Kindes-und Jugendalter [Giftedness in childhood and adolescence]* (2nd ed., pp. 358-447). Göttingen: Hogrefe.

Plucker, J. A., & Barab, S. A. (2005). The importance of contexts in theories of giftedness: Learning to embrace the messy joys of subjectivity. In R. J. Sternberg & J. E. Davidson (Eds.), *Conceptions of giftedness* (2nd ed., pp. 201-216). New York, NY: Cambridge University Press.

Pólgar, L., & Farkas, E. (1989). *Nevelj zsenit [Bring up genius].* Budapest: Interart.

Renzulli, J. S. (1986). The three-ring conception of giftedness: A developmental model for creative productivity. In R. J. Sternberg & J. E. Davidson (Eds.), *Conceptions of giftedness* (1st ed., pp. 53-92). New York, NY: Cambridge University Press.

Renzulli, J. S. (2005). The three-ring conception of giftedness: A developmental model for promoting creative productivity. In R. J. Sternberg & J. E. Davidson (Eds.), *Conceptions of giftedness* (2nd ed., pp. 246-280). New York, NY: Cambridge University Press.

Rheinberg, F., Bromme, R., Minsel, B., Winteler, A., & Weidenmann, B. (2001). Die Erziehenden und Lehrenden [The educating and teaching staff]. In A. Krapp & B. Weidenmann (Eds.), *Pädagogische Psychologie* (4th ed.). Weinheim: Beltz.

Shavinina, L. V. (2004). Explaining high abilities of Nobel laureates. *High Ability Studies, 15*(2), 243-254.

Simonton, D. K. (2005). Genetics of giftedness: The implications of an emergenic-epigenic model. In R. J. Sternberg & J. E. Davidson (Eds.), *Conception of giftedness* (2nd ed., pp. 312-326). New York, NY: Cambridge University Press.

Spearman, C. (1904). "General intelligence" objectively determined and measured. *American Journal of Psychology, 15*, 201-293.

Stern, W. (1916). Psychologische Begabungsforschung und Begabungsdiagnose [Psychological giftedness research and diagnostics]. In P. Petersen (Ed.), *Der Aufstieg der Begabten [The rise of the gifted]* (pp. 105-120). Leipzig: Teubner.

Sternberg, R. J. (1985). *Beyond IQ: A triarchic theory of human intelligence.* New York, NY: Cambridge University Press.

Sternberg, R. J. (2005). The WICS model of giftedness. In R. J. Sternberg & J. E. Davidson (Eds.), *Conceptions of giftedness* (2nd ed., pp. 327-342). New York, NY: Cambridge University Press.

Subotnik, R. F., & Rickoff, R. (2010). Should eminence based on outstanding innovation be the goal of gifted education and talent development? Implications for policy and research. *Learning and Individual Differences, 20*(4), 358-364.

Trautwein, U. (September 2010). *Die Leistungsentwicklung steht im Mittelpunkt? Welche Lern- und Bildungsziele Lehrkräfte an unterschiedlichen Schulformen wichtig finden [Focus on performance development? Which learning and educational goals teachers assign importance in different school types].* Paper presented at the 47. Kongress der Deutschen Gesellschaft für Psychologie, Bremen, Germany.

Winner, E. (1997). *Gifted children: Myths and realities.* New York, NY: Basic Books.

Winner, E., & Martino, G. (1993). Giftedness in the visual arts and music. In K. A. Heller, F. J. Mönks, A. H. Passow & A. Harry (Eds.), *International handbook of research and development of giftedness and talent* (pp. 253-281). Elmsford, NY: Pergamon Press.

Ziegler, A. (2005). The Actiotope model of giftedness. In R. J. Sternberg & J. E. Davidson (Eds.), *Conceptions of giftedness* (2nd ed., pp. 411-436). New York, NY: Cambridge University Press.

Ziegler, A. (2009). *Hochbegabung [Giftedness]*. München: Reinhardt.

Ziegler, A. (2010). Individuelle Begabungsförderung in Lernsoziotopen [Individual fostering of gifts in learning sociotopes]. In C. Fischer & C. Fischer-Ontrup (Eds.), *Individuelle Förderung multipler Begabungen* (pp. 16-27). Münster: LIT.

Ziegler, A., & Phillipson, N. S. (in press). Towards a systemic theory of gifted education. *High Ability Studies*.

Ziegler, A., & Stöger, H. (2009). Begabungsförderung aus einer systemischen Perspektive [A systemic perspective on gifted education]. *Journal für Begabtenförderung, 9*(2), 6-31.

Ziegler, A., & Stöger, H. (2011). Expertisierung als Adaptions- und Regulationsprozess: Die Rolle von Bildungs- und Lernkapital [Expertisation as adaption and regulationprocesses: The role of educational and learning capital]. In M. Dresel (Ed.), *Motivation, Selbstregulation und Leistungsexzellenz [Motivation, self-regulation, and performance excellence]* (pp. 131-152). Münster: LIT.

Bettina Harder

An Empirical Validation of the Actiotope Model of Giftedness

Abstract

A system-theoretical approach like the actiotope model of giftedness (Ziegler, 2005) is difficult to model mathematically. In order to prove its validity empirically, structural equation modeling represents a suited statistical method, even if systemic demands for interactivity cannot be fully met. A longitudinal study with 3 measuring points during the first 2 grades of grammar school and assessments of 350 students, provides the data for the examination of (1) construct and (2) predictive validity of the actiotope model. The results were as follows: (1) Factor analysis confirms the assumed highly interactive structure of the actiotope, though satisfactory model fit (according to standard fit criteria) cannot be achieved due to methodological constraints. (2) The actiotope model's predictions of achievement levels approach significance over the measuring points resulting in a marginally significant prediction of achievement at measuring point 3, indicating that school based actiotopes at the beginning of grammar school first have to develop.

1   Theoretical Background

For decades models of giftedness have been subdued to processes of reexamination and further development which has already lead to several changes of perspective (cf. Harder, 2012). Lately it seems like another paradigmatic shift is about to happen due to the flaws of theories and also practical implementations of gifted education (Ziegler & Phillipson, 2012). A systemic perspective on the emergence of expertise performance has been proposed to offer a better understanding for so far unexplainable phenomena (e.g., Ziegler & Phillipson, 2012; Ziegler & Stöger, 2009). The problem this perspective is the complexity of modeling a systemic process which follows some characteristic rules (Ziegler & Stöger, 2009): Many starting situations can result in the desired outcome (equifinality). System development is highly dependent on context (context dependency) and on changes of other system parts (interdependency, co-evolution). Nevertheless systems are complex networks that react in an ordered fashion (networking) which does not follow linear decision processes but sudden, qualitative changes (phase transitions). Furthermore excellent performance is based on many levels of a system not only on single highly developed aspects (multilevel complexity). Still, the actiotope model (Ziegler, 2005) attempts to model such a process by means of functionally defined constructs instead of traditional conceptualizations like those used in other current models of giftedness (e.g., motivation or non-cognitive factors). The actiotope model assumes four components, five mechanisms and two system states that interact constantly to result in performance of varying levels of expertise. The model itself is described elsewhere (Ziegler, 2005) and will only be summed up in the relevant aspects for the study described hereafter.

The actiotope is the space in which a person acts (cf. sociotope, biotope). This space is defined by four components: the person's action repertoire (all possible actions), their goals, and their subjective action space (all actions subjectively considered possible in the given context) as well as the environmental conditions for the action in question. These four functional constructs interact strongly e.g., goals are picked in accordance with the current action repertoire to reach the next level of competence if the individual perceives a chance for the successful completion of the developmental step under the environmental circumstances and the subjective evaluation of personal capabilities. Progression towards higher levels of competence is mediated by several mechanisms or necessary conditions within the person and the environment. These comprise the capability to recognize when an action has been successful, the availability of conditional knowledge for certain actions (when to use which action), the generation of different action variations to extend the action repertoire and thereby optimize ones' reactions in a given situation, the anticipation of future challenges to prepare oneself and the availability of efficient feedback and Feedforward loops. The interaction of components and mechanisms must be viewed against the background of the complete system which should be modifiable and stable to favor expertise acquisition. Stability is crucial for the func tioning of the whole system (e.g., a secure home situation) while total stability would be detrimental for the process of expertise acquisition as new actions and thereby learning would be prevented. Modifiability on the other hand enables the development of the actiotope towards higher levels and thus is equally essential.

Emphasis must be laid on the assumption that all parts of the model depend on each other and interact. While other models like Gagné's or Heller's moderator models (Gagné, 2005, 2009; Heller, Perleth, & Lim, 2005) suppose unidirectional influences from one variable to another, a systemic model implies bidirectional and multivariate effects. Thus, it is impossible to understand the process by investigating isolated variables. In the same sense it is highly artificial to group variables into higher order constructs like non-cognitive factors or even motivation as the comprised variables are very unlikely to interact in the same way but rather selectively. Even a functional grouping like the aforementioned division in components, mechanisms and system states is questionable as not only mechanisms interact with each other but work in combination with components and the condition of the whole system. Subsequently, a strongly interacting system is subdued to constant changes which allow the adaptation to new environmental conditions. The assessed state of an actiotope is thus always a snapshot of the current situation. If the environment poses constant basic rules and demands for the demonstration of competence in the domain the actiotope can progressively adapt to these conditions and develop necessary behaviors to get along optimally (ordered reaction within the system).

These assumptions were tested in a longitudinal study in the school context. Precisely, the development of students' actiotopes for school achievement was investigated in the two years following transition to secondary school[1]. This allowed the investigation of construct and predictive validity of the actiotope model ac-cording to the following hypotheses also taking into account the development of the construct and its predictive power over time.

Construct validity of the actiotope model:
H1: The actiotope is best described as a non-hierarchical, strongly interactive system. Higher order constructs are assumed to diminish construct validity while selective interactivity should increase construct validity.
H2: Interactivity within the actiotope should vary over time due to changes in the interplay of the different variables to ensure the adaptation to currently relevant conditions.

Predictive validity of the actiotope model:
H3: Due to snapshot-like assessments of current system states predictive validity for school achievement is expected to be low.

---

[1] This chapter is based on an article submitted for publication.

H4: actiotope adaptations to the new school environment during the first year are supposed to improve the prediction of school achievement.

2   Method

The study is part of a larger longitudinal project investigating different types of classes and their impact on the development of gifted students. For the present study three measuring points were taken into account. The assessments of actiotope variables and school achievements started at the beginning of grammar school and were repeated after one and two years (end of fifth grade and end of sixth grade).

Participants came from 16 classes in six different schools in the south of Germany. The sample consisted of N = 350 children of whom 25 % attended extra classes for the gifted. It is therefore a selection of high-ability students with grammar school being not only the highest form of secondary education but also including students from gifted classes. The age of the sampled students at the beginning of the study was M = 10.65 years (SD = 0.51), boys were slightly overrepresented with 60 % of participants being male.

The actiotope was assessed by a 50-item questionnaire (Ziegler, 2008) presenting the students with statements to which they had to indicate their agreement on a scale from 1 (disagree totally) to 5 (agree totally). The items covered the actiotope components subjective action space, goals and environment (action repertoire must be assessed objectively, see section below), the five mechanisms (recognition of success, conditional knowledge, generation of action variations, anticipation and feedback) and the two system state characteristics modifiability and stability with five items each. All ten scales were Rasch-analyzed to ensure item quality. Reliabilities of the Rasch-scores ranged from 0.71 to 0.86 (comparable to Cronbach's α) with the exception of the environment-scale which was below 0.70.

School achievement was assessed by standardized tests in German, English (first foreign language) and mathematics. In German text understanding was assessed with two published instruments (Bäuerlein, Lenhard, & Schneider, 2010; Souvignier, Trenk-Hinterberger, Adam-Schwebe, & Gold, 2008). For English and mathematics tests had to be developed for the study in a prestudy phase (Harder & Ziegler, 2009; Weiß & Schneider, 2009). Achievement tests were also Rasch-analyzed which resulted in satisfying reliabilities of 0.77 to 0.95. Achievement test scores were used both as dependent variables for the predictions of the actiotope and as the indicator of the action repertoire. The latter must be assessed objectively to measure all possible actions instead of only those represented in subjective action space which could be derived from a self-report instrument.

To test the aforementioned hypotheses confirmatory factor analysis and structural equation modeling was used in Mplus (Muthén & Muthén, 1998-2011). The actiotope and school achievement were modeled as latent constructs using the Rasch-scales of the tests and questionnaires as indicator variables. All models were calculated parallel for measuring point 1 and 2 to identify changes over time. To answer the question of construct validity different models were built: First a non-hierarchical model (actiotope as single latent factor) was compared to a hierarchical model using the higher order constructs 'components', 'mechanisms' and 'system state' as additional latent factors resulting in a second order confirmatory factor analysis (both analyses without interactions between variables). Second and as an alternative to the higher order constructs the formerly subsumed variables were allowed to interact selectively by means of residual correlations (interactive model). These correlations were only implemented between variable pairs within one of the higher order constructs paralleling the more rigid subsuming into higher order constructs. In the sense of system theory all interactions should be enabled which unfortunately is impossible due to model estimation demands (underidentified model). For the examination of predictive validity the actiotope factor was used to predict achievement (also as a latent factor) at the next measuring point.

3   Results

3.1   Construct Validity: Structure of the Actiotope and Its Change over Time

The following figures show the estimated models (standardized factor loadings, residual variances and correlations) with their indices of model fit. Indices that fulfill the commonly demanded cutoffs (cf. Geiser, 2010; Hu & Bentler, 1999; Reinecke, 2005) are set in bold type. As can be seen no model fully meets the demanded standards which will be discussed later. Still the comparison of the different models allows distinctive conclusions.

H1 states that the actiotope should be best modeled in a non-hierarchical and interactive fashion. Let's first have a look at the non-hierarchy-assumption. Figure 1 and 2 show the models without hierarchy and with higher order factors (both without interactions). Their fit indices are very similar which suggests to prefer the model with less constraints, that is the non-hierarchical model. The tendency towards better fit in the models of measuring point 2 for the non-hierarchical model throughout all fit indices also favor the non-hierarchical variant. Figure 3 shows the non-hierarchical model with residual correlations between variables instead of subsuming them to higher order constructs like in the hierarchical model before. The allowance of individual interactions between the indicator variables instead of grouping them into one factor yielded very promising results: For measuring point 1 the interactive model showed the best fit compared to the other two variants throughout all indices with RMSEA and SRMR on acceptable levels and CFI close to the cutoff-value of 0.95. For measuring point 2 the superiority of the interactive model was not that clear (Figure 3, right side compared to Figure 1, right side) as many residual correlations remained insignificant. Subsequently the interactive model showed the best AIC, CFI and SRMR while the non-hierarchical model in Figure 1 shows the better BIC, TLI and RMSEA for measuring point 2. Taken together these results favor the interactive model, for measuring point 1 more clearly than for measuring point 2.

H2 assumes the interactivity within the actiotope to change over time. A look at the differences between the two interactive models (Figure 3, left and right side) for the measuring points confirms this hypothesis. Figure 3 provides evidence for shifts of interactions as well as changes in factor loadings. The most prominent among the latter is the increasing factor loading of the action repertoire which reaches marginal significance for measuring point 2. With regard to interaction shifts one can record that only three out of nine residual correlations remain significant at measuring point 2 whereas one formerly non-significant correlation (between anticipation and conditional knowledge) reaches significance at measuring point 2. These shifts indicate rather big changes within the actiotope. However, to complete the picture of correlation shifts the knowledge of all residual correlations would be necessary which was impossible to model due to methodological constraints.

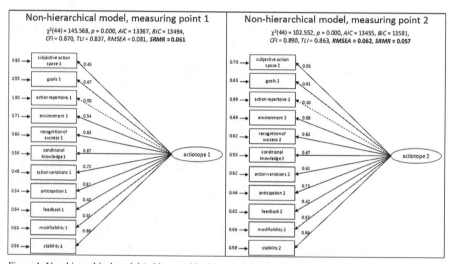

Figure 1: Non-hierarchical model (without residual correlations) for measuring point 1 (left side) and measuring point 2 (right side). Solid lines represent significant, broken lines non significant factor loadings/residual variances

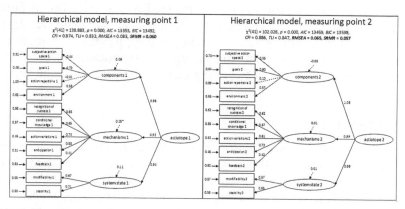

Figure 2: Hierarchical model (without residual correlations) for measuring point 1 (left side) and measuring point 2 (right side). Solid lines represent significant, broken lines non significant factor loadings/residual variances

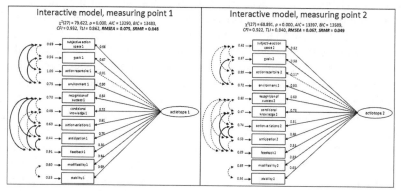

Figure 3: Interactive model (non-hierarchical) for measuring point 1 (left side) and measuring point 2 (right side) with residual correlations within the higher order constructs. Solid lines represent significant, broken lines non significant factor loadings/residual variances/correlations, m stands for marginally significant

3.2 Predictive Validity: Prediction of School Achievements and Prediction's Change over Time

H3 assumed low predictive validity for the actiotope model concerning future achievement but with a tendency towards better predictions for measuring point 3 when the students' actiotopes have been adapted to the new environment (H4). The predictive validity of the actiotope was modeled with the interactive model (cf. Figure 3). A regression of the latent achievement at time t on the latent actiotope factor at time t-1 was added to the model. Compared to the model without achievement prediction fit indices deteriorated so that none of them met the acceptance criteria (for actiotope measuring point 1: CFI = 0.560, TLI = 0.322, RMSEA = 0.170, SRMR = 0.121; for actiotope measuring point 2: CFI =

0.676, TLI = 0.500, RMSEA = 0.110, SRMR = 0.107). Bad fit indices constitute the first indicator of low validity for the prediction model. This is further supported by the regression coefficients which did not surmount the significance level. For measuring point 1 resulted $\beta = 0.00$, $p > 0.10$, for measuring point 2 the regression coefficient turned marginally significant with $\beta = 0.18$, $p < 0.10$ explaining 3 % of the achievement variance. These results confirm both hypotheses H3 and H4.

4   Discussion

The presented study attempted to demonstrate the validity of the actiotope model of giftedness. The hypotheses derived from the systemic nature of the actiotope model have been widely confirmed by the results of the study and enable some important conclusions about the validity of the actiotope model.

To test the actiotope theory's construct validity three variations of interactivity have been modeled. Taken together the results suggest that the interactive non-hierarchical model is best suited to describe the interplay of the variables. Hierarchical, higher order constructs are inflexible in a way that they do not represent the individual interactions between single aspects of the actiotope. The model with residual correlations better fulfilled this requirement allowing for selective interactivity between actiotope elements (H1). Thus empirical data confirmed the systemic assumption of complex and simultaneous interaction between the multiple aspects of person and environment in the context of school performances. The interactive model also served well for depicting changes over time which are left unknown in the hierarchical model. Interactions shifted between the two measuring points (H2). At the beginning of grammar school mechanisms and components are strongly interacting aside from their common variance that is already subsumed in the actiotope factor whereas at the end of fifth grade the picture looks totally different. Now environment and goals are left to be intertwined aside of the general actiotope while the other components are better integrated in the complete actiotope state. For mechanisms similar effects were observed while also one new residual correlation between conditional knowledge and anticipation reached significance. It is difficult to interpret residual correlations as in reality neither a distinction between main and residual relationships can be made nor can the correlative structure be generalized to other groups. Interactions are supposed to be very individual so the observed changes are the common trend in the investigated sample and demonstrate its specific development whereas another group of students might show different tendencies in interaction shifts. The crucial point is that changes occur over time which emphasizes the importance of considering selective interactivity in models of giftedness and thereby also in practice. Teachers, parents and other persons that support the educational development of students should be aware of the very specific interplay. Knowing the functional structures and their interactions which are necessary to adapt the student's actiotope to a new environment like secondary school opens new possibilities of fostering. Practitioners should keep components, system state and the mechanisms responsible for a successful adaptation to new demands in mind when guiding students through changing environmental conditions.

Regarding the predictive validity of the actiotope model the results also confirmed expectations. The assessment of the actiotope only captured the momentary situation hence its predictive validity was low (H3). A snapshot of a highly dynamic system is at first glance unsuited to predict performances that are accomplished almost one year later. Especially after transition to grammar school the students' actiotopes undergo major changes due to higher demands for concentrated work, self-regulation in learning and working, time management, quality of performances and many other aspects. For example the corresponding action repertoire first must be built up which was indicated by the better integration of this variable into the actiotope factor for measuring point 2 (as the action repertoire is not measured by the same questionnaire as the other variables it is not that closely related to them which renders the increase in factor loading over time even more impressive). The transition to grammar school poses a challenge for the existing interplay of actiotope variables. Not only the action repertoire must be extended but also feelings of anxiety or inadequacy or, on the positive side, excitement and perceived support of the home and school environment influence student's goals and subjective action space and so on. After some time one can expect this new interplay of variables to be installed and to enable the students' functioning in standard grammar school situations which makes the actiotope more predictive for later achievements (H4). It seems that until the end of fifth grade students have made some progress towards such an adapted state of their actiotopes as predictions reach marginal significance. Still, this predictability is very low which probably origins from the constant process of adapting to the manifold of new demands that continue after the starting year. Future research might unravel if a higher general adaptation after a longer period of time leads to better predictions.

These very different results for construct and predictive validity become clearer with the distinction of explaining processes vs. products. Owed to its highly dynamic nature the actiotope model is especially suited for the description and explanation of the developmental process. Analysis revealed strong changes in the complex interplay of actiotope variables and suggests a detailed description of interaction. This perspective can enable a deeper understanding of the process and thereby help to support learners in a holistic, co-evolutionary development. Predictions of long-term results or products on the other hand are difficult with the process oriented information assessed in the questionnaire. For the prediction of the overall evolution of a system surrounding conditions and their possibilities to adapt to the actual developmental step should be known. Constant favorable conditions like environmental support (e.g., learning possibilities, high quality instruction) as well as personal capabilities (e.g., time to spend on the domain, self-reflection and self-regulation) play a crucial role for the development on the long run (cf. Ericsson, Roring, & Nandagopal, 2007; Shavinina,

2004). These conditions have not been assessed in this study. Ziegler and Stöger (2011) conceptualized these conditions in form of sociotopes (different environments) and capitals (internal and external resources) for learning processes which provide a promising basis for future research.

Last, a methodological note seems to be indicated regarding the limitations of modeling a systemic theory with the given possibilities in modern psychological analysis procedures. Structural equation modeling is currently one of the most powerful strategies of analysis in the standard repertoire but it still fails at several points. First, it cannot represent the full extent of interactivity proposed by a systemic theory. This leads to constraints in modeling which for their part result in inaccuracies and thus worsen fit characteristics (like the missing consideration of all residual correlations in the interactive model did). Second, falling back on residual correlations is only a limited solution as normally factors are supposed to explain all systematic variance and residuals are desired to be independent. High dependencies lead to estimation problems (obvious in the worse fit indices of the interactive model at measuring point 2, see Figure 3). Third, complex methods of analysis almost exclusively rely on linear statistics. However system theory suggests sudden, often qualitative changes which consequently cannot be modeled adequately. A solution might lie in neuronal network models (Haykin, 1998; Posey & Hawkes, 1996) which are currently developed but not yet in common usage.

References

Bäuerlein, K., Lenhard, W., & Schneider, W. (2010). *LESEN 6-9, Lesen ermöglicht Sinnentnahme - Leseverständnistest für 6. bis 9. Klassen [LESEN reading comprehension test for 6th to 9th grade]*. Test battery in preparation.

Ericsson, K. A., Roring, R. W., & Nandagopal, K. (2007). Giftedness and evidence for reproducibly superior performance: An account based on the expert performance framework. *High Ability Studies, 18*(1), 3-56.

Gagné, F. (2005). From gifts to talents: The DMGT as a developmental model. In R. J. Sternberg & J. E. Davidson (Eds.), *Conceptions of giftedness* (2nd ed., pp. 98–119). New York, NY: Cambridge University Press.

Gagné, F. (2009). Building gifts into talents: Detailed overview of the DMGT 2.0. In B. MacFarlane & T. Stambaugh (Eds.), *Leading change in gifted education: The festschrift of Dr. Joyce VanTassel-Baska* (pp. 61-80). Waco, TX: Prufrock Press.

Geiser, C. (2010). *Datenanalyse mit Mplus. Eine anwendungsorientierte Einführung [Data analysis in mplus. A application oriented introduction]*. Wiesbaden: Springer.

Harder, B. (2012). Towards a systemic theory of giftedness. In H. Stoeger, A. Aljugaiman, & B. Harder (Eds.), *Talent development and excellence* (pp. 13-29). Münster, Germany: LIT.

Harder, B., & Ziegler, A. (2009). *Englisch Leistungstest für 5.-7. Jahrgangsstufe[English achievement tests for 5th to 7th grade].* Test battery in preparation.

Haykin, S. (Ed.). (1998). *Neural networks: A comprehensive foundation* (2nd ed.). New York, NY: Macmillan College Publishing.

Heller, K. A., Perleth, C., & Lim, T. K. (2005). The Munich model of giftedness designed to identify and promote gifted students. In R. J. Sternberg & J. E. Davidson (Eds.), *Conceptions of giftedness* (2nd ed., pp. 147-170). New York, NY: Cambridge University Press.

Hu, L., & Bentler, P. M. (1999). Cutoff criteria for fit indexes in covariance struture analysis: Conventional criteria versus new alternatives. *Structural Equation Modeling, 6*, 1-55.

Muthén, B. O., & Muthén, L. K. (1998-2011). Mplus Version 6.11. Base program and mulitlevel add-on. [Computer program]. Los Angeles, CA: Muthén & Muthén.

Posey, C. L., & Hawkes, L. W. (1996). Neural networks applied to knowledge acquisition in the student model. *Information Sciences, 88*(1-4), 275-298.

Reinecke, J. (2005). *Strukturgleichungsmodelle in den Sozialwissenschaften [Structural equation models in the social sciences].* München: Oldenbourg

Shavinina, L. V. (2004). Explaining high abilities of Nobel laureates. *High Ability Studies, 15*(2), 243-254.

Souvignier, E., Trenk-Hinterberger, I., Adam-Schwebe, S., & Gold, A. (2008). *FLVT 5-6: Frankfurter Leseverständnistest für 5. und 6. Klassen [Frankfurt reading comprehension test for 5th to 7th grade].* Göttingen: Hogrefe.

Weiß, C., & Schneider, W. (2009). *Mathematiktest für 5. bis 7. Jahrgangsstufe [Maths achievement tests for 5th to 7th grade].* Unpublished test battery, Julius-Maximilians-University, Würzburg, Germany.

Ziegler, A. (2005). The actiotope model of giftedness. In R. J. Sternberg & J. E. Davidson (Eds.), *Conceptions of giftedness* (2nd ed., pp. 411-436). New York, NY: Cambridge University Press.

Ziegler, A. (2008). *Fragebogen zur Erfassung des schulischen Aktiotops [Questionnaire to assess the actiotope in the school context].* Unpublished questionnaire, University of Ulm, Germany.

Ziegler, A., & Phillipson, N. S. (2012). Towards a systemic theory of gifted education. *High Ability Studies.*

Ziegler, A., & Stöger, H. (2009). Begabungsförderung aus einer systemischen Perspektive [A systemic perspective on gifted education]. *Journal für Begabtenförderung, 9*(2), 6-31.

Ziegler, A., & Stöger, H. (2011). Expertisierung als Adaptions- und Regulationsprozess: Die Rolle von Bildungs- und Lernkapital [Expertisation as adaption and regulationprocesses: The role of educational and learning capital]. In M. Dresel (Ed.), *Motivation, Selbstregulation und Leistungsexzellenz [Motivation, self-regulationa and achievement excellence]* (pp. 131-152). Münster: LIT.

Xiaoju Duan & Anjulie Arora

Gender and Cross-cultural Differences in STEM: An Investigation Based on the Actiotope Model of Giftedness

Abstract

The underrepresentation of women in STEM careers is a worldwide problem. Despite increases in opportunities, women increasingly opt for non-scientific careers. Over decades, scientists and researchers have postulated various theories to explain the observed gender differences in abilities and attitudes towards science and related disciplines. However, the developmental timeline and causes behind these gender disparities remain largely unclear. In this study, a total of 476 high school students between the ages of 12-13 years, from Germany and India were administered the Actiotope Questionnaire; in an attempt to investigate gender differences on scales of interest, Self-confidence, STEM activity, Future job choices, and Achievement in science and mathematics. In addition, the Actiotope Model was empirically tested. Exploratory statistical analysis including t-tests and ANOVAs did reveal some gender and cross-cultural differences amongst some, but not all scales investigated. Results regarding whether the Actiotope Model is relevant to explaining inter-individual differences amongst girls and boys were inconclusive. It was found however, that the Actiotope Model is more useful in explaining inter-individual differences among German students than Indian students.

1   Introduction

The question regarding gender differences in science and mathematics is still an important research topic for scientists worldwide. Women continue to be underrepresented in careers in Science, Technology, Engineering and Mathematics (STEM). According to a report released by the National Science Foundation in 2007, women made up 11% of engineering workforce in the United States of America and only 26% of women entered occupations as mathematicians and computer scientists (NSF, 2007). Moreover, women are underrepresented in academic positions at the university and research institutions. It was suggested that women working in science, engineering and technology were 29% less likely to obtain tenure than their male colleagues (Ginther & Kahn, 2009).

To better address the issues such as the increasing under-representation of women in STEM careers, it is vital to study and determine what might cause the underlying differences in attitudes and interest (Brotman & Moore, 2008).

Evidence suggests that high school boys tend to display more positive affect and interest towards science than girls do (Dawson, 2000). Despite much investigation into the differences in interest and attitudes towards science between boys and girls, it remains unclear as to the specific development. Therefore, it is important to further the exploration on the role that interest and attitudes towards science among high school students has on future occupational choices.

In addition to varying interest and attitudes displayed by girls and boys towards science, studies also consistently show that girls are less exposed to extracurricular science activities than boys are, which is particularly true for physical science activities (Catsambis, 1995; Jones, Howe, & Rua, 2000). However, the impact of less exposure to extracurricular science activities among girls on their Future job choices and interest in STEM fields, remains largely unexplored.

Another important psychological construct to consider is Self-confidence. Literature often refers to students' self-perceptions of their academic abil-ities as Academic Self-concept, Self-confidence or Self esteem (Santiago & Einarson, 1998). There is significant evidence suggesting that despite indications of narrowing gender differences in achievement in science and mathematics world-wide (OECD, 2009), girls continue to report feeling less confident about their abilities in science and mathematics.

According to some researchers, such achievement related beliefs; begin to develop early and to get enhanced as the girls go through school. Subsequently, such behaviour can become crucial in determining the persistence of women to remain in STEM fields in the future (Eccles, Bonnie, & Jozefowica, 1999). As a response to the growing underrepresentation of women in STEM, it is vital to continue to research the combination of factors stated above among high school students.

The underrepresentation of women in STEM careers, though increasingly a worldwide phenomenon, is a greater cause of concern in some countries than in others. Thus, in investigating gender differences in STEM careers, we should also bear in mind that the conditions of scientific learning differ throughout the world (Scantlebury & Baker, 1998).

Why are women underrepresented in STEM careers? Scientists have postulated several theories to explain gender differences in science and math careers. Some researchers argue that gender differences in the social roles of men and women have undergone evolutionary changes, whereas other scientists highlight cognitive abilities such as verbal, visuospatial and quantitative abilities (Halpern et al., 2007). Some of the most popular theories to explain gender differences in mathematics and science achievement have been sociological ones (Else-Quest, Hyde, & Lynn, 2010). Apparently, the questions regarding gender differences in STEM careers remain complex. The Actiotope Model of Giftedness used in this study is yet another model which attempts to explain the gender differences in STEM careers.

Most Scientists would undoubtedly agree that any living system is constantly developing and evolving. This process of co-evolution occurs within a living system, but alongside the environment which contains them. Arguably, the development of high ability follows a similar pattern, where an individual's actions are continuously evolving within a particular talent domain or environment (Ziegler, 2005a). According to the Actiotope Model, excellence is the result of self-organization and the ability to adapt to highly complex systems (Ziegler, 2005a; Ziegler & Stoeger, 2005).

The Actiotope Model is comprised of four components: action repertoire, subjective action space, goals, and the environment (Ziegler, 2005a; Ziegler & Stoeger, 2005). The action repertoire consists of all possible actions an individual is capable of executing at a given point in time. The Subjective Action Space represents a selected group of actions chosen to acquire a particular goal (Ziegler, 2005a; Ziegler & Stoeger, 2005).Goals have the following three primary functions: they are involved in the selection of alternative actions when necessary; they energize action by acting as a driving force for actions; and they provide direction to the action during its execution (Ziegler, 2005a; Ziegler & Stoeger, 2005). The environment is another component which can explain why some actions are not incorporated into the subjective action space. In the Actiotope Model the talent domain is considered part of the environment, an area where the individual is eventually able to execute all the actions after going through a rigorous learning process (Ziegler, 2005a; Ziegler & Stoeger, 2005). All the components of the Actiotope Model make up a system characterized by multiple interactions among the components (Ziegler, 2005a; Ziegler & Stoeger, 2005).

Perhaps, the Actiotope Model can shed light on the problem of gender differences by looking more closely into the learning strategy that girls and boys employ in studying science and mathematics. Possibly, boys and girls differ in their action repertoire, in the goals they set up or in subjective action space.

This study had three purposes: firstly, to explore gender and cross-cultural differences, on scales of Interest, Self-confidence, Involvement in STEM activities, Future job choices and Achievement in science and mathematics; secondly, to examine whether the Actiotope Model of Giftedness can explain inter-individual differences among girls and boys from Germany and India; on the scales of Interest, Self-confidence, Involvement in STEM activities, Future job choices and

Achievement in science and mathematics; lastly, to investigate whether the Actiotope Model of Giftedness is equally useful in explaining inter-individual differences among German and Indian students.

2   Method

2.1   Participants

A total of 476 high school students, from two different countries, between the ages of 12-13 years took part in this study. Of these participants 243 students (121 boys, 122 girls) were from Germany. The remaining 233 students were from India (119 females, 114 males).

2.2   Overview of the Instrument

The Actiotope Questionnaire used in this study was developed by Ziegler (Ziegler, 2005a, 2005b; Ziegler, Dresel, & Schober, 1998; Ziegler & Stoeger, 2008). Ten scales were used to measure corresponding components of the Actiotope Model, namely, Subjective Action Space, Goal, Environment, Correction, Application, Action variety, Anticipation, Feedback, Modification, and Stability. Four scales were used to measure Interest, Self-confidence, Involvement in STEM activities, and Future job choices respectively. Each scale has a minimum of 5 items. All items on the questionnaire were measured on a 5-point Likert scale, ranging from 1 *completely dis-agree* to 5 *completely agree*. All scales had a Cronbach's Alpha greater than 0.6, except the scale for Environment which had lower reliability of 0.48. Hence, results for the scale environment should be interpreted with caution. Achievement was calculated as the mean of the most recent report card grade results for the subject of mathematics, physics, chemistry and biology. Grades were scaled inversely, the lower the grade, the better. The highest grade possible was 1, and the poorest was 6.

2.3   Procedure

The data used in this study was collected from two schools; one in Germany and the other in India. On a day fixed with school administrators and teachers, students were asked to fill out the questionnaire. The questionnaire was anonymous. The researcher was blinded to the identity of the participants at all times.

3   Results

Data compilation and analysis was done using SPSS18.0. Explanatory analysis, including t-tests and ANOVA's were performed. Correlations matrixes and multiple regression analysis were also conducted.

Research Question 1: Do gender differences exist among German and Indian students?

Table 1: Gender differences amongst German Students

Variable	Gender	M	SD	t	p
Interest	Boy	4.43	0.82	-3.68	.001*
	Girl	4.82	0.85		
Self-confidence	Boy	3.59	1.07	-3.50	.001*
	Girl	4.10	1.20		
STEM activities	Boy	2.07	0.66	-1.72	.087
	Girl	2.22	0.66		
Job choices	Boy	3.98	1.04	1.12	.265
	Girl	3.84	0.95		
Achievement	Boy	2.55	0.71	-0.01	.994
	Girl	2.55	0.80		

Note. *p<.05

Table 2: Gender differences amongst Indian Students

Variable	Gender	M	SD	T	P
Interest	Boy	4.45	0.54	-1.32	.189
	Girl	4.54	0.55		
Self-confidence	Boy	3.98	0.76	0.91	.367
	Girl	3.89	0.81		
STEM activities	Boy	3.84	0.81	-0.01	.995
	Girl	3.84	0.97		
Job choices	Boy	3.74	0.78	-0.26	.793
	Girl	3.77	0.93		
Achievement	Boy	2.32	0.95	0.49	.622
	Girl	2.25	1.05		

Note. *p<.05

Results from a t-test indicated that girls in Germany on average displayed significantly higher values for Interest in STEM than boys. Such a significant effect for girls was also found for the scale of Self-confidence as compared to boys. No significant gender differences among German students were found on the other scales (Table 1). With regards to Indian students, no significant gender differences were found on all the scales (Table 2).

Research Question 2: Do differences exist among German and Indian students?

Results of t-tests (Table 3) indicate that Indian students on average reported significantly higher involvement in STEM activities as compared to German students. It was found that German students on average had significantly higher achievement scores in science and mathematics as compared to In-dian students. With regards to the scales of Interest, Self-confidence, Future job choices, results indicate that the differences between German and Indian students were not significant, $ps > .05$.

Table 3: Differences in Interest, Self-confidence, STEM activities, Future job choices and Achievement by country

Scales	Country	N	M	SD	t	p
Interest	Germany	242	4.62	0.85	1.95	.052
	India	233	4.50	0.55		
Self-confidence	Germany	240	3.85	1.17	-0.99	.323
	India	233	3.94	0.78		
STEM activities	Germany	241	2.14	0.66	-23.47	.001*
	India	233	3.84	0.89		
Job choices	Germany	237	3.91	1.00	1.82	.069
	India	233	3.75	0.85		
Achievement	Germany	240	2.55	0.75	3.22	.001*
	India	233	2.29	0.75		

Note. *p<.05

Table 4: Main and interaction effects of Gender and Country; on Interest, Self-confidence, STEM activities, Future job choices and Achievement

	Gender		Country		Interaction	
	F	p	F	p	F	p
Interest	14.19	.001*	4.26	.039*	5.42	.020*
Self-confidence	3.87	.050*	2.15	.143	8.96	.003*
STEM activities	0.55	.458	540.64	.001*	0.54	.464
Job choices	0.50	.481	2.74	.099	1.10	.295
Achievement	0.01	.922	11.35	.001*	0.79	.374

Note. *p<.05

Further analysis of the data was done by conducting a 2-way factorial analysis of variance (ANOVA) to measure further the interaction effects of Gender and

Country on each of the dependent variables. The detailed data was given in Table 4.

Research Question 3: Can the Actiotope Model explain inter-individual differences amongst girls and boys from Germany and India?

A correlation matrix (Table 5) for all participants of the study was provided.

Table 5: Correlation matrix for all Participants

	1	2	3	4	5	6	7	8	9	10	11	12	13	14
1.Subjective Action Space														
2.Goal	,23**													
3.Environment	,05	,45**												
4.Correction	,31**	,28**	,32**											
5.Application	,46**	,35**	,27**	,47**										
6.Action variety	,17**	,45**	,33**	,41**	,38**									
7.Anticipation	,14**	,43**	,42**	,45**	,41**	,53**								
8.Feedback	,03	,30**	,30**	,27**	,21**	,41**	,41**							
9.Modification	,44**	,36**	,25**	,35**	,51**	,23**	,30**	,10*						
10.Stability	,33**	,21**	,23**	,47**	,43**	,26**	,29**	,18**	,39**					
11.Interest	,17**	,57**	,48**	,35**	,32**	,42**	,42**	,32**	,33**	,30**				
12.Self-confidence	,42**	,25**	,18**	,53**	,47**	,31**	,39**	,20**	,44**	,50**	,29**			
13.STEM activity	,11*	,41**	,25**	,20**	,18**	,47**	,34**	,36**	,09	,07	,21**	,25**		
14.Job choices	,37**	,11*	,01	,17*	,37**	,15**	,11*	,03	,27**	,17**	,09	,18**	,06	
15.Achievement	-,27**	-,16**	-,06	-,23**	-,20**	-,10*	-,12**	-,10*	-,27**	-,24**	-,10*	-,33**	-,23**	-,02

A Stepwise Regression Analysis was done to see how well specific components of the Actiotope Model can explain inter-individual differences amongst boys and girls; with regards to the scales of Interest, Self-confidence, STEM activity, Future job choices and Achievement. The regression analysis involved five steps. In Step 1, dependent variables were regressed on Subjective Action

Space, Goal and Environment. In Step 2, the interactions between Subject, Goal and Environment were added to the model. In Step 3, Modification and Stability were included. In Step 4, the interaction of Modification and Stability was added. Finally, all the other components in the Actiotope Model, Correction, Application, Action Variety, Anticipation and Feedback were added to the models in Step 5. For the purpose of this study only data from the final step (step 5) is provided. Detailed regression results for German boys and girls on every variable were provided in Table 6 and data of Indian were shown in Table 7. Results from the regression analysis indicate that the Actiotope Model can explain inter-individual differences amongst German and Indian girls and boys.

Table 6: Regression Analysis for German

	Interest		Self-confidence		STEM-Activity		Job-Choices		Achievement	
	Boy	Girl	Boy	Girl	Boy	Girl	Boy	Girl	Boy	Girl
R^2	0.57	0.62	0.61	0.61	0.46	0.34	0.29	0.31	0.4	0.35
Predictors β										
SAS	0.30*									
Goal		0.60*	0.31*						-0.29*	
Environment		0.22*		-0.18*						
SAS*Goal						0.32*				
SAS* Environment			0.18*		0.22*					
Goal*Environment										
SAS*Goal*Environment										-0.33*
Modification			0.20*	0.20*						
Stability				0.29*						-0.28*
Modification*Stability					0.19*				-0.25*	
Correction			0.19*	0.18*	0.25*					
Application	0.22*		0.25*		0.25*		0.30*	0.51*		
Action variety					0.33*		0.24*		0.27*	
Anticipation			-0.23*		0.22*				-0.23*	
Feedback										

Note. *p<.05; SAS is an abbreviation for Subjective Action Space

Table 7: Regression Analysis for Indian

Predictors β	Interest		Self-confidence		STEM-Activity		Job-Choices		Achievement	
	Boy	Girl	Boy	Girl	Boy	Girl	Boy	Girl	Boy	Girl
R²	0.44	0.66	0.44	0.49	0.22	0.41	0.32	0.25	0.2	0.13
SAS							0.36*	0.21*		
Goal	0.21*	0.28*								
Environment					0.22*					
SAS*Goal										
SAS* Environment		-0.35*							-0.26*	
Goal*Environment							0.28*			
SAS*Goal*Environment										
Modification		0.16*		0.19*					-0.24*	
Stability				0.25*	0.21*					
Modification*Stability										
Correction	-0.19*		0.30*						-0.27*	
Application	0.33*							0.22*		
Action variety						0.28*				
Anticipation			0.38*							
Feedback										

Note.*p< .05; SAS is an abbreviation for Subjective Action Space.

Research Question 4: Is the Actiotope model more useful in explaining differences in Germany or India?

Regression analyses indicate that the Actiotope Model explains similar percentages of Interest in STEM in both countries. Detailed regression results for both countries were shown in Table 8.

Table 8: Regression Analysis for cross-cultural differences.

Predictors'β	Interest German	Interest Indian	Self-confidence German	Self-confidence Indian	STEM-Activity German	STEM-Activity Indian	Job-Choices German	Job-Choices Indian	Achievement German	Achievement Indian
R²	0.55	0.49	0.58	0.39	0.34	0.28	0.22	0.16	0.31	0.12
SAS			0.23*						0.19*	-0.21*
Goal	0.47*	0.22*			0.16*					
Environment	0.19*		-0.12*							
SAS*Goal										
SAS*Environment		-0.29*								
Goal*Environment			0.14*							
SAS*Goal*Environment								0.18*		
Modification		0.13*	0.20*							
Stability			0.19*	0.20*				-0.26*	-0.19*	
Modification*Stability										
Correction			0.23*	0.21*						
Application			0.16*			0.23*			-0.16*	
Action variety	0.12*	0.21*				0.22*	0.36*	0.21*		0.24*
Anticipation				0.26*						
Feedback	0.10*									

Note.*$p<.05$; SAS is an abbreviation for Subjective Action Space.

4   Discussion

This study was conducted to determine whether gender and cross-cultural differences exist among high school students from Germany and India on scales of Interest, Self-confidence, STEM activity, Future job choices and Achievement. In addition, an attempt was made to explain observed inter-individual differences among girls and boys from both countries through the Actiotope Model of Giftedness. The findings of this study will be discussed systematically in three aspects: Gender differences, Cross-cultural differences and Inter-individual differences.

4.1   Gender Differences

A large body of evidence indicates that boys show more interest in science and science-related disciplines than girls (Dawson, 2000; Jones et al., 2000). In contrast to previous studies, it was found in this study that girls from Germany and India displayed slightly greater interest in STEM than boys on average. This difference was found to be significant in Germany but not in India, which was quite unexpected. However, this might be the result of prior relevant experiences not controlled in this study.

Self-confidence is also a psychological construct that has been researched extensively. Many empirical studies have indicated that girls display lower Self-confidence and self-concept regarding their abilities in science and mathematics as compared to boys (Andre, Whigham, Hendrickson, & Chambers, 1999; Marsh, Trautwein, Lüdtke, Köller, & Baumert, 2005). In this study we found that girls in Germany reported to have significantly higher Self-confidence related to STEM fields compared to boys. However, such a significant gender difference in Self-confidence was not observed among Indian boys or girls. The higher values in Self-confidence among German girls were really surprising. Some researchers indicated that the constructs of achievement and self-concept are interrelated, and that higher grades usually mean higher Self-confidence (Marsh et al., 2005). It is possible that German girls who took part in this study were performing well in subjects related to STEM and achieving high grades, which may have influenced their reported Self-confidence.

Results from an exploratory t-test indicated that no significant gender differences existed in both countries on the scales of STEM activity, Future Job choice and Achievement.

4.2   Cross-cultural Differences

This study found no significant differences between German and Indian students on the scales of Interest, Self-confidence and Job choices. However, significant differences were found between German and Indian students on the scales of involvement in STEM activities and Achievement.

It was expected that German students would report higher involvement in STEM activities than Indian students because of cultural and environmental differences. In India, it is uncommon for students to take part in extracurricular activities related to STEM fields. In western countries like Germany, students have more access to a wide range of scientific programs and their regular visit to scientific research facilities and museums are encouraged. But contrary to expectation, German students reported less STEM activities. The possible reason is different standard used by two countries' students. Maybe a German student would think carrying out a STEM experiment once a week is not a big deal, while an Indian student thinks it is an important activity and worth to memorize and report it.

Contrary to expectations, this study found that German students achieved higher grades in science and mathematics compared to Indian students. Recent PISA investigations indicated that Korean students had the best performance among OECD countries in 2009 science and mathematics performance assessment. The partner countries including Shanghai China, Singapore, and Hong Kong China, ranked second and third respectively (OECD, 2009). India was not an OECD member country. However, considering the strong performance of Asian students in science and mathematics, Indian students were expected to have higher achievement scores than German students in science and mathematics. Even though German students had higher achievement scores in this study, the results are not conclusive and do not necessarily suggest that students from Germany are better at science and mathematics than Indian students. The observed differences in achievement need to be analyzed with some caution, given the marked difference in educational system of the two countries. In this study, achievement was measured on the basis of the grades on the last report card in Mathematics, Physics, Chemistry and Biology. Even for the same subject studied by students from Germany and India, there were considerable differences in the curriculum and topics that students were tested on.

4.3   Inter-Individual Differences

The Actiotope Model of giftedness was used to explain inter-individual differences among girls and boys from Germany and India; on scales of Interest, Self-confidence, STEM activity, Future job choices and Achievement. It was predicted that the Actiotope Model would better explain the inter-individual differences among girls from the two countries than among boys. Results indicated no clear pattern to support this prediction. The findings were complex to interpret as different components of the Actiotope Model were important in explaining differences in Interest, Self-confidence, STEM ac-tivity, Future job choices and Achievement amongst girls and boys.

No conclusions could be drawn regarding whether the Actiotope Model better explained inter-individual differences in Interest, Self-confidence, STEM activities, Future job choices and Achievement among girls or boys. However, data from regression analysis indicate that the explained variance for each of the 5 variables investigated in this study was always higher among students from Germany than among students from India. These findings do suggests that the Actiotope Model is more useful in explaining Interest, Self-confidence, STEM activities, Future job choices and Achievement among students from Germany than from India. Although the model appeared to be more useful in Germany, different sets of predictors were found to be important in explaining the observed variances. Therefore, it remained inconclusive as to which components of the Actiotope Model were really crucial in explaining the observed differences on each of the scales investigated.

4.4   Limitations

There are several limitations which need to be considered when interpreting the data and drawing conclusions. The questionnaire had 15 scales with a minimum of 5 items to measure each scale. Such a large number of scales and items made the study complex and data analysis difficult. The questionnaire needs to be simplified by reducing the number of scales and items before it is used again in a cross-cultural comparative study. For the purpose of this study, 12- to 13-year old students were chosen to participate. We speculate that older children about to graduate from high school may have a more stable opinion regarding aspects such as Future job choices in STEM.

4.5   Future Outlook and Research

Although components of the Actiotope Model did help the further understanding of the behaviour of girls with respect to Interest, Self-confidence, involvement in STEM activities, Future job choices and Achievement in science and math; there is not enough evidence to suggest that the model is useful in explaining the problem of underrepresentation of women in STEM careers. In order to further explore this issue, all components of the model need to be investigated. Moreover, this study should be repeated with an older group of participants. Researchers should also consider conducting a longitudinal investigation, which can help bring more clarity to the timeline of the development of such aspects as interest and Self-confidence related to STEM.   This study did not attempt to explain gender differences among girls and boys via the Actiotope Model, requiring more exploration in subsequent studies. As the explanation of gender differences between girls and boys is crucial to understand the problem of underrepresentation of women in STEM careers, continued cross-cultural comparisons of the model are essential to increase the Actiotope Model's empirical support in interpreting gender difference.

References

Andre, T., Whigham, M., Hendrickson, A., & Chambers, S. (1999). Competency beliefs, positive affect and gender stereotypes of elementary students and their parents about science versus other school subjects. *Journal of Research in Science Teaching, 36*, 719-747.

Brotman, J. S., & Moore, F. M. (2008). Girls and Science: A reviw of four themes in the science education literature. *Journal of Research in Science Teaching, 45*(9), 971-1002.

Catsambis, S. (1995). Gender, race, ethnicity and science education in the middle grades. *Journal of Research in Science Teaching, 32*, 243-257.

Dawson, C. (2000). Upper primary boys' and girls' interest in science: Have they changed since 1980? *International Journal of Science Education, 22*, 557-570.

Eccles, J. S., Bonnie, B., & Jozefowica. (1999). Linking Gender to Educational, Occupational, and Recreational Choice: Applying the Eccles et al. Model of Achievement -Related Choices. In W. B. Swann, J. H. Langlois & L. A. Gilbert (Eds.), *Sexism and Stereotypes in Modern Society: The Gender Science of Janet Taylor Spence* (pp. 153-191). Washington D.C.: American Psychological Association.

Else-Quest, N. M., Hyde, J. S., & Linn, M. C. (2010). Cross national patterns of gender differences in mathematics: A meta-analysis. *Psychological Bulletin, 136*(1), 103-127.

Ginther, D. K., & Kahn, S.. (2009). Does science promote women? Evidence from academia 1973-2001. In R. B. Freeman & D. L. Goroff (Eds.), *Science and Engineering Careers in the United States* (pp. 163-194). Chicago: University of Chicago Press.

Halpern, D. F., Benbow, C. P., Geary, D. C., Gur, R. C., Hyde, J. S., & Gernsbacher, M. A. (2007). The Science of Sex Differences in Science and Mathematics. *Psychological Science in the Public Interest, 8*(1), 1-51.

Jones, M. G., Howe, A., & Rua, M. J. (2000). Gender differences in students' experiences, interests and attitudes towards science and scientists. *Science Education, 84*, 181-192.

Marsh, H. W., Trautwein, U., Lüdtke, C., Köller, O., & Baumert, J. (2005). Academic self-concept, interest, grades and standardised test scores : Reciprocal effects models of causal ordering. *Child Development, 76*(2), 397-416.

NSF (2007). *Employed women 16 years and older as a percentage of selected occupations*. Arlington, VA: National Science Foundation.

OECD (2009). *PISA 2009 Results: What students know and can do: Student performance in reading, mathematics and science*. Paris: Organization for Economic Co-Operation and Development.

Santiago, A. M., & Einarson, M. K. (1998). Background characteristics as predictors of academic Self-confidence and academic self-efficacy among graduate science and engineering students. *Research in Higher Education, 39*(2), 163-198.

Scantlebury, K., & Baker, D. (1998). Gender issues in science education research: Remembering where the difference lies. In S. K. Abell & N. G. Lederman (Eds.), *Handbook of Research on Science Education* (pp. 257-285). Lawrence Erlbaum Associates.

Ziegler, A. (2005a). The Actiotope Model of Giftedness. In R. J. Sternberg & J. E. Davidson (Eds.), *Conceptions of Giftedness* (pp. 411-436). Cambridge: Cambridge University Press.

Ziegler, A. (2005b). *Actiotope Questionnaire*. Uni Paper Nr-17. University of Ulm. Ulm.

Ziegler, A., Dresel, M., & Schober, B. (1998). *Messung motivationsbezogener Schüler(innen)merkmale [Measurement of students motivation.]*. Ludwig-Maximilians-Universität, Munich.

Ziegler, A., & Stoeger, H. (2005). The role of counseling in development of gifted students' actiotopes: Theoretical background and exemplary application. In S. Mendaglio & J. S. Peterson (Eds.), *Models of Counseling Gifted Children, Adolescents and Young Adults* (pp. 253-283). Waco, TX: Prufrock Press.

Ziegler, A., & Stoeger, H. (2008). Effect of role models from films on short term ratings of intent, interest and self-assessment of ability by high school youth: A study if gender-stereotyped academic subjects. *Psychological Reports, 102*(2), 509-531.

Magdalena Kist

Sociotopes, Actiotopes, and English Achievement

Abstract

In the focus of this chapter are the factors that influence second language learning and school performance (as an indicator of the outcome of the learning process). In an empirical study an attempt is made to define these factors more closely and look at them from a systemic perspective. Firstly a short overview of theories of the development of (school) performance and foreign language learning is given. Secondly the sociotope theory that serves as theoretical basis for the empirical study represented in this chapter is explained in detail. Thereby sociotopes are typical situation clusters that either are conducive, neutral or detrimental for learning. Thirdly the method and the results of an empirical study with 96 seventh grade students are reported. In this study it was investigated whether achievements in second language instruction can be predicted by actiotope and sociotope variables. The basic assumption of the research was confirmed, namely that the explanation of achievements has to take systemic variables into account. Finally conclusions from these results are outlined.

1   Predictors of performance in second language instruction

Learning a second language is influenced by many factors which haven't been precisely defined yet. There is no definite theory about the structure, the formation and the development of foreign language competence. But it is commonly accepted that "The acquisition of language is, no doubt, a thoroughly social phenomenon. (…) In fact any acquisitional situation is extremely complex in terms of the number of factors that may constitute the total situation. It can reasonably be assumed that the total number of such factors is infinite. (…) It is nonetheless necessary that it be determined how these many factors interact with respect to how human beings learn languages (Wode, 1981, p.26)." But although the number of influencing factors is indefinite it can not be questioned that internal as well as external factors influence achievement in the learning process (Ellis, 1985). An indicator for the result of this learning process is the school achievement. But also the construct of school achievement underlies different determinants. For several years now the pedagogical psychology has been trying to determine predictors of school achievement. In the centre of attention of recent studies are frequently cognitive, motivational and affective determinants or the learning environment at school or at home (Helmke & Weinert, 1997; Helmke & Schrader, 2001a). But due to the multiple determination based on the variety of factors involved in the process this hasn't been achieved so far. Nevertheless there is a scientific consensus that the individual as well as his/ her surrounding have an impact on school achievement (Heller, 1997; Krapp, Prenzel, & Weidenmann, 2001; Helmke & Schrader, 2001b) but in how far these determinants take effect is not clarified. Even if we don't know so far what influences the learning process of a foreign language and its outcome in terms of school performance, it became clear that it is necessary to understand the system of the individual and his/her external environment and then single determinants of performance, functioning in reciprocal dependency, can be defined. The Actiotope Theory (Ziegler, 2005) as an action theory which has already been presented in detail (this volume) shows that there is a bidirectional interdependency between the actions of an individual and the environment. That means that the actions a person fulfills in order to learn something contribute to the learning outcome. It is assumed that for the explanation of performance in a special domain (like second language learning) the environment an individual interacts with must also be taken into consideration in order to determine how performance can be predicted. This implies that the performance in second language instruction should be considered from the perspective of a systemic theory. As the environment consists of multiple components such as resources, settings, social actors etc. it is necessary to configure different sub-categories. Easily conceivable are sociotopes as such sub-categories (Ziegler, 2010).

2   Sociotope Theory

"Sociotope" designates the contextual conditions of individual actions (Ziegler, 2010). Sociotopes are situation clusters. With regard to learning processes and influencing factors on performance they can be distinguished whether they are conducive, neutral or detrimental for learning.

Table 1: Typology of sociotopes (referring to Ziegler, 2010)

Objective Action Space	Normative Action Space		
	Learning is considered as		
	positive	negative	neither nor
Learning is possible	Learning Sociotope	Restrictive Sociotope	Infrastructural Sociotope
Learning is not possible	Thematic Sociotope	Antagonistic Sociotope	Competitive Sociotope

Table one shows that sociotopes consist first of an objective action space. From this it follows that specific actions, considered from an objective perspective, are possible to fulfill in a sociotope. But only a few are actually accomplished. Second the sociotope exhibits the normative action space. This aspect takes into account that the individual learns during his/her lifetime which actions are usually approved of. The above-mentioned sociotopes can be analyzed on the basis of two questions:

Which actions within the scope of the learning process are possible to accomplish (implementations of opportunity for actions)?

How strong is the normative pressure of the specific sociotope that actions which are conducive for the learning process are accomplished (Ziegler, 2009, p.24)?

In this context it is important to make clear that the individual itself plays a substantial role. The realization of implemented and institutionalized actions in his/ her subjective action space is depending on the respective person.

Learning Sociotopes are designed for the progress in learning. They are highly effective and well suited for the individual needs of each learner. They facilitate learning. Therefore the objective action space admits actions which are conducive for the learning process. The normative action space includes actions which lead to advanced learning. Infrastructural Sociotopes enable actions which can lead to a learning progress but they are facultative. In most cases this type of sociotope serves as a basis for the accomplishment of specific actions. Thematic Sociotopes are characterized by the positive encouragement for learning through social actors. This leads to the point that a specific domain is esteemed. But there are no objective possibilities for a learning process. Competitive Sociotopes prohibit learning processes but an explicit rejection does not exist.

In contrast to the Antagonistic Sociotope in which the engagement in the domain or the tracking of learning targets is sanctioned or respectively declined. Also in Restrictive Sociotopes actions underlying the learning process are limited and receive no support.

It becomes apparent that learning processes and their results, that means the visible performance in a specific domain, obviously correlate with the sociotopes a learning person interacts with. That means that the environment contributes in a large part to the learning outcome. For this reason it is in the focus of the empirical study represented below. With regard to the performance in English as a first foreign language it has to be hypothesized that the achievement in English is predictable on the basis of actiotope- and sociotope variables. Moreover should it be possible to distinguish the high performing from the average performing children with the help of these variables. Differences in the performance issue firstly from the accessibility of an environment which is conducive for learning and secondly from the components, mechanisms and the attributes of the respective actiotope. Both of them correlate with a student's performance in English.

3   Method

Participant
A sample of 96 children attending an urban secondary school participated in the study. It consists of 42 boys and 54 girls learning English as first foreign language.

Procedure
The data was collected with the help of two instruments. A standardized test measuring language skills in English (Harder & Ziegler, 2009) and a questionnaire where the instruments utilized. All testing took place in the classrooms and lasted 45 minutes. First the students had to work on the standardized test subsequently they completed the questionnaire. The children were tested in groups which were formed by the respective classes.

Instruments
Standardized English Test: In order to gain a realistic assessment of the actual performance in English of each pupil they had to work on a standardized test. It gathers the following fields of language competence: word-production, vocabulary, orthography, phonetic knowledge,reading comprehension, and grammar. This test boasts a reliability of Cronbach's alpha $\alpha = .86$ and guarantees an efficient testing. The test implementation only takes 20 minutes as each exercise has a time limit.

Questionnaire: The Questionnaire consists of 16 scales with 80 items. The function is to gather data underlying the analysis of the actiotope and the sociotopes. It is designed in a forced choice answering shape with a four-step

Likert-Scale. It consists of the following answer options: 1 = not correct, 2 = rather not correct, 3 = rather correct and 4 = correct.

The first part of the questionnaire refers to the actiotope of the respective pupil. The scales are based on mechanisms, components and characteristics of the Actiotope Model of Giftedness (Ziegler, 2005). That implies that there are ten scales with five items per scale (one item of each scale is presented as an example below). The scales are: Subjective Action Space ("Frequently I realize that I've evaluated my foreign language skills wrong"), Goals ("It is important to me to improve my foreign language skills"), Learning Environment ("It is important to my teachers that I show good performances in foreign language instruction") Correctness ("Usually I know whether I've learnt enough for a test or not"), Applicability ("It is difficult for me to apply my knowledge in foreign languages to different tasks"), Variation of Actions ("I always try to find new procedures of solution in the foreign language learning"), Anticipation ("I always try to prepare myself early enough for the foreign language instruction so that nothing unexpected happens"), Feedback ("My teachers always tell me what I have to improve in my foreign language learning"), Modifiability ("It would be easy for me to learn more in foreign languages") and Stability ("I am content with my foreign language learning").

The Learning Environment which plays an important role is examined in detail with the help of the sociotope scales. In doing so the current sociotopes should be identified. The scales correspond to the sociotope theory: Learning Sociotope, Infrastructural Sociotope, Restrictive Sociotope, Antagonistic Sociotope, Thematic Sociotope and Competitive Sociotope. The reliability of the questionnaire is Cronbach's alpha $\alpha = 0.62$.

Analysis

In order to answer the question which predictors on the basis of the sociotope and actiotope variables do exist a regression analysis with stepwise regressions has been calculated (pin = 0.05, pout = 0.10). To find out whether these predictors are valid for high performers as well as for average performers a t-test for independent samples and a binary logistic regression have been administered. In the t-test the sample was divided into groups depending on their performance on the standardized English test. This lead to two groups: the group of high performance (N=19) resp. the upper 20% and the group of average performance (N=77) or the lower 80%. The 80/20 rule of Gardner (2003) underlies this classification and says that 20% of the people are able to show higher performances than the average.

In the binary logistic regression the subject group was divided into two performance groups, which encompasses the upper 20% and the lower 80%. In the next step a binary logistic regression was calculated. The actiotope and sociotope variables served as predictors and the group variable as dependent variable.

4   Results

The objective of the empirical study was to determine predictors of the achievement of foreign language instruction. It became clear that this is only possible with considering external and internal factors influencing the learning process. In this context the question was whether an approach is possible on the basis of actiotope and sociotope variables. Therefore it was first important to find out if there are correlations between actiotope- and sociotope variables and the performance in English. Correlations showed that there definitely is a connection between these variables. The scales Subjective Action Space ($r = .44$), Applicability ($r = .34$) and Stability ($r = .31$) correlate with English achievement. Therefore the knowledge about the actions which are possible to accomplish, the applicability of actions out of the action repertoire as well as the stability of the actiotope are strongly associated with the performance in English.

With regard to the sociotope variables a negative correlation between the performance in the standardized Englishtest and the Learning Sociotope ($r = -.21$) and also the Restrictive Sociotope ($r = -.21$) is reported. This negative correlation is not according to expectations because this implies that spending less time in a Learning Sociotope contributes to good performances. But this could also be an indication that environments that are supportive for learning processes do not necessarily directly influence performance. A negative correlation between the Restrictive Sociotope and the performance meets expectations. The less time a person spends in a surrounding which is detrimental for learning processes the better the performances get.

5   Predictors of English language proficiency

Table 2: Results of the Regression analysis. Standardized β-weights, T-value and significant p-values for predicting English language proficiency (only significant predictors reported)

Predictor	β	ΔR^2	p
Subjective Action Space	.47	0.19	.001
Anticipation	.35	0.10	.001
Antagonistic Sociotope	-.24	0.04	.01
Applicability	.24	0.03	.03

The results in Table two show that there are four factors on the basis of actiotope und sociotope variables which can predict the language proficiency. The strongest predictor, the Subjective Action Space cleared 19% of the variance. Anticipation, Antagonistic Sociotope and Applicability generated incremental explained variance of 10%, 4% and 3%. The explained variance came to $R^2 = 0.36$, what is a substantial explained variance with regards to the reliabilities of the predictors.

On the basis of these results pupils who are able to show average to good performances are characterized as follows: they learn in an anticipative way with regards to a high applicability of their knowledge and they contrive means and ways to cope with difficult learning situations. Furthermore they spent less time with people who reject learning of foreign languages. The results lead to the question in how far do these predictors hold true for pupils showing high performances.

6   Influencing factors on the performances of high and average performing students

It becomes obvious that there are fundamental differences in the performance in the English test. The mean values of the overall performance differ about .20 between the 20% of high performing pupils and the 80% of average performing pupils. High performance ($M =.46$, $SD =.06$) in the context of this test means, regarding the mean value, that almost half of the exercises could be solved in a correct way. The average performance ($M = .26$, $SD =.06$) lies clearly lower.

Performance must be related with the actiotope and sociotope variables. For this purpose the peculiarity of the characteristics, mechanisms and components of the actiotope as well as of the different forms of sociotopes is compared between the average and the high performing students on the basis of the mean value and the standard deviation initially in a descriptive analysis.

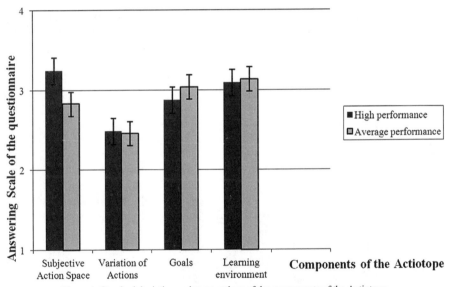

Figure 1: Standard deviation and mean values of the components of the Actiotope

Figure one shows that on a descriptive level the variation of actions and the learning environment seems to be almost equal in both groups. The average performers tend to show a clearer goal definition than the high performers. But only the difference between de Subjective Action Space of high performers and average performers with t(94) = 3.05, $p < 0.01$ is significant.

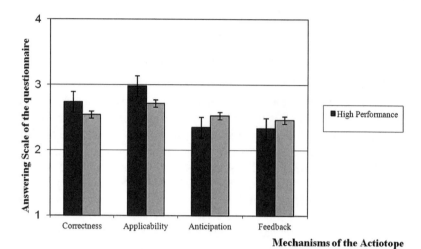

Figure 2: Standard deviation and mean values of the mechanisms of the Actiotope

Figure two shows that the correctness of actions seems to be more distinct with high performers. But anticipation and feedback tend to be lower when showing high performance. Statistically significant is the Applicability with t(93) = 1.78, $p < 0.05$.

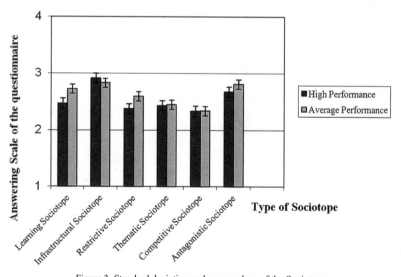

Figure 3: Standard deviation and mean values of the Sociotopes

Figure three shows that only the Infrastructural Sociotope of high performers seem to be different from the average performers. With regard to the Thematic Sociotope and the Competitive Sociotope only small differences between the mean values become apparent. The Learning Sociotope as well as the Antagonistic Sociotope of average performers could be distinct. But significant is only the Restrictive Sociotope $t(92) = -2.0$, $p < 0.05$. Descriptives indicate differences between the two performance groups concerning the components, mechanisms and types of sociotopes. But also the characteristics of an actiotope namely modify-ability and stability differ between the performance groups. Stability got significant with $t(92) = 2.73$, $p < 0.01$. On the basis of a t-Test for independent samples these differences can statistically be secured and from these results we gain the picture of a prototypical high performer. He/ She posesses a high Subjective Action Space and he/ she is able to use his/her knowledge in different contexts and is therefore able to manage difficult situations. But yet the stability of the actiotope is high. With regard to the environment it seems to be important that the learner spends less time in an environment that is detrimental for learning.

These data show that there are definitely differences between the actiotope and sociotope variables of high and average performers. But it seems interesting to determine factors that can predict to which group one belongs. Thereby the predictors which differentiate high performers from average performers were focused in the following.

7   Predictors of performance of high performing students

Four predictors on the 5% level could be determined. Two additional predictors are marginally significant with a significance level less than .10. Significant are the predictors Subjective Action Space (*Wald* = 3.92, *p* < 0.05), Variation of Actions (*Wald* = 2.92, *p* < 0.05), Anticipation (*Wald* = 5.51, *p* < 0.05) and Antagonistic Sociotope (*Wald* = 3.23, *p* < 0.05). Marginally significant are Correctness (*Wald* = 1.70, *p* < 0.10) and Restrictive Sociotope (*Wald* = 2.66, *p* < 0.10). With *Wald* = 29.56, *ß* = 1.42, *p* <.001 it becomes apparent that a good sorting by means of the independent variables is possible. *Cox & Snell R²* as well as *Nagelkerkes R²* serve as so called Pseudo-*R²*-coefficients which can be applied to evaluate the model fit. They are .29 respectively .47. That indicates substantial possibilities of prediction.

These results show that a high performing pupil can control his/ her learning process (Subjective Action Space) and the process is more efficient (rich in variation of actions, anticipative with classification of the results). Furthermore the learning takes place in supportive environments (these pupils rarely stay in Antagonistic and Restrictive Sociotopes). As the sample was divided in an asymmetric way it is not possible to get a better result of classification as the overall percentage of 80.6%.

8   Conclusions

With the aid of the main leading questions of this empirical study the conclusions based on the data analysis are summarized as follows:

Do the actiotope and the sociotope variables correlate and is it possible to define the environment, which is part of the Actiotope Model of Giftedness, on the basis of the Sociotope Theory? Feedback, Learning Environment and Variation of Actions correlate highly with the different forms of sociotopes. The Antagonistic Sociotope, the Infrastructural Sociotope as well as the Learning Sociotope correlate frequently with the actiotope variables. This results in the confirmation of the hypothesis that the environment variable in the Actiotope Model of Giftedness can be defined in greater detail with the help of the Sociotope Theory. As a consequence the influence of the environment on an individual can be observed in a more specific way. The combination of those theoretical approaches, of the Actiotope Model of Giftedness and the Sociotope Theory, is essential for the systematic analysis of the realization of school performance.

Is it possible to explain achievement in English with the help of actiotope and sociotope variables? In a regression analysis four predictors explaining achievements in English could be determined: Subjective Action Space, Anticipation, Antagonistic Sociotope and Applicability. These results show, that performance in English is based on the following factors:

The learner's Subjective Action Space is well developed, that means that a great number of actions are feasible

The learner chooses appropriate and effective actions out of the personal action repertoire which contains a lot of different actions

The learner is able to act and learn in an anticipative way

The learner spends little time in environments in which learning isn't possible and is evaluated in a negative way.

These predictors also confirm that the development of English performance is attributable to endogenous and exogenous factors. In addition this ratifies the assumption that school achievement always must be seen from a systemic perspective. These predictors give evidence which factors are involved in the process of development of school achievement. This is relevant for the conception of affirmative actions.

Is it possible to distinguish between high performers and average performers on the basis of actiotope and sociotope variables? Differences between those two performance groups are confirmed with regard to their actiotope and their learning environment. Data shows that high performers have a larger Subjective Action Space and a more stable Actiotope. They can apply a specific action in a more effective way and above all they spend less time in Restrictive Sociotopes. By means of the above-named factors high performers can be distinguished from average performers.

Which predictors for high performance on the basis of actiotope and sociotope variables do exist? The results of the regression analysis show that the probability of showing high performances is influenced by four factors. In common with the results of the linear regression analysis Subjective Action Space, Anticipation and Antagonistic Sociotope also turn out to be convenient predictors to identify high performers. In addition the variation of actions is another significant predictor. That means that the learner is able to vary the actions according to the respective context. Of marginal importance is that the learner realizes which actions are effective and lead to a defined goal and that the learner spends little time in environments where learning would be possible but is evaluated as negative.

The reults of the empirical study lead to the assumption that the above-named actiotope variables are better shaped with high performers. Moreover data shows that both the Actiotope Model of Giftedness and the Sociotope Theory are adapted for analyzing the achievement of foreign language instruction from a systemic perspective. The combination of the Actiotope Model of Giftedness with the Sociotope Theory is appropriate to gather the multiple determination of school performance and to consider the different influencing factors. It is important, especially for teachers, to be aware of the dynamic within the surroundings in which students learn and develop the foreign language skills and also their knowledge in general. It is necessary that teachers create learning environments which take this into account especially for the purpose of an individual learning facilitaton. Data also showed that there are predictors for high performance and on their basis high performers can be identified and differentiated from the average performers. But it is not enough to identify the high performers even more relevant is to nurture the mechanisms, characteristics and components which are specific for the actiotope of high performers as well to create types of sociotopes which are supportive for learning. The same applies to the average performers. In this way it might be possible to facilitate every student in the most effective way.

References

Ellis, R. (1985) *Understanding Second Language Acquisition.* Oxford: Oxford University Press.

Gardner, H. (2003). Three distinct meanings of Intelligence. In R.J. Sternberg; J. Lautrey & T.I. Lubart (Eds.), *Models of Intelligence. International Perspectives* (pp 43-54). Washington D.C.: American Psychological Association.

Harder, B., & Ziegler, A. (2009). *Englisch Leistungstest für 5.-7. Jahrgangsstufe.[English Achievement Test for 5th to 7th grade].* Testinventory in prep.

Heller, K.A. (1997). Individuelle Bedingungsfaktoren der Schulleistung: Literaturüberlick. [Individual determinants of school achievement. A literature overview] In F.E. Weinert & A. Helmke (Eds.), *Entwicklung im Grundschulalter [Development in the Elementary school age]* (pp.183-201). Weinheim: Beltz.

Helmke, A., & Weinert, F.E. (1997). Bedingungsfaktoren schulischer Leistung [Determinants of school achievement]. In F.E. Weinert (Ed.), *Psychologie des Unterrichts und der Schule [Psychology of Instruction and School]*. Enzyklopädie der Psychologie, Serie Pädagogische Psychologie (pp.71-176). Göttingen; Bern: Hogrefe.

Helmke, A., & Schrader, F.W. (2001a). Determinanten der Schulleistung [Determinants of school achievement]. In D.H. Rost (Ed.) *Handwörterbuch Pädagogische Psychologie [Concise Dictionary Pedagogical Psychology]*(pp.81-91). Weinheim: Beltz.

Helmke, A., & Schrader, F.W. (2001b). Jenseits von TIMSS: Messungen sprachlicher Kompetenzen, komplexe Längsschnittstudien und kulturvergleichende Analysen. Ergebnisse und Perspektiven ausgewählter Leistungsstudien [Beyond TIMMS. Measurements of language competence, complex longitudinal studies and cross cultural analyses. Results and perspectives of selected achievement study] In F.E. Weinert (Ed.), *Leistungsmessungen in Schulen [Performance measurement in schools]* (pp.237-250). Weinheim und Basel: Beltz.

Krapp, A, Prenzel, M., & Weidenmann, B. (2001). Geschichte, Gegenstandsbereich und Aufgaben der Pädagogischen Psychologie [History, subject area and tasks of Pedagogical Psychologie]. In A. Weidenmann & B. Krapp (Eds.), *Pädagogische Psychologie [Pedagogical Psychology]* (pp.1-29). Weinheim: Beltz.

Wode, H. (1981). *Learning a Second Language. An Integrated View of Language Acquisition.* Tübingen: Narr.

Ziegler, A. (2005). The actiotope model of giftedness. In J.E. Davidson & R. Sternberg (Eds.) *Conceptions of giftedness* (pp.411-434). Cambridge, UK: Cambridge University Press.

Ziegler, A. (2009). "Ganzheitliche Förderung" umfasst mehr als nur die Person: Aktiotop- und Soziotopförderung [Holistic Facilitation includes more than the individual. Actiotope- and Sociotope Facilitation]. *Heilpädagogik Online* (8), 5-24.

Ziegler, A. (2010). Lernsoziotope. Zur Ausschöpfung der Lernpotenziale gehört eine anregende Lernumwelt [Learning Sociotopes. An inspiring environment is necessary for the exhaustion of Learning Sociotopes]. In *Rückblick und Ausblick. 10 Jahr Jubiläum Stiftung für hochbegabte Kinder [Review and Prospect. 10th anniversary of the foundation for gifted children]*. Retrieved from:
    http://www.hochbegabt.ch/documents/3/broschuere_10_jahr_jubil%C3%A4um.pdf

Katharina Schurr

Counseling at the 'State-Wide Counseling and Research Center for the Gifted at Ulm University' (LBFH)1 – A Case Study

Abstract

The 'State-Wide Counseling and Research Centre for the Gifted at Ulm University' (Germany) diagnoses, counsels and promotes gifted children and adolescents. The theoretical approach is described in the ENTER-Model (Ziegler & Stoeger 2004; Grassinger 2009) and based on the Actiotope Model of Giftedness (Ziegler 2005, 2008, 2009, 2011). The systemic counseling approach aims at implementing an optimal, individually tailored learning process in regard to the gifted child or adolescent to promote his/her development towards higher levels of expertise. Therefore it requires a comprehensive knowledge of the client's Actiotope comprising personal and environmental characteristics. Based on this information, a learning track is constructed to reach the individual goals (make up for deficits, extend competences in all relevant areas) and is put into practice with the counselor's support. The complete counseling process will be illustrated by means of the case study of 6;4 year old Leon.

---

[1] LBFH: Landesweite Beratungs- und Forschungsstelle für Hochbegabung, rebuilt at the University Erlangen-Nürnberg

Introduction

Counseling of the gifted is often understood to be a "diagnosis without subsequent promotion". Counseling at the 'State-Wide Counseling and Research Center for the Gifted at Ulm University' offers - besides diagnosis - also a promotion in form of an individual learning track. The counseling is based on the Actiotope Model of Ziegler (2005). Its systemic perspective, progressive adaption and holistic view are essential for the counseling model described in this chapter.

In the first part of this chapter I will explain the theoretical approach of the counseling center. The ENTER-Model (Ziegler & Stoeger 2004, 2009; Grassinger 2009) is described as a model which comprises all reasons of counseling gifted children and adolescents. ENTER subdivides the counseling in five phases: Explore, Narrow, Transform, Evaluate and Review. The first two phases are part of an extensive diagnosis and the other three phases constitute and assess the learning track. Grassinger's (2009) ENTER-Triple L-Model comprises three counseling levels. In the second part of this chapter I will give an example of a counseling case. It illustrates the application of the systemic counseling approach within the framework of the ENTER-Triple L-Model.

1   Theoretical approach of counseling

Counseling at the 'State-Wide Counseling and Research Center for the Gifted at Ulm University' is based on the Actiotope Model of Giftedness (Ziegler, 2005). The systemic approach, its components, the holistic view and the progressive adaption is described in a previous chapter by Harder in this book and will not be outlined further here. In the following sections the main focus will be the counseling process based on this approach.

Counseling is a process of interaction between counselor and client, with the aim at improving willingness to help themselves, self-control ability and action competence (Barthelmeß, 2001; Nestmann, 1992). These abilities will help to improve the current situation with regard to the specific environment of the person seeking advice. He/she should be able to develop appropriate strategies and implement them when faced with challenges, problems and pending decisions.

1.1   Reasons for counseling

In regard to gifted children, they should be counseled for primary, secondary and tertiary preventive reasons (Caplan, 1964), thereby solving problems before they arise or become too large.

- *Primary preventive reasons*

Many parents contact the counseling center because they are confused about the otherness of their child in comparison to the peers (Wittmann, 2003). They report that their child is bored in kindergarten or at school, is not challenged and behaves conspicuously. Their primary focus is on diagnosing talent, collecting information and providing appropriate promotion opportunities (Elbing, 2000; Schilling et al., 2002). Parents hope to find information pertaining e.g. to early enrollment, skipping a class and appropriate schools.

- *Secondary preventive reasons*

Secondary prevention counseling deals with current problems, which jeopardize the Actiotope of the child. Underachievement is the most frequent cause of counseling (Elbing, 2000). Also, attention deficits, perfectionism, depression and refusing to learn (Elbing, 2000; Wittmann, 2003) are among the secondary tasks of counseling.

In the social sector highly gifted children can be isolated. Parents report that their child has difficulties in dealing with peers or is a victim of mobbing. Furthermore, the teacher student relationship can be problematic.

The environment often reacts ignorantly when confronted with giftedness. When parents confront teachers with the subject of their child's giftedness and the necessary support, they do not always find understanding among teachers. Therefore the clients seek advice from the counselor in this regard and also on educational matters.

- *Tertiary preventive reasons*

Giftedness when understood as having high-level basic or innate skills is not the only predictor for future performance excellence. According to Ericsson, Roring and Nandagopal (2007) at least 10.000 hours of efficient training are necessary to achieve excellence. This training must be done professionally and requires great effort and motivation on the part of the learner. The term *deliberate practice* has been specially marked by Ericsson, Krampe and Tesch-Römer (1993). *Deliberate practice* stands for the effective learning efforts with professional feedback. A key predictor for the achievement of performance excellence is outstanding learning opportunities (Ziegler & Perleth, 1997). The tertiary preventive counseling task promotes the learning process with the aim at achieving excellence.

1.2   ENTER – A Model of Counseling

The initial letters of the acronym ENTER stand for Explore, Narrow, Testing, Evaluate and Review. These terms designate phases in the diagnostic process and can be applied with any theoretical framework. Accordingly, the Actiotope Model of Giftedness constitutes a framework for ENTER (Ziegler & Stoeger, 2004, 2007). The systemic approach considers the individuality of the client, his/her goals and his/her environment in a holistic manner.

Grassinger (2009) developed this identification approach to the ENTER-Triple L- Model and implemented the counseling of gifted children and adolescents according to this model at the 'State-Wide Counseling and Research Center for Giftedness' at Ulm University. Diagnosis and counseling of Grassinger's EN-

TER- Triple L-Model aim at improving the adaption between individual and environment for an effective learning track, in short: The diagnosis is designed to promote. The counseling is carried out on three levels as shown in the following illustration.

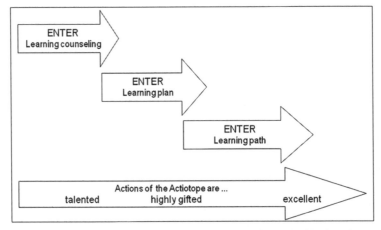

Figure 1: The ENTER-Triple L-Model by Grassinger (2009), translated by the author

If the child needs more promotion, suffers due to mobbing, shows signs of underachievement or other performance hindrances then *learning counseling* is indicated. This kind of counseling aims at promoting the child in cognitive, social and emotional ways, so that it can perform talented actions. Thus *learning counseling* possibly constitutes the beginning of a lengthy learning process with the aim at attaining high achievements within a domain.

The *learning plan* is useful if the child displays well above average talented actions and should be applied intensively over several months. This type of counseling helps an individual to develop highly gifted actions in his/her domain.

The *learning path* aims at achieving excellent actions in a domain. It supports the client and his/her Actiotope over a period of several years with the expectation of publications and awards in the academic section (Grassinger, 2009).

1.3   The ENTER-Phases of the *learning counseling* by Grassinger (2009):

At the 'State-Wide Counseling and Research Center for the Gifted at Ulm University' most clients start off with Grassinger's *learning counseling* because children rarely have shown gifted actions in a domain when first seeking professional advice. The clients usually seek counseling for primary or secondary preventive reasons. That is why this process of learning counseling is described in detail and exemplified by a case study. Each of the ENTER-Phases in *learning counseling* includes a specific diagnosis and counseling tasks which are summarized in figure 2.

Explore	• Initial contact by telephone • General data from parents' perspective of the Actiotope by questionnaire • General data from educator's perspective of the Actiotope by questionnaire
Narrow	• L- and Q-data of the Actiotope by parents interview • L- and Q-data of the Actiotope by child interview and T-data by intelligence and other tests • Preparation of a learning track towards talented actions
Transform	• Presentation of results from the diagnostic phase and the previous learning track in form of a psychological report • Determining the following learning track in a talk with the family • Where applicable: Instruction of a portfolio • Summary of agreements and discussed distribution of tasks between the individuals involved
Evaluate	• Parents and child meetings for the formative evaluation of the implementation of individual promoting measures • Where applicable, presentation of selected products from the portfolio by the child with feedback by the counselor • If necessary further discussions with persons from the child's environment, such as educator, ...
Review	• Possibly, further presentation of selected learning products from the portfolio by the child and feedback through the counselor • Summary evaluation of existing promotion measures • Outlook to future promotion possibilities, such as *Learning plan* • Feedback from parents and child regarding the counseling event • Documentation by the counselor

Figure 2: Enter-Phases by Grassinger, 2009; translated by the author

▪ *Explore-Phase*

First, a comprehensive L- (life) and Q- (questionnaire) data (Cattell, 1973; Ziegler & Stoeger, 2003) collection is required to record, the components of the Actiotope of the individual. Also data of the system quality, e.g. flexibility and stability, and the development of the Actiotope is collected. This data from different perspectives will be ascertained by the initial telephone contact and by the following parents' and educators' questionnaire.

The initial telephone contact gives information about contact data and particularly about the reason for counseling. Also the clients receive information about the counseling process and the aims at the counseling. A guide for the initial contact on the phone is a half standardized interview. Due to the fact that the counseling should be done on the basis of trust, the first contact affords an empathic behavior on the part of the counselor (Grassinger, 2009). For clinically relevant counseling reasons, such as ADHD disorder or depression, the counselor passes on the addresses of competent psychiatric and therapeutic facilities.

The L- and Q-data in the form of open and closed questions are recorded in the parents' questionnaires. In addition to general L-data about the child and the parents there are questions about specific characteristics of the child and its environment and about past history. The third part of the questionnaire identifies accomplishments and requirements, learning habits and performance, interpersonal and psychological area, and data about school and family. Furthermore the parents' record all of the child's activities during the week in this questionnaire. Likewise to get a diversity of perspectives of the child's Actiotope, the educator of the kindergarten or the teacher fill out a similar structured questionnaire. Moreover the parents are requested to bring previous psychological opinions if available, like school reports and special performance records to the first meeting in the counseling center (Grassinger, 2009).

- *Narrow-Phase*

In the Narrow-Phase of the ENTER-Triple L-Model further L-, Q-, and T (test)-data are recorded. The difference to the Explore-Phase is the increased focus on the reason for counseling. Further amnesic explorations occur in a parent-counselor interview during the first meeting in the counseling center. Grassinger (2009) recommends for this interview checklists regarding the Actiotope.

In the framework of the child's or adolescent's interview further L-data regarding the Actiotope are collected. More Q- and T-data are recorded by two different IQ-tests, and if necessary by further concentration tests and questionnaires on the learning behavior or motivation. In all these measures the counselor observes the child's or adolescent's behavior in interaction with parents and especially his/her performance behavior during the test situation.

The Narrow-Phase aims at an individually tailored learning track on the basis of the Actiotope of the child or adolescent. Based on the experience of Grassinger (2009) the complete process of collecting narrowed diagnostic information takes between four and six hours. The following meeting (Transform-Phase) should be scheduled in approximately two weeks.

- *Transform-Phase*

In a status-oriented diagnosis the goal would be achieved after knowing the diagnosis results. This is, according to Stöger (2009) not the case with the dynamic view of the Actiotope Model of Giftedness. According to the results of the psychological assessment based on the Explore- and Narrow-Phases, the counselor discusses and develops a variety of promotion possibilities and their implementation within the family life in cooperation with the parents. The aim is to expand the Actiotope in the direction of talented actions. The counselor pays attention to the co-adaption of the components of the Actiotope, for instance the ability to understand and support on the part of the parents and the environment, and the goals and needs of the child/adolescent (Grassinger, 2009).

The elder child/adolescent (pupil or student) learns how to research a topic in a scientific manner in order to acquire learning strategies and to expand the action repertoire. Thus, he/she is shown how to create a learning portfolio. The research process and the documentation by the child/adolescent in his/her own words should continue over four weeks with a daily exercise and the parents' task is to support and motivate their child. All the information is to be collected and structured and furthermore the child/adolescent is encouraged to give a presentation, e.g. a power point presentation, an essay or a poster. The presentation will take place in the next counseling meeting.

At the end of the Transform-Phase, an individual learning track is established. Parents choose the appropriate promotion measures to implement at home and write them down. The counselor also notes the measures and makes an appointment for the evaluation phase with the parents in about eight weeks.

- *Evaluate-Phase*

The aim of the formative Evaluate-Phase is to support and encourage the learning track developed in the Transform-Phase. Therefore further interviews with parents and child/adolescent are necessary. If the child/adolescent has prepared a presentation, now is the time to hold it. The counselor follows the lecture and gives his/her feedback regarding strategies and content at the end. The further elaboration of the same or a new topic is suggested. The parents contribute information about motivation and learning behavior during the making of the portfolio.

An informative interview with the child/adolescent takes place in the Evaluate-Phase. Depending on the results agreed upon during the Transform-Phase, the interview deals with e.g. the portfolio, learning in advance, the implementation of other measures. The child/adolescent reports about his/her experience with motivation, emerging problems, invested time, sources of information, emotions, and he/she also receives feedback from the counselor.

In the Evaluate-Phase further conversations with educators could be essential; thereby the environment of the client is involved. These conversations occur mostly by telephone. This way the educator can be informed about suitable promotion measures.

The Evaluate-Phase comprises one to four sessions in the span of several weeks each and the counselor can also be contacted by telephone, if problems should emerge. The Evaluate-Phase ends with an appointment for the Review-Phase (Grassinger, 2009).

- *Review-Phase*

The Evaluate- and Review-Phase of the ENTER model also influences the adaption of the counselor's Actiotope. He/she is involved in a systemic way within the Actiotope of the client and through feedback he/she can improve his/her counseling. The Evaluate-Phase shows him/her if the chosen learning track was followed successfully and the Review-Phase gives feedback about the usefulness of the chosen methods (Stöger, 2009).

In the last phase of the ENTER-Triple L-Model all ways of learning leading to talented actions are summarized and evaluated. The parents and the child/student report on their learning experience, learning behavior and the knowledge acquired in their area of interest. The content of the portfolio also can provide useful information about the learning progress. Finally, the counselor refers to other appropriate opportunities for the advancement of the gifted and gives an outlook to the *learning plan*, the next step of the ENTER-Triple L-Model.

2   Diagnosis and counseling, illustrated by a case study: Leon, 6;4

The systemic perspective requires that all relevant aspects be recorded in the Actiotope of the child in order to get a holistic and individual view. A high quality diagnosis must be wide-ranging over a prolonged period of time and requires diverse methods and perspectives. Relevant areas include cognitive skills, learning and working behavior, motivation, social behavior and learning environment. How this can be realized is exemplified in the following by the case of counseling Leon.

2.1   ENTER: Explore

The parents of the 6;4 year-old Leon contacted the counseling center with a request for talent diagnosis and advice for further promotion. In order to get more information on Leon's Actiotope the counselor sent a parent questionnaire and an educator questionnaire to the family.

The questionnaire revealed the case history and Leon's strengths and problems. Leon lived together with his parents and his 4 ½ years old brother in a provincial town. The mother recorded high abilities in memory, language fluency and reasoning in the early childhood development. Also the fine-motor skills were advanced. Leon was a healthy, sensitive child with a great thirst for knowledge. At the age of 18 months, his brother was born and Leon reacted with jealousy.

When he was three years old Leon entered kindergarten. Leon showed social difficulties, such as isolating himself. When Leon felt unchallenged, he acted like a clown. Leon preferred drawing, doing handicrafts and had an interest in books, geography, and technical constructions. His high level of detailed knowledge made a positive impression on the educator. Furthermore Leon's exceptional ability to concentrate and his perseverance were unusual for his age. A diagnosis of giftedness was recommended to the parents by the educator of the kindergarten. But an advanced school enrollment at the age of 5 was not taken into account because of his social problems.

So, primary preventive reasons of counseling were prevalent because of the boredom of the child and the desire of the parents for diagnosis. A learning track should promote his cognitive competences and enable Leon to perform talented actions. Furthermore Leon's social problems constitute a secondary preventive reason for counseling.

2.2   ENTER: Narrow

About two months after the initial contact the diagnostic meeting took place at the counseling center. At nine o'clock in the morning, Leon arrived together with his father and mother. The counselor explained the diagnostic schedule and started with a warm up game.

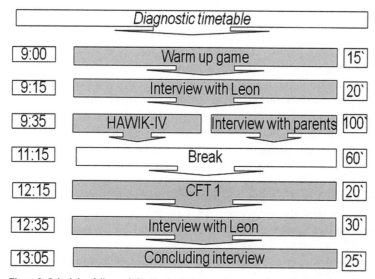

Figure 3: Schedule of diagnosis by Harder 2010; transformed and translated by the author

The interviews covered different aspects regarding Leon's and his parents' Actiotope. Parallel to the interview with the parents the intelligence test HAWIK-IV[2] was conducted with Leon. After an hour's break, Leon completed the CFT1[3] test. Later he gave a detailed report of the kindergarten and he also was consulted about psychological issues such as fears and wishes. The first meeting ended with a concluding interview with both parents and Leon.

---

[2] HAWIK-IV: Hamburg-Wechsler-Intelligenztest für Kinder (Petermann & Petermann, 2007), German version of the Wechsler Intelligence Scales for Children

[3] CFT1: Culture Fair Intelligence Test (Weiß & Osterland, 1997)

The following information concerning Leon's Actiotope was compiled. At the age of one year Leon could already name all brands of tractors and with one and a half years he already spoke three-word-sentences. When Leon was three years old, he attended the kindergarten. But Leon was isolated, the older children did not want to play with him, they even beat him and Leon had no interest in the younger ones. He often acted the part of a clown. The only friend he had had in kindergarten was already in school. In dealing with conflict situations and emotions, Leon couldn't speak about his problems, the right strategies were still missing. He also felt stressed, when he had to stop a favorite activity with flow experience and when his thirst for knowledge was not quenched. He would then respond with withdrawal behavior.

Musical education was provided for with a group of young children and the mother already thought about letting Leon take single piano lessons. Leon got along well with his younger brother, quarrels and jealous behavior were in the normal range. He enjoyed playing football or cycling outside. Because the parents ran their own handicraft business, there was little time for additional support during the week. But Sunday was the family-day with common activities, for example visiting a museum, castle or sporting activities outdoors.

Leon's favorite books, appropriate for children aged 10, were about the universe, biology, geography and technology. He also liked to build airplanes and tractors with Lego bricks. Furthermore the boy had a long attention span when working on puzzles, painting or crafting. Nevertheless he could read and write all letters and many words. Leon also could count, add and subtract fast and confidently up to 20.

In the test HAWIK-IV Leon reached an overall performance IQ of 127 (PR = 96.4) and was thus above average in his age group. Leon's endurance waned in the afternoon that is why the overall score in the CFT1 test was IQ = 109 (PR = 73).

At the end of the meeting the next appointment was scheduled.

2.3   ENTER: Transform

Approximately two weeks later Leon's parents came to the LBFH for counseling. First, the psychological report with all results of the tests were shown and explained. Then different promoting measures were discussed. According to the diagnosis results social behavior and cognitive competences should be promoted. In order to improve his social abilities Leon should learn strategies for solving conflicts. The counselor suggested practicing change of perspective and role plays for a better understanding. The ability to express emotions could be trained through rituals like mutual day reflection. It was also essential to have contacts with peers. Therefore the counselor recommended regular meetings with peers as well as older children and like-minded friends. The situation in regard to his clownish behavior was also to be improved by reflection and an increase of social behavior options.

Thinking and learning competences were to be promoted through high quality games, like memory games, chess, Sudoku, puzzle riddling, etc. Self-directed learning should be promoted and the counselor explained how. The right setting of goals, proper planning of the learning process and reflection of one's own learning behavior with evaluation of the achievement of the objectives were important strategies. Knowledge-building through journals, learning-CDs, internet, museum and selected TV shows was initiated by the counselor. Leon's interest and motivation could be strengthened through praise and the counselor gave examples.

Furthermore the systemic perspective requires the involvement of the people within the client's environment. Therefore the parents were instructed by the counselor about favorable attribution and the reflection of their feedback behavior. To optimize the learning environment, the cognitive challenge should be increased. The kindergarten could provide preschool learning material. The goal should be to work with the learning material about 20 minutes every afternoon. This would extend Leon's knowledge, give structure in his daily routine and prepare Leon's learning attitude in respect to school. He should also be given enough space for creative handicraft. Furthermore, Leon should be given single piano lessons.

All these measures were discussed with the parents and they decided which promoting actions fit in their family situation and these were to be realized within the next weeks. A new appointment was agreed upon in two months. Leon did not need to prepare a portfolio, because he couldn't read or write fluently yet.

2.4   ENTER: Evaluate

During this third meeting, the counselor asked, how the progressive adaption of Leon's Actiotope had developed. What new phenomena had arisen?

The counselor had suggested a daily reflection in the evening. But according to his mother Leon spoke only about positive events. The problems with other children remained unmentioned. The mother tried a role play, but Leon did not like it. He wanted to solve his social problems with his peers himself. The counselor understood this to be an attempt on Leon's part at being independent and that the mother should support this. Leon still played the part of the clown and the agreed upon stop-signal didn't work.

Furthermore Leon's mother described also about his positive development in kindergarten. The educator supported Leon by giving him challenging learning materials and enough space for creative handicraft. The other children admired Leon's exceptional results. In addition, he received single piano lessons and the mother watched over the daily fifteen-minute practice sessions. On enrollment day at school, Leon worked concentrated and fast. He performed all exercises correctly. Leon was looking forward to school.

For further promoting with the aim at talented actions the counselor underlined the importance of bringing more structure into Leon's daily routine. His goal should be to work about 20 minutes every afternoon. The parents should continue already started promoting measures and the next appointment was scheduled five months later, when Leon would already be going to school.

2.5   ENTER: Review

At the Review-appointment Leon had attended school for three weeks and had no problems integrating himself in the group of classmates. According to the class teacher, Leon participated well and displayed a good understanding of the subject matter. Leon finished his homework in more or less 10 minutes, while the other pupils needed more than an hour. To further his cognitive development the counselor suggested participation in academic competitions. The motivation for piano practice deteriorated, but Leon wanted to continue the lessons. He preferred to play the piano pieces by memory. To further his motivation the counselor suggested choosing more appealing pieces and demonstrating his success by recording his playing. The daily schedule was not yet internalized. Thus the counselor recommended a consistent education and a visualized schedule, which could help Leon to organize all tasks by himself. He should be involved, when the plan was compiled to strengthen his responsibility and self-organized learning competences.

The parents gave feedback about counseling and the gain they had received. Last but not least the counselor pointed out, that she will continue to be available for further questions.

3   Discussion

The results of the parents' feedback questionnaire and an interview by phone showed all reasons for counseling had been taken into consideration. The parents appreciated the detailed diagnosis of aptitude. Now, they understood Leon better and could respond appropriately. They received many suggestions on how they can encourage their son. All proposals to promote Leon were well understood and many of them were carried out. The integration into the class went over smoothly without any social problems. Leon enjoyed the lessons in school and the teacher supplied him with additional learning materials. Thus he didn't feel bored and Leon's Actiotope was stable.

The *learning counseling* also considered the four components of the Actiotope. Leon could expand his action repertoire and by applying his knowledge also his subjective action space. The individual tailored learning track with its progressive adaption supported the goal which was to enable Leon to execute talented actions. The systemic perspective included all relevant fields and persons, such as parents, sibling, peers, educators, class and school.

References

Barthelmess, M. (2001). *Systemische Beratung* [Systemic counseling]. Weinheim, Germany: Beltz.

Caplan, G. (1964). *Principles of preventive psychiatry.* New York: Basic Books.

Cattell, R. B. (1973). *Die wissenschaftliche Erforschung der Persönlichkeit* [*The empirical investigation of personality*]. Weinheim: Beltz.

Elbing, E. (2000). *Hochbegabte Kinder: Strategien für die Elternberatung* [*Gifted children: Strategies for parents counseling*]. München, Germany: E. Reinhardt.

Ericsson, K.A., Krampe, R.T., & Tesch-Romer, C. (1993). The role of deliberate practice in the acquisition of expert performance. *Psychological Review, 100,* 363-406.

Ericsson, K.A., Roring, R.W., & Nandagopal, K. (2007): *High Ability Studies 18,* 3-56.

Grassinger, R. (2009). *Beratung hochbegabter Kinder und Jugendlicher [Counseling of gifted children and adolescents].* Vol. A: Talentförderung – Expertiseentwicklung – Leistungsexzellenz [Promotion of Talent – Developement of Expertise – Performance of excellence] (Eds. K. A. Heller & A. Ziegler).Münster, Germany: LIT-Verlag.

Harder, B. (2010). *Beratung an der LBFH (Landesweite Beratung- und Forschungsstelle für Hochbegabung an der Universität Ulm),* [Counseling at the LBFH (Nationwide Counseling and Research Center for giftedness at the University of Ulm)], Seminar of Stöger, H., Universität Regensburg.

Nestmann, F. (1992). Beratung [Counseling]. In R. Asanger & G. Wenninger (Eds.), *Handwörterbuch Psychologie [Dictionary Psychology],* (pp. 78-84). Weinheim: Psychologie Verlags Union.

Stöger, H. (2009). Die Identifikation Hochbegabter basierend auf einem systemischen Begabungsansatz und deren Relevanz für Begabte mit heilpädagogischem Förderbedarf [The Identification of the gifted based on a systemic aptitude approach and their relevance for gifted students with therapeutic educational needs]. *Heilpädagogik online, 8,* 35-63.

Schilling, S.R., Graf, S., Hanses, P., Pruisken, C., Rost, D.H., Sparfeldt, J.R., & Steinheider, P. (2002). Klare Informationen für Betroffene. [Clear informtion for persons concerned]. *Reportpsychologie, 27*(10), 642-647.

Wittmann, A.J. (2003*). Hochbegabungsberatung. Theoretische Grundlagen und empirische Analysen [Counseling of giftedness. Theoretical principles and empirical analyses].* Göttingen, Germany: Hogrefe.

Ziegler, A. (2005). The Actiotope Model of Giftedness. In R.J. Sternberg & J. Davidson (Eds.), *Conceptions of giftedness* (pp. 411–436). New York: Cambridge University Press.

Ziegle A. (2008) *Hochbegabung [Giftedness]*. München: UTB.

Ziegler, A. (2009). Ganzheitliche Förderung umfasst mehr als nur die Person: Aktiotop- und Soziotopförderung [Holistic promotion comprises more than just the person: Promotion of the Actiotop and Sociotop]. *Heilpädagogik online, 2*, 5-34.

Ziegler, A. (2011). Analysekategorien zur Bewertung von Lernumwelten: Sociotope und Bildungskapital [Categories of analysis for the assessment of learning environments: Sociotope and capital of education]. In U. Ostermaier (Ed.), *Hochbegabung, Exzellenz und Werte. Positionen in der schulischen Begabtenförderung [Giftedness, excellence and values. Positions of the promotion of gifted students in school]* (pp. 119-138). Dresden: Thelem.

Ziegler, A., & Perleth, C. (1997). Schafft es Sisyphos, den Stein den Berg hinaufzurollen? Eine kritische Bestandsaufnahme der Diagnose- und Fördermöglichkeiten von Begabten in der beruflichen Erstaus- und Weiterbildung vor dem Hintergrund des Münchner Begabungsmodells [Does Sisyphus manage to roll the stone up the mountain? A critical assessment of diagnosis and funding opportunities of the gifted in initial vocational education and training in the context of the Munich model of talent]. *Psychologie in Erziehung und Unterricht, 44*, 152-163.

Ziegler, A., & Stoeger, H. (2003). ENTER – Ein Modell zur Identifikation von Hochbegabten [ENTER – a model for the identification of talented persons]. *Journal für Begabtenfoerderung, 4*, 8-21.

Ziegler, A., & Stoeger, H. (2004). Identification based on ENTER within the conceptual frame of the Actiotope Model of Giftedness. *Psychology Science, 46*, 324-342.

Ziegler, A., & Stoeger, H. (2007). The role of counselling in the development of gifted students' Actiotopes: Theoretical background and exemplary application of the 11-SCC. In S. Mendaglio & J. S. Peterson (Eds.), *Models of Counselling* (pp. 253-286). Waco, TX: Prufrock Press Inc. Waco, TX.

Ziegler, A., & Stoeger, H. (2009). Begabungsförderung aus einer systemischen Perspektive [A systemic perspective on gifted education]. *Journal für Begabtenförderung, 9*(2), 6-31.

Shane N. Phillipson

Putting the Actiotope Model of Giftedness to the Scientific Test: Commentaries on Harder, Duan and Arora, Kist, and Schurr

Abstract

The actiotope model of giftedness represents a paradigm shift in the way that development of exceptionality can be understood. Instead of focusing on traits, the model takes an actiotope as the unit of study, with interactions amongst the four components described as a system. Hence, exceptionality is the product of a system rather than individual. The four studies in this commentary represent the some of the first tentative steps in testing the veracity of the model and its usefulness to guide the counseling process of a child indentified as having the potential for exceptional achievement. The four studies highlight the methodological difficulties inherent in the study of systems. However, the studies demonstrate that the model can be amenable to empirical studies, leading to refinements in the protective belt.

1   Introduction

The actiotope model of giftedness (AMG) was first described in Ziegler (2005) to redirect what Ziegler described as a degenerating domain of research, specifically an understanding of the basis and development of exceptional human achievement. Rather than attempting to find giftedness in the individual, Ziegler argued that exceptional achievement is the outcome of a system involving the individual and their environment in the context of a particular domain. As with all systems, exceptional achievement can never be guaranteed; rather, the probability that exceptionality will occur increases when the system is operating at optimal levels. Importantly, exceptional achievement can only occur as the system evolves in response to changes within the individual and the environment. In the AMG, the system evolves through a series of disequilibria.

Three of the four components of the AMG are situated within the individual. The first component is the action repertoire (AR), consisting of all possible actions available to the individual. The second and third components are the subjective action space (SAS) and goals (G). The SAS refers to the individual's subjective assessment of their AR and, hence, determine which of the skills and/or knowledge are actually used. The SAS helps to explain the relationship between self-esteem and self-concept, for example, and academic achievement. Last, goals direct the individual into expanding the AR and, hence, are an important aspect of the AMG. Here, goal orientation theory (Cheng & Phillipson, in press) and broad models of motivation can be used to explain the bases of an individual's behavior, particularly when engaged in learning activities.

In broad terms, as new learning goals are set, the environment needs to change in order to accommodate the expansion of the AR. Alternatively, a change in environment initiates the development of new learning goals, and hence, the expansion of the AR. Third, it is also possible that an expanding AR initiates a change in the individual's goals and/or environment, leading, again, to a further expansion of the AR. Finally, an assessment of whether or not an action is available and, if implemented, will lead to success is the function of the SAS. Accordingly, the SAS must develop along side the other three components if exceptionality is to be achieved.

In contrast to trait models of giftedness, the AMG does not focus on the individual traits such as intelligence, creativity nor motivation, for example. Rather, the AMG focuses on the interactions between the four components and the conditions that enable the system to develop exceptionality. Although the specifics may differ, a *learning* environment is a necessary but insufficient condition for exceptionality.

An important feature of the AMG is that an individual's actiotope alternates between periods of relative stability, punctuated by transitional periods of change. Hence, the actiotope is modifiable although it is difficult to predict the duration of either the period of stability and/or change. Furthermore, the unit of focus in the AMG is the individual unit rather than cohorts of individuals, arguing that it is difficult to generalize systems. When focusing on aciotopes, strategies for both the identification (Stoeger & Ziegler, 2004) and counseling (Ziegler & Stoeger, 2007) of students with the potential for exceptionality need to take into account all four components.

2   The AMG as a research tool

In order for a theory to direct research, the theory must have an internal structure consisting of four components (Lakatos, 1974). The first component forms the *hard core* of the theory of the structure, containing the basic assumptions underlying the theory. This *hard core* includes knowledge, terminology and experimental paradigms that are implicitly agreed upon by the scientists working with the theory.

By definition, the *hard core* is unchangeable. If the contents of the *hard core* are a source of disagreement, then the antagonist is working outside the paradigm. According to Chalmers (1994), however, it is often difficult for a scientist to articulate the precise nature of the paradigm within which they are working unless the paradigm is seriously questioned. The issue is confounded if a number of different theories share a common term or label to describe key elements in their *hard core*. The scientists using the AMG as the theoretical framework, for example, have agreed, implicitly or otherwise, the basic assumptions and terminology of the AMG.

Along side the basic assumptions of the structure, is the *protective belt* of the theory, consisting of "...explicit auxiliary hypotheses...[and] ... assumptions underlying the description of the initial conditions and ... observation statements" (Chalmers, 1994, p. 81). Chalmers described the protective belt as protecting the *hard core* from being falsified. In other words, evidence to the contrary can be attributed to deficiencies in the auxiliary hypotheses, the assumptions in the initial conditions or observations rather than to problems with the *hard core*.

The two remaining components of the structure are the two *heuristics* of the theory. The *positive heuristic* is that part of the structure that provides impetus for strengthening the auxiliary hypotheses surrounding the *hard core*. It should offer ways to implement the research programme by describing mathematical models and experimental techniques.

On the other hand, the *negative heuristic* serves to protect the *hard core* from modification thereby reinforcing the paradigm in which it is constructed. Chalmers attributes *positive heuristics* with the additional feature of fertility, where the degree of fertility is the extent that the *positive heuristic* " ... contains within it objective opportunities for development ... " (p. 125) that scientists may not recognize initially.

3   Harder - *Empirical Validation of the actiotope model of giftedness*

Harder's paper accepts the AMG's *hard core* and tests the auxiliary hypothesis of non-hierarchical, non-linear and highly interactive relationships, reflecting the features of systems. Harder's thesis is that structural equation modeling offers an indirect way to validate the AMG. However, her approach is somewhat unusual in that recognizing that the AMG predicts interactivity and non-linearity amongst the components, a *poor* fitting SEM is a desirable outcome.

Harder's study involved measuring aspects of an individual's actiotope at different times reflecting changes in their school development, based on the Actiotope Questionnaire described in Ziegler and Stoeger (2008). Harder used their academic achievement as reflecting their action repertoire and estimated their subjective action space, goals, and environment, together with five mechanisms necessary for the adaptation of an actiotope (recognition of success, conditional knowledge, generation of action variations, anticipation and feedback), together with the measures of system modifiability and stability, using a 50-item self-report questionnaire. Moreover, the responses to the self-report questionnaire were Rasch analyzed and the Rasch scores used to generate structural equation models at the different times.

All structural equation models were poorly fitting although the interactive and non-hierarchical models were less poorly fitting than the hierarchical models. These results were taken by Harder to confirm that individual actiotopes are not generalizable even when the environment seems outwardly similar.

Harder's argument depends on the availability of high quality data, particularly when the argument depends on poorly fitting structural equation models. The use of Rasch scores (logits) helps to meet some of the basic data requirements for structural equation models, including the use of interval data. However, the reported reliabilities of .7 to .86 for the ten scales are not indicative of high quality data.[1] Hence, it is possible that the poorly fitting models reflect the quality of the data rather than the interactivity and the non-hierarchical nature of the relationships between the components.

Clearly, Harder's conclusions need to be replicated with particular attention to the quality of the data. As she pointed out, however, it is better to use analytic techniques that can directly confirm the existence of interactivity and non-hierarchical relationships between the four components of the AMG, rather than rely on techniques that imply the absence of non-interactivity and hierarchical relationships. Accordingly, Harder recognizes that new methodologies such as neuronal networks may be used to model systems.

Harder makes some tentative but important steps into a difficult experimental paradigm. Nevertheless, Harder's study begins the task of developing the heuristics needed to develop the protective belt of the AMG.

---

[1] Other indicators of the fit of the data to the Rasch model include infit and outfit scores. These indicators were not reported in Harder. In Rasch modeling, it is important to identify and remove both ill fitting items in each of the tests, and/or poorly fitting cases, based on these indicators.

4   Duan and Arora - *Gender and Cross-cultural Differences in STEM: An Investigation based on the actiotope model of giftedness*

Duan and Arora's study focused on the under-representation of girls in Science, technology, engineering and mathematics (STEM). Noting that there are some cross-cultural differences in this under-representation, comparisons between students from Germany and India were also examined. In this study, the AMG was used to determine whether the under-representation of girls could be explained by differences in one or more of the four components of the AMG (subjective action space, goals, environment and action repertoire), the five mechanisms necessary for the adaptation of the actiotope (recognition of success, conditional knowledge, generation of action variations, anticipation and feedback), together with the measures of system modifiability and stability.

As in Harder, this study was based on the Actiotope Questionnaire described in Ziegler and Stoeger (2008). In addition, Duan and Arora measured student interests, self-confidence, involvement in STEM activities and future job choices. The 476 students from India and Germany completed all self-report measures using a 5-point Likert scale and the raw scores used in a number of parametric statistical tests such as ANOVA.

Although testing the ability of the AMG to account for the under-representation of girls in STEM, Duan and Arora have accepted the hard core of the AMG. In testing the predictive ability of the AMG they are exploring and characterizing the protective belt of the AMG and their results will not threaten the *hard core* in any way.

The first noteworthy result was that the German students reported higher levels of academic achievement than Indian students – a result in contrast to expectations. On the other hand, this conclusion is not based on a common test of academic ability but rather school-based reports. One likely explanation of these results is that there are significant differences in academic standards and expectations.

The results showed gender differences favoring girls in Germany for both interest in and self-confidence for STEM subjects.[2] On the other hand, no gender-based differences were found for Indian students. In terms of cross-cultural differences, Duan and Arora reported more German students being involved in and achieving greater academic success in the STEM activities compared to Indian students. The possible reasons for the increased interest and self-confidence of German girls and the cross-cultural differences in involvement and achievement were explored in the next section of their study.

Step-wise regression of components of the AMG against interest, self-confidence, STEM activities, job-choices and achievement showed that goals

---

[2] Note that Duan and Arora only reported significant differences for interest, although Table 2 seemed to show significant differences in both interest and self-confidence.

play a very important role for German girls in developing both an interest and being involved in STEM activities. In contrast, goals played an equally important role for both Indian boys and girls. Interestingly, job-choices in STEM were predicted by subjective action space for both boys and girls. When investigating cross-cultural differences, Duan and Arora found that goals were the most important predictor of interest in STEM.

In basing their study on the AMG, Duan and Arora seems to have ignored the individual focus and systems nature of the AMG. Rather, they assume that there is sufficient alignment in gender-based and cultural actiotopes to ensure regularity in the responses. Only when there is regularity in the responses is it possible to detect differences in the responses using parametric tests such as ANOVA and to test linear relationships using regression analysis.

Duan and Arora did not report any data that characterized their data in any way, so assumptions of normality and homoscedasticity were not tested. Given that Likert scales generate ordinal data the requirement for interval level data when using parametric tests was also not met. Nevertheless, the report of significant differences in responses and the success of regression models indicate that the actiotopes may be similar across a large number of individuals. In other words, Duan and Arora may have evidence that individual actiotopes may be more similar than they are different, adding another dimension to the protective belt of the AMG.

5   Kist - *Predictors of performance in second language instruction*

A key component of the AMG is the environment, providing the external context of the individual (Ziegler, 2010). Ziegler termed the external context sociotopes and recognized the distinction between objective action space (broad environmental conditions) and normative action space (local environmental conditions). Under ideal conditions, a learning socitope is viewed as the ideal environment for knowledge acquisition.

Kist's study examined the role of different types of sociotopes in the acquisition of a second language (English) by German students.   Her empirical study aimed to uncover the sociotopes that lead to second language acquisition. As for the previous studies, Kist used the Actiotope Questionaire (Ziegler & Stoeger, 2008), corresponding to the components, mechanisms and characteristics of the AMG. In addition, Kist used a learning environments questionnaire to identify the students' sociotopes, including learning, infrastructural, restrictive, antagonistic and, thematic and competitive sociotopes.

The acquisition of English was measured using a standardized test of English, assessing word-production, vocabulary competency amongst other skills. The reported reliability for the language acquisition test was .86. Apart from the language test, all scales generated ordinal data, being based on a Likert scale. In contrast to previous studies, Kist reported the use of a 4-point rather than a 5-point scale.

As a first step, Kist divided the students into two groups, based on their language acquisition, namely high performance (top 20% of scores) compared to average performance (lower 80% of scores). The responses by students within each group were used in subsequent regression analyses.

As a first analysis, Kist reported that a regression analysis showed that a student's subjective action space, anticipation and applicability positively predicted language proficiency, with an antagonistic actiotope negatively predicting language proficiency, helping to account for 36% of the variability in scores. On the other hand, there were no relationships between the other sociotopes and language acquisition. Kist interpreted this result to indicate that, in general, it is far more important to *not* spend time with others who reject learning than to be with those that support learning.

When comparing high and average performing students, Kist found that the subjective action space, applicability of the actiotope and infrastructural sociotope were the only differences. She interpreted this finding as high performers spend less time in environments that are detrimental for learning, their subjective action space is geared positively toward language acquisition and that they are able to use their knowledge in difficult situations.

This interpretation was confirmed when binary logistic regression was performed in order to compare the regression coefficients from the two groups. Kist demonstrated that for high performing students, language acquisition was predicted by subjective action space, variations, anticipation and antagonistic sociotopes. Kist interpreted this result to mean that high performing students are better able to access their action repertoire and are more efficient in being able to mange their actions. Furthermore, avoidance of antagonistic sociotopes is far more important than any of the other sociotopes.

Many of the methodological issues in Duan and Arora's study are echoed in Kist's study, including a better characterization of the data set and the use of ordinal responses in parametric tests. Again, however, the results tentatively confirm the usefulness of the AMG in predicting the bases of academic achievement. Furthermore, the results suggest that there may be greater regularity amongst individual actiotopes than implied by the systems nature of the AMG.

6   Schurr - *Counseling at the 'State-Wide Counseling and Research Center for the Gifted at Ulm University': A case study*

One of the first practical applications of the actiotope model of giftedness is in counseling students identified with the potential for exceptional achievement (Ziegler & Stoeger, 2007). Involving a 5-step process, the ENTER model of counseling includes the phases known as Explore, Narrow, Transform, Evaluate and Review. Schurr describes a further application of the ENTER model involving a 6-year old boy.

Schurr describes the theoretical basis of the ENTER counseling model, highlighting the focus on the individual, including assessment of their subjective action space, action repertoire, goals and environment. Hence, an important aspect of the counseling involves the child's parents. The outcomes of the counseling process are recommendations for a learning path that involves the key members of the child's environment, including the child's parents.

The child was referred to the counsellors by the child's parents. Despite showing evidence of "giftedness" the parents reported their son as showing behavioral difficulties such as clowning and preferences for solitude. Using the results of a series of tests, the counselors recommended a focus on strategies that improved his social abilities and cognitive competencies, including strategies that promoted perspective taking, role play expression of emotions and reflection. To develop the thinking and learning competencies, the strategies recommended included the use of high quality games such as memory games, chess, Sudoki and word puzzles. Furthermore, self-directed goals were developed, as were planning skills and self-reflection.

Knowledge building was developed through the use of journals, museum and selected TV programmes, and self-confidence developed through the use of appropriately implemented praise. A learning environment was also promoted at both home and kindergarten, including the learning of piano, the introduction of the preschool curriculum material and a structure to his daily routine.

The holistic approach to counseling depended on the active involvement of his parents, peers and siblings. Accordingly, his parents were involved at every stage of the counseling process. The end result of the counseling process was generally positive, although Schurr provided few details.

This application of the actiotope model of giftedness is based on the contents of the hard core of the model. In providing a theoretical basis for counseling and showing a successful outcome, the likelihood that the model will be used again increases, thereby increasing its popularity. As Chalmers (1994) argued, a scientific model increases its acceptance as the preferred model partly because of the sheer number of adherents.

However, the strategy is both labor intensive and extends over a considerable period of time. Future research should focus on comparing the costs and benefits of this strategy with other counseling strategies. Such research, however, should bear in mind that the AMG is a probabilisitic model and exceptional outcomes cannot, by defninition, be guaranteed.

7   Conclusion

The four studies represent an important development in the acceptance of the actiotope model of giftedness as the preferred scientific model for understanding the development of exceptionality. Despite the methodological difficulties in testing a system model, Harder, Duan and Arora, and Kist demonstrate that it is possible to apply conventional analytic techniques to strengthen the protective belt of the actiotope model of giftedness. More importantly, it provides a heuristic to further technical advances in methodologies.

Building on the counseling strategies outlined in Ziegler and Stoeger (2007), Schurr describes a counseling case study involving a young boy, indicating that the AMG provides sufficient detail to be of practical use. Whether or not the strategies are able to increase the probability of exceptional achievement is yet to be determined

References

Chalmers, A. F. (1994). *What is this thing called science?* (2nd ed.). Queensland: University of Queensland Press.

Cheng, R., & Phillipson, S. N. (in press). Goal orientations and the development of subjective action space in Chinese students. In S. N. Phillipson, H. Stoeger & A. Ziegler (Eds.), *Giftedness in East Asia: Explorations in the actiotope model of giftedness*. London: Routledge.

Lakatos, I. (1974). Falsification and the methodology of scientific research programmes. In I. Lakatos & A. Musgrave (Eds.), *Criticism and the growth of knowledge*. (pp. 91-196). Cambridge: Cambridge University Press.

Stoeger, H., & Ziegler, A. (2004). Identification based on ENTER within the Conceptual Frame of the actiotope model of giftedness. *Psychology Science, 46*(3), 324 – 341.

Ziegler, A. (2010). Lernsoziotope. Zur Ausschöpfung der Lernpotenziale gehört eine anregende Lernumwelt [Learning Sociotopes. An inspiring environment is necessary for the exhaustion of learning sociotopes]. In *Rückblick und Ausblick. 10-jähriges Jubiläum der Stiftung für hochbegabte Kinder [Review and Prospect. 10th anniversary of the foundation for gifted children]*. Retrieved from: http://www.hochbegabt.ch/documents/3/broschuere_10_jahr_jubil%C3%A4um.pdf

Ziegler, A. (2005). The actiotope model of giftedness. In R. Sternberg & J. Davidson (Eds.), *Conceptions of giftedness* (pp. 411-434). Cambridge, UK: Cambridge University Press.

Ziegler, A., & Stoeger, H. (2007). The role of counselling in the development of gifted students' actiotopes: Theoretical background and exemplary application of the 11-SCC. In S. Mendaglio & J. S. Peterson (Eds.), *Models of Counselling* (pp. 253-286). Waco, TX: Prufrock Press.

Ziegler, A., & Stoeger, H. (2008). Effect of role models from films on short term ratings of intent, interest and self-assessment of ability by high school youth: A study of gender-stereotyped academic subjects. *Psychological Reports, 102*(2), 509-531.

II. Developmental Aspects of Giftedness and Early Fostering

Marion Porath

Understanding the Social Context of Learning: Gifted Students' Perspectives

Abstract

This study explored how gifted elementary school students understand the social context of learning. Research tasks designed to reflect gifted students' school experiences were the basis for interviews with children about the thoughts and feelings that may have motivated the actions of the children and teachers portrayed in the tasks. A clear age-related progression was evident, showing development in thinking from action-based rationales for behaviour to explanations that incorporated intentions and, in the most mature responses, personality variables. The children's responses offer a view of how they mentally represent the social world of school. The content and developmental progression of their representations, and the interview method used to elicit their responses, have implications for how we understand and support gifted children educationally.

1   Introduction

We know little of how children of exceptional ability understand the thoughts and intentions of peers and teachers. These thoughts and intentions underpin interactions amongst children, their peers, and their teachers in learning environments, influencing academic motivation (Harter, 1996; Junoven & Wentzel, 1996) and predicting academic achievement (Caprara, Barbaranelli, Pasterelli, Bandura, & Zimbardo, 2000). Positive relationships with peers and teachers promote academic motivation and achievement. Among learners considered gifted, however, these relationships are often impacted by misunderstanding, or lack of understanding, of advanced development (Keating, 1991). One of the contributing factors to lack of understanding is the nature of developmental profiles of gifted learners. There is considerable intra- and inter-individual variability across academic and social domains (Matthews, 1997). If this variability is not appreciated and understood, children's academic and social needs may be affected.

Gifted children may be exposed to curricula and instructional strategies that are inappropriately challenging for their level(s) of academic development. That is, instructional options may not be *optimally matched* (Robinson & Robinson, 1982) to their need for curriculum that is deep, broad, and meaningful and instruction that is geared to their pace of learning. Lack of an optimal match may result in decreased motivation to learn – even among a population noted for their exceptional intrinsic motivation (Gottfried, Gottfried, Bathurst, & Guerin, 1994; Winner, 1996) – and/or behavioural problems (Keating, 1991; Neihart, 2007).

2   Understanding Thoughts and Intentions in Relation to Actions

The central developmental task in social understanding is the ability to link thought and action (Porath, 2003). This ability is key to understanding others' thoughts and/or feelings and actions in a coordinated way, and is especially relevant to helping children understand and cope with the myriad of relationships they encounter in school – to make meaning of their interpersonal experiences at school. Meaning making involves the systematic linkage of events and mental states (Perner, 1991) or, as Bruner (1986) described it, the united consideration of two landscapes – the landscape of *action* and the landscape of *consciousness*.

Schools and classroom are complex settings in which success requires that children understand the intentions of their teachers and peers. Gifted children's school experiences may present particular challenges to understanding the actions and intentions of others. Knowing how gifted learners perceive aspects of their school life is critical to informing optimal educational support (Harter, 1996). Their mental representations are tools for understanding development, yet are rarely considered; the approach is underused in developmental (Dweck

& London, 2004) and educational research (Bruner, 1996). Current work in giftedness emphasizes the importance of learners' perspectives in defining directions for education (Hymer, Whitehead, & Huxtable, 2009), highlighting the need to explore the nature of gifted learners' perspectives on their education.

This research explored two questions: How do children understand the roles that peers' and teachers' thoughts and intentions play in situations that impact their learning? Are there changes in their understanding as they mature? The study reported here is part of a larger study of gifted learners' understandings of learning and teaching and the 'social literacy' important to school success across childhood and adolescence (e.g., Porath & Lupart, 2009; Porath, Lupart, Katz, Ngara, & Richardson, 2009; Porath, Ngara, Lai, Fogel, & Lupart, 2010).

2. 1   Theoretical framework

Because of its articulation of the structure and content of children's representations of the academic and social dimensions of school, and the developmental course of these representations, Case's (1992; Case & Okamoto, 1996) neo-Piagetian theory was chosen as the theoretical framework for the study. Previous work within this framework mapped developmental changes in children's conceptions of the social world of schooling (Porath, 2003), describing how young children's understanding of why peers and teachers act, think, and feel the way they do develops from action-based reasoning to reasoning that incorporates understanding of others' mental states. It also described the strong relationship between this reasoning and how children understand the social dynamics in their classrooms.

2.2   Social structures of mind

The key construct in Case's (1992) theory is the "mind's staircase," or the increasingly complex structures of mind that develop over time. These structures share a common form – a form that becomes increasingly complex and abstract as children mature - but develop independently from each other. These *central conceptual structures* are the explanatory mechanisms underpinning the development of mathematical, logical, and social thought, for example. The *structural* aspect of thought can be likened to a "blueprint" of the relations that develop among foundational aspects of thought. These relations are semantic, describing the core meanings derived from the coordination of foundational concepts, making the structures *conceptual*. Structures are considered *central* to domains because they provide the conceptual framework for understanding a wide range of related tasks within domain (Case, 1992; Case & Okamoto, 1996).   A central social structure has been identified (Case, 1992; Fischer, Hand, Watson, Van Parys, & Tucker, 1984; Goldberg-Reitman, 1992; McKeough & Griffiths, 2010; Porath, 2003, 2009), one that is relevant to children's understanding of others' intentions.

Social structures of mind are characterized by different levels of thought. In early childhood, children articulate their understanding of their social world in „scripts" that involve recitations of actions in sequence, such as the events that happened at a birthday party – what Bruner (1986) termed the „landscape of action.". They also are well aware of emotions – the „landscape of consciousness" (Bruner, 1986) and can discuss them, but do not „merge" these two capabilities (Case & Okamoto, 1996). By about age 5 or 6, children become capable of uniting the two landscapes, action and consciousness, in their explanations of others' behaviours and intentions. Throughout middle childhood, they become increasingly sophisticated in their explanations of others' intentions, coordinating multiple thoughts, feelings, and judgments in explaining why others do what they do. In adolescence, explanations become „psychological" in that notions about the type of person one is are included in interpretations of their own and others' behaviour and inten-tions. Further details on these levels of thinking are included in the section on scoring.

3   Method

Participants were 42 elementary school children (21 girls; 21 boys) identified as gifted learners who attended schools in two large cities in western Canada. As is typical in Canada, the children were identified either by their teachers, formal testing, or some combination of the two. Gifted education services ranged from in-class provisions to pullout programs to self-contained classes for gifted children. There were 6 participants in Grades 1 and 2 (average age 7 years, 10 months); 12 participants in Grades 3 and 4 (average age 9 years, 1 month); and 24 participants in Grades 5 and 6 (average age 10 years, 5 months). Participants were grouped by grade to facilitate developmental analysis. The research consisted of two phases.

3.1   Phase 1

The first phase of the research involved observations of educational settings that included gifted children. The major focus of these observations was to discover the situations that arise for gifted children in meeting the demands of school. Digitally videotaped observations were done in each setting to determine children's approaches and reactions to academic tasks (e.g., engagement, reluctance, avoidance) and interactions with teachers and peers around academic tasks and social interactions. Field notes were also taken to supplement the videotapes. Videotapes and notes were analyzed to inform the design of ecologically valid research tasks.

Research tasks

The format of the research tasks was based on previous social developmental research (Porath, 2003). Tasks included illustrated stories and a semi-structured interview to tap understanding of peers' and teachers' intentions in school-related situations. From the analysis of videotapes and notes, factors that either supported or challenged learning were noted. For example, meaningful and supportive peer-to- peer interactions and aesthetically pleasing classrooms that provide learning guidelines, easy access to materials, and physical and educational organizational support appeared to facilitate engagement with learning. Mismatch of ability and assigned tasks, lack of encouragement of social understanding, and teacher control were examples of factors that challenged learning (Phillips & Porath, 2005; Porath, Lupart, Phillips, Song, & Belzile, 2004). Scripts were written for three child-to-child and three child-to-teacher learning situations and line drawings were commissioned to go with the scripts. (see Appendix for examples).

3.2   Phase 2 – Task administration

The researcher or a graduate research assistant interviewed each child individually in a room at their school. Each interview was digitally tape recorded and then transcribed for analysis. Notes on interview responses also were taken to aid in transcription. The tasks were administered with other research tasks in the larger project. The three child-child tasks were administered in the first of two interview sessions; the three teacher-child tasks were administered in the second session.

3.3   Scoring

Transcripts were reviewed multiple times by four research assistants; reviews included crosschecks on scores assigned and clarification of each person's interpretation of scoring criteria. Discussion of areas of disagreement took place among the four research assistants and the researcher. Final scores were assigned once consensus was achieved.

For each participant, responses to the interview questions were considered together as a "unit" and scored following the guidelines in Tables 1 and 2. To achieve a particular level score, responses had to include at least one exemplar of thinking associated with that level. The scoring guidelines were based on the developmental progression in social narrative identified by McKeough (1992; McKeough, Davis, Forgeron, Marini, & Tuk, 2005; McKeough & Genereux, 2003), a progression informed by Case's (1992; Case & Okamoto, 1996) theory. In early childhood, children's explanations for events draw on the "landscape of action" (Bruner, 1986). By about the age of 6, as they enter middle childhood, children's explanations begin to draw on their own and others' intentions, uniting the "landscape of action" with the "landscape of consciousness" (Bruner, 1986) in a preliminary fashion. Thus, *intentional* thinking develops and becomes increasingly sophisticated as children mature (McKeough, 1992) (see Table 1). At around the age of 12, children become capable of being more "psychological," including dimensions of personality in their explanations of events.

Table 1: Intentional structure scoring

Level	Criterion	Score
Level 0 (Pre-intentional)	Response is a "sequence of events that are temporally, causally, or referentially related and that occur exclusively in the physical world of action and events" (McKeough et al., 2005, p. 249). There is a simple reiteration of the actions occurring in the story. Explanations refer only to the story events.	0
Level 1 (Uni-intentional)	Response includes "explicit or implicit reference to mental states" (McKeough et al., 2005, p. 249) (thoughts, feelings) that motivate action in the world of school. Explanations include a thought, feeling or intention associated with the event.	1
Level 2 (Bi-intentional)	"Additional mental states are mentioned or implied" (McKeough et al., 2005, p. 249). Two or more related thoughts, feelings, and/or intentions are coordinated with the story event in the child's explanation.	2
Level 3 (Integrated intentional)	Criteria for Level 2 in an integrated, well-planned sense to the response. One response has more significance than the others, thereby "broadening the characters' intentions" (McKeough et al., 2005, p. 249).	3

Thinking at this stage can be described as *interpretive*, with interpretations of behaviour becoming increasingly more sophisticated throughout adolescence (McKeough & Genereux, 2003) (see Table 2).

Participants were in the age range typically associated with middle childhood where intentional thinking is most common. However, criteria for interpretive thinking were included in the scoring guidelines to guard against a ceiling effect.

The following excerpts from the interview responses of a girl aged 8 years, 6 months includes evidence of uni-intentional thinking. The child's responses are in italics and references to mental states are in bold type. She was responding to a story about two girls, Kira and Danielle, who explained their problem solving process in a science project to their classmates.

And what are the other children thinking?

That maybe they should do that.

Maybe they should do that, sure. Why do you think that?

*Because **they probably want their rovers to be powerful**....*

And what do Kira and Danielle do next?

Probably put batteries and stuff in their rovers.

Okay and why do you think that?

Cause in the story it says that they'll add some batteries and motors.

And what are Kira and Danielle thinking then?

*That their rover might go **where they want it to**....*

Another 8-year-old girl demonstrated bi-intentional thinking in this excerpt from her response to the story about Ms Little's class (see Appendix).

What is Ms. Little thinking?

About how everybody's doing.

Why?

Because she ... because she wants everybody to understand what they're doing.

How does Ms. Little feel?

Proud of her students.

Why?

Cause they're doing good at their work.

A boy aged 9 years, 2 months demonstrated integrated intentional thinking in the following excerpt taken from his response to a story about a student, Josh, who had difficulty writing but loved to draw.

How does Josh feel? Why do you think so?

*He feels **nervous** when ... he probably feels nervous like when he's asking or before he asked if he's going to write because **he's not very good at it**. And he probably **feels really excited** once he says that's he gets to draw since **he's good at it and he likes it**. So then he probably **feels even more excited** when he sees the objects since it seems like they **feel really interested** in it.*

Table 2: Interpretive Structure Scoring

Level	Criterion	Score
Level 4 (Uni-interpretive)	The focus of the response "shifts from the characters' actions and mental states to why particular mental states are held" (McKeough et al., 2005, p. 249), taking personality into account rather than the situation. "A constellation of mental states create[s] a psycho-logical profile or [personality] trait that is represented across time and situations" (McKeough et al., 2005, p. 249). This constellation/profile, in this study, includes the kind of teacher one is.	4
Level 5 (Bi-interpretive)	"Additional traits [are] represented, such that a dialectic is created wherein the interaction of two states or traits lead to further psychologically oriented complications" (McKeough et al., 2005, p. 249).	5
Level 6 (Integrated interpretive)	The "dialectical relation between states or traits act[s] as an integrating device lending a greater sense of coherence" (McKeough et al., 2005, p. 249) to the response.	6

A girl aged 10 years, 7 months, demonstrated uni-interpretive thinking in the following excerpt from her response to the story about Lucy and Thomas (see Appendix).

How does Thomas feel? Why?

*Thomas feels...probably **kind of proud of himself** cause what, from what it sounds like he, **he thinks he's, um, maybe, possibly better, in a subconscious way**.*

What does Lucy do next? Why?

*Um, she probably says...that's a hard question. **It totally depends on who she is**, so I don't, I'm sorry but I don't know who she is. I mean **if she was a polite person** she would say, "Oh thank you very much." **If she wasn't so polite** she's like, "Yeah well you're not perfect either you couldn't even find pictures on the web."*

What is Lucy thinking then? Why?

*She's probably thinking, she's either thinking sarcastically, "Oh yeah you're so perfect" or, or um, "Oh wow that's really great, thanks I can't believe I missed those." Again **this is a very personality based question.***

4 Results

The average scores (SD) by grade group were 1.89 (.36) for Grades 1 and 2, 2.33 (.46) for Grades 3 and 4, and 2.57 (.38) for Grades 5 and 6. When compared to theoretical predictions for age (Grades 1 and 2 – 2.00; Grades 3 and 4 – 2.5; Grades 5 and 6 – 3.00), the average scores were close to expectations. No participant scored at the pre-intentional level. Several scored at the uni-interpretive level; these scores were achieved across grade groupings and tasks, indicating some intra-individual differences in responses to the stories.

Average scores were analyzed using oneway ANOVA. A significant group difference was found, $F(2, 39)=7.198$, $p=.002$. This result was confirmed via a repeated measures analysis of variance, with the within-subject variable of responses to the six picture stories and the between-subjects factor of age group. The condition of sphericity was met, Mauchly's $W=.707$, $p=.566$. There were no significant within-subjects effects but the between-subjects effect was significant, $F(2,38)=7.488$, $p=.002$. Post hoc comparisons were not done due to the unequal group sizes.

As can be seen in Figure 1, there is a linear developmental progression in intentional thinking and a limited amount of variability by task. Level of understanding varied little between tasks focused on child-to-child interactions and those focused on child–to-teacher interactions.

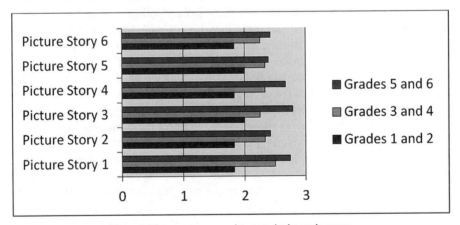

Figure 1: Mean scores across picture stories by grade groups

5   Discussion

This study offers a view of how students identified as gifted perceive the social aspects of school. Their mean scores on the tasks are similar to levels of social understanding expressed by children not identified as gifted (e.g., McKeough, 1992). No direct comparison of the complexity of their responses is possible, given the study design; however, as in other studies of gifted children's performance on neo-Piagetian tasks, what is distinctive about their responses is the complexity and sophistication of expressiong. That is, it is what gifted children *do with* the level of thinking available to them that is distinctive (Porath, 2006).

The research was limited by unequal sample sizes, especially in the youngest age group, and its cross-sectional design. Subsequent research could track students' development of social understanding in the school setting longitudinally, using a comparison of students not identified as gifted, to acquire a fuller sense of how development of social understanding evolves over time and how intellectual ability influences that development. While tasks were designed in an ecologically valid manner with enough scope in the questions to allow a generative approach to studying gifted children's mental representations of the social context of school, it may be more meaningful to situate students' discussions in real events in their own schools and classrooms. On the other hand, participants brought their own experiences to bear in answering the questions, supporting the efforts in Phase 1 to situate the story scenarios in the real world of schools. Their responses give us insights into how gifted children understand social-educational contexts and provide directions for research and practice grounded in children's perspectives (Bruner, 1996; Hymer et al., 2009).

Case's (1992; Case & Okamoto, 1986) theoretical framework, as instantiated in McKeough's (1992; McKeough et al., 2005; McKeough & Genereux, 2003) work on the development of social structure provided a meaningful way to analyze participants' mental representations of the roles that peers' and teachers' thoughts and intentions play in situations that impact their learning and to track the changes in their understanding related to age. The participants' responses were also informative in contributing to our knowledge of how thinking transitions from one level of thought to higher order understanding. For example, some of the youngest children in the sample gave action-based explanations on some tasks when they were clearly capable of "being intentional" on other tasks. Experience and context matter in the type of thought expressed, and may matter more as children begin to acquire a new level of thought. That is, they are more likely to demonstrate more sophisticated thinking on tasks where the content is familiar to them and revert to simpler ways of making meaning when the task is unfamiliar (Case, 1992; Fischer & Bidell, 1998).

Other children, across ages, demonstrated understanding on some tasks that was more sophisticated than would be expected from theoretical predictions (see examples below under "Educational implications"). Analysis of children's mental representations within a developmental theoretical framework provides informa- tion critical to optimal support of children's learning and social development (Dweck & London, 2004).

There was some intra-individual variability in the children's responses, although it was not statistically significant. Few children scored at the same level across all six tasks; most showed variability in the nature of one level above or below the mean for their age group, consistent with research in the neo-Piagetian tradition on children of both average and significantly above average abilities (Case, 1992; Case & Okamoto, 1996; Fischer & Bidell, 1998; Porath, 1996, 1997, 2003). Children may have had more or less experience with some scenarios, more or less motivation to discuss some scenarios (Case, 1992), and/or profiles of ability that may or may not have matched those portrayed in the scenarios, a factor that may affect the degree to which they related to the story characters. They may also have felt more or less supported in responding to the task, a factor that can influence dem-onstration of optimal level of understanding (Fischer & Bidell, 1998). This variability, and the factors that may contribute to it, should be taken into account when considering educational implications.

6   Educational Implications

The examples presented in this section suggest how teachers could use children's understandings to support students in clarifying their understanding and organizing "more meaningful structures of understanding" (Schwartz & Fischer, 2010, p. 149).

This young boy, aged 7, interviewed at the end of Grade 1, coordinated story events with a number of mental states at several points, indicating that he was capable of bi-intentional thinking. With appropriate scaffolding, he could be helped to more complete understandings of situations where he reverted to action-based explanations and where his understandings of thinking and feeling seem to be confounded. As Schwartz and Fischer (2010) point out, "Interviews that focus on the student's experiences can help them question their ideas and support new   understandings" (p. 152). Adding questions that focus on students' own experiences could be helpful here, as could classroom activities and/or discussions focused on thoughts and intentions in relation to behaviours.

> How do the kids in Ms. Little's class feel? Why do you think they feel that way?
>
> *Um, really excited. Cause the presentation might be fun.*
>
> What are the kids in Ms. Little's class thinking? Why do you think so?
>
> *I got another one for the one before that - they might be a little afraid. Cause some people are scared of presentations. Some of them are really, really proud in their presentation and some of*

them are really, really proud in their second presentation. Or, I mean some of them might be scared of the presentation.

What is Ms. Little thinking? Why?

She'd still be proud of the class. Cause she is ... she might be the happiest teacher in the whole school.

How does Ms. Little feel? Why?

Really, really excited. Why do you say why? I just said! (I know. There a lot of whys, aren't there?) *Yeh!* (So if you think it's the same reason that you've already given me just let me know, OK?) *OK, I will!*

What do you think the kids will do next? Why do you think so?

They will ... they will do ... actually they'll probably do... they will probably do the presentation the next day. Cause that might be ... cause after they might... are they in kindergarten?

What are they thinking then? Why?

They're thinking like a very very proud person. Two verys, OK?

How do they feel then? Why?

Um ... I said it! Excited. (Same reason?) *Yeh.*

In the second example, excerpts are presented from responses of a girl aged 10 years, 7 months to the story of David whose work was criticized by his teacher. Further discussion would, first, aid in consolidating her sophisticated ability to interpret others' actions in light of personality as well as intention. Stability and longevity of optimal skills, such as this child's appear to be, are influenced by supportive context and scaffolding (Schwartz & Fischer, 2010). Second, support and scaffolding would give her a strong foundation from which to construct more sophisticated interpretive responses (McKeough, Okamoto, & Porath, 2002).

What do you think he is thinking about?

He's probably, he's probably resenting the teacher cause you know, I've done that a couple of times myself, but he's probably angry and upset that the teacher's being so not understanding. And I mean, if there's, there's the rational sense probably in him that maybe I rushed a bit and I should go figure out what the right answers to these questions are but a lot of the time that's probably overcome with the "man I'm so angry at her."

Why do you think he's thinking that?

Well, because, from the, well the pictures tell, cause he could be one of those teacher's pet guys who's like, "Ok I'll do that, all the way!" But he's obviously not, and um, he's probably thinking that because the teacher, a lot of what you think about somebody is based on what they say to you, and a lot about what you think about what you're doing is based on how good that subject is to you...not that it can come up and pat you on the shoulder, but you know, luck has a lot to do with it, whether or not you apply yourself has a lot to do with what you think of the subject by what results you get. So, he's not feeling good probably, because he doesn't like the subject now, because of course somebody was mean to him about it, about it or he's, he's perceptive that somebody was mean to him about it, so....

How does Ms. Dumont feel?

She feels, probably, well I don't know her she's just a piece of paper but, my thoughts would be that she feels disrespected maybe, um, possibly not useful because you know she's trying to teach this kid stuff and he's not paying, she feels he's not paying any attention which of course might not be true he might just not of learned all of it cause you know there's at least seven questions it's not that bad to get less than half of them wrong....

Interviewing, conceived of in the way Schwartz and Fischer (2010) do as "an inviting dialog where students [can] experiment with their views" (p. 173), provides the opportunity for teachers to understand how children understand their learning and others' roles in that learning. This is an important foundation for designing learning experiences for all children, but particularly for gifted children, whose needs are often misunderstood. Interviewing also offers children the opportunities to challenge, build, and extend their understandings to the full extent of their zone of proximal development.

References

Bruner, J. (1986). *Actual minds, possible worlds*. Cambridge, MA: Harvard University Press.

Bruner, J. (1996). *The culture of education*. Cambridge, MA: Harvard University Press.

Caprara, G. V., Barbaranelli, C., Pastorelli, C., Bandura, A., & Zimbardo, P. G. (2000). Prosocial foundations of children's academic achievement. *Psychological Science, 11,* 302-306. doi:10.1111/1467-9280 .00260

Case, R. (1992). *The mind's staircase: Investigating the conceptual underpinnings of children's thought and knowledge*. Hillsdale, NJ: Erlbaum.

Case, R., & Okamoto, Y. (1996). The role of central conceptual structures in the development of children's thought. *Monographs of the Society for Research in Child Development,61*(1-2, Serial No. 246).

Dweck, C. S., & London, B. (2004). The role of mental representation in social development. *Merrill-Palmer Quarterly, 50*, 428-444. doi:10.1353/mpq.2004.029

Fischer, K. W., & Bidell, T. R (1998). Dynamic development of psychological structures in action and thought. In W. Damon & R. Lerner (Eds.), *Handbook of child psychology. Volume 1: Theoretical models of human development* (5th ed., pp. 467-561). New York, NY: Wiley.

Fischer, K., Hand, H. H., Watson, M. W., Van Parys, M., & Tucker, J. L. (1984). Putting the child into socialization: The development of social categories in preschool children. In L. Katz (Ed.), *Current topics in early childhood education* (Vol. 5, pp. 27–72). Norwood, NJ: Ablex.

Goldberg-Reitman, J. (1992). Young girls' conception of their mother's role: A neo-structural analysis. In R. Case (Ed.), *The mind's staircase: Exploring the conceptual underpinnings of children's thought and knowledge* (pp. 135–152). Hillsdale, NJ: Lawrence Erlbaum.

Gottfried, A. W., Gottfried, A. E., Bathurst, K., & Guerin, D. W. (1994). *Gifted IQ: Early developmental aspects. The Fullerton longitudinal study*. New York, NY: Plenum Press.

Harter, S. (1996). Teacher and classmate influences on scholastic motivation, self-esteem, and level of voice in adolescents. In J. Juvonen & K. R. Wentzel (Eds.), *Social motivation: Understanding children's school adjustment* (pp. 11-42). New York, NY: Cambridge University Press.

Hymer, B., Whitehead, J., & Huxtable, M. (2009). *Gifts, talents and education: A living theory approach*. Chichester, UK: Wiley-Blackwell.

Junoven, J., & Wentzel, K. (Eds.) (1996). *Social motivation: Understanding children's school adjustment*. New York, NY: Cambridge University Press.

Keating, D. P. (1991). Curriculum options for the developmentally advanced: A developmental alternative to gifted education. *Exceptionality Education Canada, 1*, 53-84.

Matthews, D. J. (1997). Diversity in domains of development: Research findings and their implications for gifted identification and programming. *Roeper Review, 19*, 172-177. doi:10.1080/02783199709553821

McKeough, A. (1992). A neo-structural analysis of children's narrative and its development. In R. Case (Ed.), *The mind's staircase: Exploring the conceptual underpinnings of children's thought and knowledge* (pp. 171-188). Hillsdale, NJ: Lawrence Erlbaum.

McKeough, A., Davis, L., Forgeron, N., Marini, A., & Fung, T. (2005). Improving story complexity and cohesion: A developmental approach to teaching story composition. *Narrative Inquiry, 15,* 241-266. doi:10.1075/ni.15.2.04mck

McKeough, A., & Genereux, R. (2003). Transformation in narrative thought during adolescence: The structure and content of story compositions. *Journal of Educational Psychology, 95,* 537-552. doi: 10.1037/0022-0663.95.3.537

McKeough, A., & Griffiths, S. (2010). Adolescent narrative thought: Developmental and neurological evidence in support of a central social structure. In M. Ferrari & L. Vuletic (Eds.), *Developmental relations among mind, brain and education. Essays in honor of Robbie Case.* (pp. 213-229). New York, NY: Springer.

McKeough, A., Okamoto, Y., & Porath, M. (2002, April). *A design for development: The legacy of Robbie Case.* Paper presented at the American Educational Research Association, New Orleans.

Neihart, M. (2007). The socioaffective impact of acceleration and ability grouping: Recommendations for best practice. *Gifted Child Quarterly, 51,* 330-341. doi:10.1177/0016986207306319

Perner, J. (1991). *Understanding the representational mind.* Cambridge, MA: MIT Press.

Phillips, L., & Porath, M. (2005, May). *The child as psychologist: The social context of learning for gifted students.* Paper presented in the symposium The child as psychologist: The social context of learning for gifted and gifted/learning disabled students. Canadian Society for the Study of Education, University of Western Ontario.

Porath, M. (1996). Narrative performance in verbally gifted children. *Journal for the Education of the Gifted, 19,* 276-292.

Porath, M. (1997). A developmental model of artistic giftedness in middle childhood. *Journal for the Education of the Gifted, 20,* 201-223.

Porath, M. (2003). Social understanding in the first years of school, *Early Childhood Research Quarterly, 18,* 468–484. doi:10.1016/j.ecresq.2003.09.006

Porath, M. (2006). The conceptual underpinnings of giftedness: Developmental and educational implications. *High Ability Studies, 17,* 145-157.

Porath, M. (2009). Fostering social expertise in early childhood. *Early Child Development and Care, 179,* 93-106. doi:10.1080/03004430600989098

Porath, M., & Lupart, J. (2009). Gifted children's representations of learner identities. *Exceptionality Education International, 19* (3), 80-96.

Porath, M., Lupart, J., Katz, J., Ngara, C., & Richardson, P. (2009). Gifted learners' epistemological beliefs. *Talent Development & Excellence, 1,* 57-66.

Porath, M., Lupart, J., Phillips, L., Song, K-H., & Belzile, L. (2004). *The child as psychologist: Report on research activities – Year 1.* Unpublished manuscript, Faculty of Education, The University of British Columbia, Vancouver, Canada.

Porath, M., Ngara, C., Lai, Y., Fogel, K., & Lupart, J. (2010). Children's understanding of teaching: A component of self-regulation? *Psychological Test and Assessment Modeling, 52,* 454-471.

Robinson, N. M., & Robinson, H. B. (1982). The optimal match: Devising the best compromise for the highly gifted student. In D. F. Feldman (Ed.), *New directions for child development: Developmental approaches to giftedness and creativity* (pp. 79-94). San Francisco, CA: Jossey-Bass.

Schwartz, M. S., & Fischer, K. W. (2010). Interviewing: An insider's insight into learning. In M. Ferrari & L. Vuletic (Eds.), *Developmental relations among mind, brain and education. Essays in honor of Robbie Case.* (pp.149-175). New York, NY: Springer.

Winner, E. (1996). *Gifted children: Myths and realities.* New York, NY: Basic Books.

Appendix

Sample Picture Stories

- *Child-Child*

Mr. Bartelli tells his class that they are going to work in pairs today to help each other complete their science fair projects. Tomorrow they are going to present their work to their parents and the rest of the school. He says, "You all know what you still need to work on, so choose a partner to work with. You can take turns helping each other."

Lucy and Thomas decide that they will work together. Lucy needs help writing her report and Thomas needs help finding pictures on the Internet to help him

complete his poster. Because Lucy's work might take a little longer, they decide
to work on the writing first.

Thomas reads Lucy's report very carefully and after awhile he says, "Lucy, I
think you need capital letters here and here. Do you think this is the right word
here? Shall we try to think of another one that would be better?"

How do you think Lucy feels about what Thomas said? Why do you think so?

What do you think Lucy is thinking about? Why do you think so?

What is Thomas thinking? Why?

How does Thomas feel? Why?

What does Lucy do next? Why?

What is Lucy thinking then? Why?

How does Lucy feel then? Why?

■   *Children-Teacher*

Ms. Little's class was in the computer lab learning how to add photos to the PowerPoint presentations they had created for their independent projects. Ms. Little showed them how to find photos on the internet and put them in their presentations.

After showing them, Ms. Little checked to see if they understood what to do. She said, "Put your arm straight up if you get it; like this / if you need some clarification; and like this --- if you want me to come and help you. OK, let's do the clarifications together."

"Now I'll come and help those who want help. Then, after choosing some photos, you might like to work together and give each other feedback. What kind of feedback could you give?" The kids in the class said, "Does the photo make sense? Does it add to the meaning of the presentation?

The class worked on their presentations. Ms. Little talked to those who wanted help; then she talked to each of them. She asked them if they had any questions or anything they would like feedback on. The recess bell rang and Ms. Little said, "I'm so pleased with the thinking you did this morning and the way you encouraged each other. We have the lab booked all morning so we'll continue to work on this but now you can take a break. If you want to keep working, just remember not to eat or drink near the computers."

How do the kids in Ms. Little's class feel? Why do you think they feel that way?

What are the kids in Ms. Little's class thinking? Why do you think so?

What is Ms. Little thinking? Why?

How does Ms. Little feel? Why?

What do you think the kids will do next? Why do you think so?

What are they thinking then? Why?

How do they feel then? Why?

—

This research was supported by a grant from the Social Sciences and Humanities Research Council of Canada.

The assistance of Lynda Phillips, Lise Belzile, Kwang-Han Song, Constantine Ngara, Jennifer Katz, Pamela Richardson, Krista Fogel, Natalie Moore, and Yuan Lai with data collection, transcription, and coding is gratefully acknowledged.

Wilma Vialle

'I don't think I'm a boy!' Social Understanding and Giftedness in Preschoolers

Abstract

Australian school systems have policies that permit accelerative options to meet the needs of students identified with gifted potential. However, practice demonstrates that this accelerative option is often negatively regarded by decision-makers and, consequently, is infrequently implemented. Reasons for not allowing early entry, for example, focus more on the child's social, emotional or physical development than their intellectual readiness. While there is research exploring this conundrum, the voice of parents is under-researched. This chapter presents the case studies of two four-year-old preschoolers who were purposively selected for the study. Both were suitable candidates for early entry, but their parents in each case were advised against early entry by preschool personnel. These case studies illustrate the complex interplay of social understanding, emotional maturity and intellectual precocity in young children. They illustrate the need for better training of Early Childhood teachers so that they can appropriately respond to the needs of such individuals.

1   Introduction

Despite the existence of policies in Australia that support the early entry of gifted youngsters into schools, practice demonstrates that this accelerative option is often negatively regarded and is infrequently implemented (Diezmann, Watters, & Fox, 2001; Gallagher, Smith, & Merrotsy, 2010; Rankin & Vialle, 1996). Accelerative practices, including early entry, remain a conundrum in education because they are strongly supported by research evidence (see, for example, Colangelo, Assouline, & Gross, 2004; Hattie, 2009) but meet with strong resistance in school settings (Vialle, Ashton, Carlon, & Rankin, 2001). Early entry, in particular, is readily recognised as beneficial to young gifted children at least in the cognitive realm (see, for example, Rogers, 1991; VanTassel-Baska, 1986). Arguments against the practice, however, tend to focus on assumptions about children's social 'readiness' for school, their emotional maturity, or their physical stature (Armstrong, 1993; Rankin & Vialle, 1996).

The separation of individuals' intellectual needs from their social-emotional needs permits these to be placed in conflict with each other. The argument proposed is that social and emotional concerns are more important for schools to satisfy than intellectual needs. Proponents of gifted education, however, point out that these needs interact with each other and therefore cannot be separated and set in opposition. Rather, the gifted child's opportunity to mix with ability-peers may also bring social and emotional benefits (Kulik & Kulik, 1997; Meininger, 1998). Indeed, some researchers have proposed that giftedness brings with it the type of thinking that allows greater social understanding, empathy and altruism (Levine & Kitano, 1998).

The parent's voice in the existing research on early entry is largely absent. One article written by an Australian parent closely documented her experiences in securing early entry for her daughter in the face of stringent opposition (Armstrong, 1993). In her paper, Armstrong commented on the inter-relationship of her daughter's intellectual needs and her social-emotional needs. She argued that her daughter's aberrant behaviours and immaturity in the school setting, as perceived by teachers, was a response to the way she was treated. Armstrong (1993) stated:

> Rosie learnt inappropriate behaviour, because she wasn't allowed to be herself—an extremely intelligent, capable individual. Instead, people judged her by her appearance—a cute, tiny little baby-faced scrap you just want to pick up and hug, and coo over….For Rosie, early entry was just what she needed. We've all benefited from her needs being met. (Armstrong, 1993, p. 100)

Armstrong's experiences have been echoed by numerous parents who have contacted my office over the last ten to fifteen years, whereby precocious youngsters gravitate more readily to older children and demonstrate more mature social skills in such circumstances. Several parents have reported that their child's unhappiness in settings without intellectual challenge have led to physical ailments, including nausea, headaches, stomach complaints and skin irritations. This was also demonstrated in a more recent study by Diezmann and colleagues, which closely detailed the parental experience of early entry.

> If we had not early entered our daughter I fear she would have remained angry, aggressive and the eczema would have continued. Another year in a situation, which was out of kilter with her ability and developmental profile, would have been emotionally undermining. Socially she may have become even more alienated from her peers due to her aggressiveness. Intellectually she would have been bored. She would have become a serious underachiever with all the resultant ramifications for her self-esteem and confidence....Our daughter is happy....It was definitely an advantage for our daughter to be enrolled in a state primary school a year younger than prescribed. (Diezmann, Watters, & Fox, 2001, p. 14)

Given the continued existence of a gap between policy and research, on one hand, and practice of early entry, on the other, this study sought to examine the cases of two preschoolers whose intellectual abilities suggested they were suitable candidates for early entry. I was particularly interested in the role played by the youngsters' social understanding, if any, in the decisions made about their education. It also sought to redress the relative lack of parental voice by investigating the parental views on their children's potential early entry. Consequently, this research examined the cases of two "May babies" at the time they turned four. In both cases, the parents were advised by school personnel to delay entry of their children to Kindergarten[1] despite the evidence that they were intellectually ready.

2   Social understanding and giftedness

There are several lines of research and theory that are relevant to this issue, each of which is worthy of extensive coverage. Given the space restraints of this chapter, I will keep the discussion of each of these areas as succinct as possible. From a theoretical perspective, I draw on Vygotsky's work in positing the importance of children's social understanding in learning and development. Vygotsky (1978) proposed that children are social from birth and that, consequently, their learning and development are *mediated* by their social interactions with others within a particular cultural context. Vygotsky stated:

> Every function in the child's cultural development appears twice: first, on the social level, and later, on the individual level; first, between people (interpsychological) and then inside the child (intrapsychological). This applies equally to voluntary attention, to logical memory, and to the formation of concepts. All the higher functions originate as actual relationships between individuals. (Vygotsky, 1978, p. 57)

---

[1] In New South Wales, Australia, preschool services are for children aged 3 to 5. Kindergarten is usually entered at age 5 and immediately precedes Year 1 of primary schooling.

For Vygotsky, then, the development of children proceeds "not from the individual to the social, but from the social to individual" (Vygotsky, 1986, p. 36). Thus, our higher mental functions, including the ability to think abstractly and undertake complex problem solving, are social in origin and depend on those mediated interactions with adults and more knowledgeable peers (Vygotsky, 1978). Wertsch (1985) argued that this notion of social mediation is the most significant component of Vygotsky's theories.

Central to Vygotsky's sociocultural theory of development is the Zone of Proximal Development (ZPD), which may be defined as the difference between the level children can attain independently and the level they can attain with the assistance of more expert others. These social interactions that occur within the ZPD are critical for children's development, and are tai- lored to the child. "The term proximal (nearby) indicates that the assistance provided goes just slightly beyond the learner's current competence, complementing and building on existing abilities" (Cole & Cole, 2001, p. 207). This differential support provided to the learner has been subsequently referred to as scaffolding (Wood, Bruner, & Ross, 1976). Further, Vygotsky theorized that what the child is able to accomplish with the help of others today, he or she will be able to accomplish independently tomorrow.

From a Vygotskian perspective, then, all good learning occurs within the child's ZPD and is socially mediated. Hence, social understanding is implicit in children's development and learning. The implication of this theory for gifted youngsters is that an appropriate school environment is one that allows children to work within their ZPD by allowing them to interact with their intellectual peers; further, such intellectually challenging environments are essential for the development of their cognitive skills and social understanding.

As indicated previously, much of the resistance to early entry on the part of educators derives from an over-emphasis on the gifted learners' physical characteristics or perceptions of their emotional maturity. Indeed, the clinical work of Silverman (2002) draws attention to the 'asynchrony' of gifted individuals, whereby their cognitive abilities outstrip their physical skills development and emotional regulation. The concept of asynchrony has even been incorporated into the Columbus Group's definition of giftedness:

> Giftedness is asynchronous development in which advanced cognitive abilities and heightened intensity combine to create inner experiences and awareness that are qualitatively different from the norm. This asynchrony increases with higher intellectual capacity. The uniqueness of the gifted renders them particularly vulnerable and requires modifications in parenting, teaching, and counseling in order for them to develop optimally. (NAGC, 2008)

In arguing the need for special provisions to accommodate for the asynchrony of gifted learners, Silverman (2002) indicated that some intellectual and personality characteristics are associated with such asynchrony. These characteristics can be observed from birth and include sensitivity, intensity, curiosity, perceptiveness, complexity, reflectiveness, and perfectionism.

The characteristics Silverman identifies echo ideas that have emerged from Dabrowski's (1972) theory of 'overexcitabilities'. Dabrowski coined this term to describe the heightened intensities experienced by many (but not all) gifted individuals and he classified them into five fields, including the Psychomotor, Sensual, Intellectual, Imaginational, and Emotional. While one or more of these intensities may be evident in gifted youngsters, the emotional overexcitability is of particular interest for the study reported herein. Emotional intensity is often evident early in a child's life and involves intense and complex feelings, and the capacity for strongly identifying with the feelings of others, which includes empathy and sensitivity toward others (Piechowski, 1991). Dabrowski and Piechowski (1977) believe that individuals with this overexcitability will display powerful emotional attachments to other people as well as to places and things. However, children with such emotional intensity may not be well understood by adults. One potential outcome of emotional intensity is that it is confused with immaturity, which in turn is seen as evidence of poor levels of social understanding. For example, research on early entrance to school has demonstrated lower levels of emotional maturity among the younger members of the class (Gagné & Gagnier, 2004). However, this applied to younger students who were *unselected*, that is, they were not provided early entry on the basis of their giftedness (Gagné & Gagnier, 2004). This research contrasts with the more positive outcomes on social-emotional measures for *selected* early entrants, that is, those students who underwent a careful screening process to ensure their intellectual readiness (Rankin & Vialle, 1996; Robinson, 2004; Rogers, 2002).

The capacity for empathy and strong emotional attachments to others, that are associated with emotional intensity, will impact gifted youngsters' social understanding and their expectations of friendship. Research has shown that gifted learners gravitate to peers on the basis of ability rather than their chronological age (Gross, 2002a, 2002b; Kervin & Vialle, 2004). Gross (2002b), for example, hypothesised that children's friendships were tied to mental age rather than chronological age and that gifted children were ahead of their age peers on the developmental trajectory of friendships. A gifted preschooler may be at the level of expecting 'intimacy and empathy' from friendship, for example, while others the same age are still at the 'play partner' level. Gross suggested that such discrepancies in the expectations of friendship are more pronounced in the early childhood years. Hence, gifted youngsters were more likely to hold different expectations of friendship, which could lead to loneliness and social isolation for these individuals early in their school careers (Gross, 2002b).

Similarly, the research reported by Kervin and Vialle (2004) concluded that the friendships of young gifted children are often based on shared interests. They describe the close friendship that existed between two seven-year-olds, Ben and Justin, despite their apparent intellectual differences. However, both boys were passionately interested (and gifted) in mathematics and science, and Ben would patiently assist Justin with the literacy skills required for the complex 'alien' games they invented and played together. In concluding, Kervin and Vialle cautioned that peer tutoring of struggling students should not be forced on gifted learners despite some reports of its benefit for the tutors (see, for example, Coenen, 2002). In Coenen's (2002) study, the positive reports by the gifted students demonstrated their social understanding and altruism rather than any academic gains.

3   Method

As indicated previously, the purpose of this exploratory study was to con- sider the social understanding of gifted youngsters in the context of an educational system that was largely resistant to the early entry of gifted individuals to formal schooling. Social understanding was the focus of the investigation because this area, coupled with emotional immaturity, was frequently cited as the reason for non-acceptance of early entrants who were intellectually ready for school. By contrast, Porath's chapter in this book (Porath, 2012) demonstrates the potential for advanced developmental patterns among gifted youngsters for social understanding. A multiple case study design was utilised and two four-year-old preschoolers were purposively selected for the study.

The site for the research was a large regional centre in the most populous state of Australia, New South Wales (NSW). Early entry into NSW public schools is enshrined in policy (NSW Department of Education and Training, 2004) but is still largely under-utilised as a strategy for meeting the needs of gifted youngsters (Diezmann, Watters, & Fox, 2001; Gallagher, Smith, & Merrotsy, 2010; Rankin & Vialle, 1996; Whan, 1993).

The two case studies were purposively selected because they met the following criteria: (1) they demonstrated intellectual precocity from an early age; (2) they were deemed intellectually capable of commencing school early; and, (3) their parents had been advised against early entry by preschool teachers. The first case, Michael, was male and the older of two children to professional parents from an Anglo-Saxon background. His parents had rejected the advice to hold their son back from school and he will attend Kindergarten in 2012. The second case, Jie-Qi, was female and the sole child of professional parents from a Chinese background. Her parents had accepted the advice to hold their daughter back in 2011 and she will enter Kindergarten also in 2012.

Data were collected through multiple semi-structured interviews with the children's parents over the course of a three-year period. These interviews were supplemented by researcher observations of the children in natural contexts, including home and in the day-care centres they attended. The data are reported in a narrative style to ensure that the parents' voices are clearly articulated.

4   Results

4.1   Michael

At the time of writing, Michael is a four-year-old boy, living with his Anglo-Saxon parents and younger sibling (aged two) in a moderate-sized regional city in Australia. He attends a preschool for two days per week and is cared for on other days by his aunt or grandparents. Michael was born six weeks premature and was delayed in meeting many of his physical milestones. For example, he did not start walking until he was about 14 months of age. At age four, though, he is still small for his age but has "caught up" his physical skills, which are now on a par with those of other children his age. By contrast, Michael's verbal skills have been precocious from an early age. By eight months, his vocabulary numbered 50 words and he was voracious in his appetite for books. His mother commented that it is his verbal precocity that has led to some social issues in the preschool environment.

Michael has been attending day-care[2] services on a one-day per week basis since he was two years of age. This was a conscious decision by the parents to expose him to other children his own age. Being a first-born child of professional parents (both parents trained as primary school teachers), his early social interactions were predominantly with adults with whom he was completely at ease. On one occasion, I attended a luncheon hosted by Michael's mother alongwith a handful of other adults. Michael was three at the time and he happily engaged all the adults in long conversations. His mother decided that it was time for his afternoon nap and she escorted him to his bedroom where he was overhead to comment, "Tell my people that I will see them when I've had my rest."

When situations arose in which he was exposed to other children, his parents noted that he naturally gravitated to older children. They determined that they needed to seek out opportunities for Michael to socialize with other children. This led to the decision to enrol him in a day-care centre as well as to enrol him in multi-age activities such as Art classes and Music classes. His mother report-

---

[2] Day-care services cater for children from birth to 5 years of age and can include a preschool environment for children aged 3 to 5. Day-care services are voluntary and separate from compulsory formal schooling, which commences at age 5.

ed that it has been a constant battle to find structured ac- tivities for Michael that are need-appropriate as opposed to age-appropriate.

Michael's preference for older friends has led to some issues in the day-care setting. Prior to his third birthday he had to endure the 'baby room' stigma, which meant that the older children with whom he wanted to play refused his advances because he was from the 'baby room'. When he was promoted to the room for the over-threes, he encountered another age division designated by the day-care teachers as the 'inventors' and the 'explorers' groups. Again, this created social issues as his membership of the younger inventors group meant that he was not supposed to mix with the older explorers and, yet, that was where his natural friendships were located.

The title of this paper, "I don't think I'm a boy", has been taken from one of Michael's conversations with his mother on the drive to the day-care centre. When he made this comment, his mother probed to see why he felt that way. His response was that he was not interested in the same things as the other boys, preferring to interact with the girls. Most of his friends until recently have been girls. His friendships are based on the sharing of similar interests, which tend to be more complex than those of his age-peers. He has sophisticated technological skill and is familiar with the latest technology, which is partly due to his father's role as an educator with the Apple company. On one occasion, I was having coffee with his mother when Michael was three years of age. His mother had just loaded some iPhone applications onto her phone and to keep the young Michael occupied she allowed him to "play" with her phone. Despite the fact that Michael had not seen the games on the device before, he quickly worked out which icons to touch and how to navigate through the games.

Michael states that he often feels misunderstood by others. He has been extremely hurt by the reactions of other children to him in the day-care centre. The other children, for example, have stated that he "talks funny", which is a reference to his fluent usage of advanced vocabulary. By way of example, he particularly loves Roald Dahl books and a few months ago called his mother a "miserable midget", which features in one of Dahl's books. Conflicts in the preschool environment are discussed with his mother who has tried to help him talk through these social issues. He has learned to express his feelings by saying, "I don't like it when you..." but is often frustrated by the failure of his peers to follow his train of thought. When his mother asked if he had told the teacher about the conflicts, he indicated that he had tried telling the teacher but "they did not hear [him]". He feels a great deal of frustration and pent-up anger, which manifests itself in clenched fists and impassioned speech. But once he has vented his frustration, he relaxes again.

The treatment he received from other children led to him reporting "feeling sick" on several occasions on the days that he had to attend the day-care centre. When his mother telephoned the doctor to make an appointment for him, one time, he confessed that he wasn't "that kind of sick". This led to the discovery that the other children had been calling him "a bully". His mother recounted their conversation on the way to day-care that morning.

Mum:	Why does Seamus call you a bully?
Michael:	Because I don't want to play his games, I want him to play my games.
Mum:	Why don't you want to play his games?
Michael:	Because they're boring. He always wants to do the same things.
Mum:	Well, what can you do today so that he won't think you are a bully?
Michael:	Well, I suppose I could play his game for a while. And then I could suggest that we play my game. And if he doesn't want to play my game, I could just go and play by myself.

Michael reports, too, that his teachers ignore him. An incident late last year illustrates this observation. Michael and his parents were having dinner at the home of his father's grandmother. After the meal, Michael's grandfather asked his own mother (Michael's great-grandmother) if he could be excused from the table. Michael was intrigued by this interchange and it became the topic of conversation with his father on the drive home. The following week, Michael's mother picked him up from the day-care centre and was told by the teacher that he had done something very strange that day. The children are rostered to eat at staggered times and Michael was in the first group to eat. However, he had remained seated at the lunch-table while the subsequent groups of children ate their lunches. When his mother asked Michael why he had remained at the table after finishing his lunch, he replied that he had asked the teachers several times, "May I please be excused from the table" but they had not responded. Hence, he waited until all the children were finished eating and the teacher instructed them to leave the table.

Michael has a marked capacity for empathy and deep levels of processing. A conversation is never a simple thing and is revisited days and weeks later, according to his mother. Michael has always enjoyed books and has observed that the fox is an evil character in many picture books. Recently, though, he has been looking at factual texts and one on animals featured a fox. This was his first realisation that the evil character of many of his stories was based on a real creature. After some thought, he expressed deep concern for the well-being of his aunt: "I'm worried about Auntie Leanne because she lives in the country and foxes live in the country." His concern was so great that his mother agreed that they could telephone his aunt and Michael said to her that "foxes are real" and therefore if she goes outside she should not "wear a chicken costume".

Michael's younger brother is a very different personality. Michael is very protective of his brother and the latter idolises Michael. This has created some frustration for Michael because Oscar wants to do everything with his brother but he is not old enough to engage in the kind of play and activities that interest Michael. Consequently, Michael sometimes experiences frustration or irritation. Two incidents illustrate this complex sibling relationship. Michael was playing with some blocks, building an elaborate construction when Oscar knocked them over. Rather than screaming at Oscar or hitting him, which might be the anticipated reaction of a three-year-old, Michael slowly turned to his mother and with one tear in the corner of his eye, asked her, "When is Oscar going to be a playmate for me?"

On another occasion, Michael's mother had taken the opportunity to have a shower while the two boys ate their breakfast. As she was dressing, Michael knocked on the door and said the neighbour was at the front door. When his mother went to the door, she was concerned to find the neighbour from several doors down the road had Oscar with her. On investigation, it transpired that Michael had decided he needed some "quiet time" so he had helped Oscar out of his high-chair, retrieved the front door key from its hiding place, unlocked the front door, and told Oscar to "go off on an adventure", closing the door behind him. Fortunately, the neighbour had spied the young adventurer and returned him home safely.

Despite the latter incident, Michael is very thoughtful in how he handles his need to be alone so as not to hurt Oscar's feelings. For example, he might suggest that Oscar spend time with their father while Michael does something different with their mother.

The dynamics of the family and Oscar replacing him as the 'cute baby' have led to Michael starting to try to find other ways to connect with family and friends. These interactions are planned to the last detail. Recently, for example, he carefully planned an iPad application 'lesson' for his 'technophobe' grandfather. This included his selection of an activity that he thought his grandfather would enjoy, rehearsing how he would explain how the application worked, the development of an example that he could show his grandfather, and then monitoring of his grandfather's completion of the ac-tivity. Recently, he carefully planned a complex 'Show and Tell' for the day-care centre, which involved a number of items he owned. He rehearsed his presentation several times the evening before. However, when the morning came, one of the items could not be located. Michael was distraught and explained to his mother that he was upset for three reasons, which he went on to enumerate.

At the age of four, Michael continues to demonstrate the capacity to reason logically and the ability to read the emotions of others. He will often comment that a child "looked like they're sad" or "we haven't seen X for a while, so we should call them to see how they are." He knows all the details of his friends at preschool: names of their entire family, birthdays, pets, where they live, and so on. He is also able to articulate his perceptions of the feelings and motives of others. His mother reports that he is now differentiating how he relates to his parents: technological and practical activities are directed toward his father while emotional issues and abstract ideas are discussed with his mother.

His teacher at the Centre suggested that they should make lunch for everyone at the Centre and guided him through the making of a chicken and chorizo casserole. Afterwards, Michael asked his teacher for a copy of the recipe and filed it at home. Some time later, when his mother indicated that some relatives were coming for dinner and she was unsure what to cook, he unearthed the recipe, saying that he thought, "Auntie Mel will really like this casserole". Once again, he drew on his observations and recollections of people to draw conclusions about their preferences.

Michael is a perceptive child as the following examples illustrate. When he was three, Michael's mother was driving the children home and called her husband to check whether he would be home in time to watch the kids so she could attend P-I-L-A-T-E-S; she spelt the word so that the children would not know what she was talking about. She then asked whether she should stop for I-C-E-C-R-E-A-M. She heard a squeal of excitement from the backseat and noted that Michael was clapping his hands enthusiastically. When she asked why, he responded, "I just know it's something good when you talk in letters!"

Shortly before his fourth birthday, Michael accompanied his brother to the doctor. When he witnessed Oscar's distress at receiving his inoculations, Michael decided to change his birthday from May to September so that he could avoid getting an injection.

Michael's best friend is a seven-year-old girl. At a recent birthday party she was absent and he was 'out of sorts' until he made friends with a nine-year-old boy. He indicated that one of the reasons he was so upset was that he wanted to seek her advice on the best lunch-box for Kindergarten. He had been researching lunch-boxes for some time and had narrowed it down to a couple of contenders. This is one illustration of his resourcefulness and orientation toward complex problem solving. His mother commented that he tends to seek out the help he needs from appropriate sources. In another example, he recently asked his aunt who is a primary school teacher to bring him some handwriting stencils and books to help him learn to read because he anticipates he will need these skills in school next year. On another occasion, he asked for Art classes because he had reached his own boundaries for improvement.

Parent advocacy has been essential to ensure that Michael is treated appropriately by his teachers. Teacher quality has been variable. The best examples have been the centre director who helped Michael with mediating his relationships with others. The director made him feel safe in the environment and listened closely to what he had to say. Many of his most severe social issues at the centre occurred when she was on leave. Another teacher, Matt, is the epitomy of "testosterone" according to Michael's mother. Matt is good at reading the boys' needs and has helped Michael negotiate this territory and it is only recently, under Matt's tutelage, that Michael has developed friendships with boys.

On the negative side, some teachers have not respected Michael's abilities and talked down to him. For example, the Centre's computer was much older than the latest technology in his home and Michael observed to his mother one afternoon that the computers at the Centre were different from theirs. When asked how they were different, it was not the age or model or physical characteristics he was referring to but the ways in which the computer was used. At home, he is allowed to use all the equipment in the house, but when he went to turn the page of a book on the computer at the Centre he was chastised because "only the teacher is allowed to touch the computer!"

Cognisant of Michael's intensity, sensitivity and intellectual precocity, his parents have spent the last year weighing up the options for his education in 2012. Most of the advice they received from teachers and friends was that they should leave him in preschool rather than enrolling him in Kindergarten. The arguments given in favour of holding him back ranged from his small stature through to his emotional "frailty". After much soul-searching, his parents decided that Kindergarten was the best option and they based this on his thirst for intellectual challenge and his need to build friendships with classmates.

Having made that decision, Michael's parents needed to choose an appropriate school that would respect his sensitivity and intensity and in which he can thrive. His mother indicated that he takes time to develop a relationship with people before he is willing to show what he can do, and so a smaller school seemed the best fit.
But none of the options available were ideal: the local Montessori school's resources and activities were too archaic; the local public schools were too overcrowded; the local independent school seemed a good match but beyond their financial resources; and the local Catholic school has expressed some antipathy toward the need for differentiating for gifted students. The parents decided that the Catholic school was the best option but they see it as an environment in which he will develop socially and they anticipate they will need to extend him intellectually at home.

4.2   Jie-Qi

At the time of writing, Jie-Qi is a five-year-old girl, living with her Chinese parents in a moderate-sized regional city in Australia. Her mother is a university academic and her father is an accountant. For the first year of her life, she was cared for by her grandmother, who speaks no English. She then attended a day-care centre full-time until her third birthday. She currently attends the preschool attached to a local independent school for two days a week and spends the re-mainder of her time at the day-care centre attached to the local University where her mother works. From an early age, Jie-Qi   demonstrated intellectual precoc-ity, fluently navigating the three languages to which she was exposed and show-ing a facility for mathematics. She also demonstrated a desire for intellectual challenge. At the age of three, for example, she requested that she be allowed to go to the independent school all the time, instead of the University centre, be-cause she could learn more.

Both parents are strongly committed to giving her a "good start in life". Jie-Qi embraces activities that allow her to exercise creativity. Since the age of three, she has been studying the violin, taking swimming lessons and attending ballet classes. When she turned four, she added Art lessons to her busy schedule. Her mother enrolled her in a class taught by a Chinese artist so that Jie-Qi could practise her Mandarin speaking at the same time. Jie-Qi's mother insists that all these activities are important for her daughter's self-discipline and to prevent her from being bored. Additional daily violin practice at home is also scheduled. Her mother commented "if she doesn't give 100% effort, I tell her she will have to stop the violin because there is no point in not doing things as well as you can. Then she works harder and she enjoys it more."

Jie-Qi seems happy to engage in the practice sessions mandated by her mother. She also demonstrates some perfectionist tendencies, as she will   voluntarily spend extra time rehearsing her violin or ballet steps, or improving her art-works. She seeks feedback and approval from her parents and if there is any sense that her 'output' is not perfect, she will start her performance from the be-ginning or go back to her drawing board. Her parents record her concerts and she watches them several times and points out to her parents where she was not perfect, stating, "I have to go practise that bit again."

Jie-Qi is a shy and reserved child when she is in the day-care and preschool en-vironments. She is also timid when confronted with novel situations but, once she has gained some experience, she rapidly gains confidence. When sur-rounded by other children, she tends to stand back and follow other children's leads but, among adults, is strong-willed and displays initiative. She enjoys close friendships with a small number of girls who attend the same preschool environments. When playing with these friends at her home, she happily fits in with whatever her friends want to do and never imposes her will on them. In settings where there are children of varying ages, Jie-Qi prefers to associate with children her own age. She is also happy to play with younger children and is attentive to their needs, demonstrating clear social understanding.

Both Jie-Qi's parents have expressed their surprise at her memory abilities and her reflective reasoning. As a three-year-old, she started regularly feeding a neighbour's cat when the neighbour was away. This stimulated a number of long conversations with her parents exploring the origins of animals and their relationship with human beings. During these conversations, she frequently referred to specific details that had escaped her parents' attention, such as the shape of the food-bowl or the arrangement of furniture in the house. She would always remember the days that she needed to feed the cat and would remind her mother or father to get the neighbour's keys from their hallway stand.

Jie-Qi has expressed a strong desire for a sibling so that she can have a play companion at home. Her discussions with her parents around this topic reveal her social awareness and her strong desire to nurture a younger sibling. She often talks about the ways in which she would teach a younger sister or brother "all about everything in the whole world".

In the latter half of 2010, Jie-Qi's parents investigated the possibility of enrolling her in Kindergarten for the 2011 school year. They were advised by the teachers at both centres to delay her entry even while they acknowledged that she was cognitively capable of Kindergarten work. The teachers based their recommendation on Jie-Qi's small physical stature and her timid and shy demeanour. Jie-Qi's parents decided to take this advice, although they indicated that a small part of the decision was that they were planning to spend a few weeks overseas during 2011 and were concerned that if she had been in Kindergarten she may have fallen behind in her work. They decided to provide additional enrichment for her, including enrolling her for several weeks in a preschool in China so that she could improve her Mandarin language skills.

5   Discussion

While there are some points of similarity between Michael and Jie-Qi, there are also distinct differences. In both cases, the children were sufficiently intellectually advanced to enter Kindergarten and both demonstrated the *intentional* thinking described in Porath's chapter (Porath, 2012) that would suggest that their social understanding was at the level expected of those in middle childhood (Porath, 2012). Both children displayed a thirst for learning that was not being met in the early childhood settings, and that may have been possible in the Kindergarten classroom. However, both sets of parents had been advised against early entry on the basis of their child's physical size and aspects of their personality. Neither of these sets of reasons is sufficient to warrant the negative advice given to the parents, nor is either of these aspects likely to change dramatically in the extra year they are forced to remain in the preschool environments.

Both children demonstrate a number of the characteristics that Silverman (2002) associated with the asynchrony of gifted individuals: sensitivity, intensity, curiosity, perceptiveness, complexity, reflectiveness, and perfectionism. Michael demonstrates all of these characteristics. Some of these characteristics, particularly his intensity and complexity, have created social difficulties for him in the day-care setting he currently attends. But he also draws on his perceptiveness and reflectiveness to find the resilience to withstand these issues.

Michael's parents were counselled against early entry because of his size and because of some of the social conflicts he had experienced in the day-care centre. The social issues he had confronted, though, were not consistently demonstrated and highly context-dependent. The teachers providing this advice assumed that he had poorly developed social skills, but he related very well to older children and was comfortable interacting with girls. He had displayed the perceptiveness to develop strategies for dealing with the taunts of the other boys in his day-care group. He would initiate conversations with his mother and the new day-care teacher, Matt, to help develop these plans for social interactions.

Michael's emotional intensity and complexity create a vulnerability for him in the school setting. He currently experiences high levels of frustration because of the treatment he receives from some children in the day-care centre but he demonstrates the capacity to manage his emotions by clenching his fists at his sides and verbalising his frustrations to Matt or to his mother. As indicated, his parents are convinced that he is in danger of disengaging from school if he is not understood and appropriately challenged. Hence, they have carefully weighed their options and selected a school that they believe will give him the social support and a greater intellectual challenge than he would get if he remained in preschool in 2012.

Jie-Qi does not demonstrate the emotional intensity displayed by Michael and she has not experienced any of the social difficulties he has faced. She is motivated to please others. She is perceptive and sensitive to others' intentions and needs and she happily adjusts to satisfy their demands and expectations.

Jie-Qi's parents were advised against entering her early in school in 2011 because of her physical size and because of the perception that she is shy and passive. Certainly, in large group settings, she does tend to hold back but this is motivated by her desire to fit in with others rather than any lack of confidence. Jie-Qi has a desire for intellectual challenge that may have made Kindergarten a better alternative in 2011. However, her parents have ensured that she remains intellectually stimulated by taking her to Europe for a holiday, enrolling her in a preschool in China for several weeks, and by continuing her daily music, dance and art sessions.

6   Conclusion

While these two case studies cannot be generalised to all gifted youngsters, they illustrate the difficulty faced in our current educational system. Despite the positive research evidence, educators continue to resist early entry for young children who are intellectually ready for school. Both Michael and Jie-Qi demonstrated levels of social understanding that were commensurate with their intellectual skills. Michael's emotional intensity did not mean that he was immature or that he could not continue to develop appropriate social skills; Jie-Qi's reticence did not mean that she could not embrace the challenges of the Kindergarten classroom.

Both sets of parents have the capacity to seek advice on the educational needs of their children, which has meant that they could digest the research evidence and weigh it up against the advice they were given by Early Childhood teachers. Not all parents have the same cultural capital to be able to do that. Hence, an ongoing priority in our educational system has to be the training of Early Childhood teachers. The current Federal government has recognized the need to improve the design and delivery of Early Childhood services and is directing much-needed resources to this sector. The establishment of university-based training courses over the last decade has increased the percentage of Early Childhood providers with teaching qualifications. However, there is still more work to be done. The inclusion of units on giftedness should also be mandatory if we are to move to evidence-based practice and away from myth-driven practice.

References

Armstrong, H. (1993). Early enrolment: A parent's perspective. In D. E. Farmer (Ed.), *Gifted children need help* (pp. 98-100). Strathfield, NSW: New South Wales Association for Gifted and Talented Children.

Coenen, M. E. (2002). Using gifted students as peer tutors: An effective and beneficial approach. *Gifted Child Today, 25*(1), 48-55.

Colangelo, N., Assouline, S. G., & Gross, M. U. M. (2004). *A nation deceived: How schools hold back America's brightest students*. Iowa City, IA: Connie Belin & Jacqueline N. Blank International Center for Gifted Education and Talent Development, University of Iowa.

Cole, M., & Cole, S. (2001). *The development of children* (4th edn). New York: Scientific American Books.

Dabrowski, K. (1972). *Psychoneurosis is not an illness*. London: Gryf.

Dabrowski, K., & Piechowski, M. M. (1977). *Theory of levels of emotional development* (Vols. 1 & 2). Oceanside, NY: Dabor Science.

Diezmann, C. M., Watters, J. J., & Fox, K. (2001). Early entry to school in Australia: Rhetoric, research and reality. *Australasian Journal of Gifted Education, 10*(2), 5-18.

Gagné, F., & Gagnier, N. (2004). The socio-affective and academic impact of early entrance to school. *Roeper Review, 26,* 128-138.

Gallagher, S., Smith, S., & Merrotsy, P. (2010). Early entry: When should a gifted child start school? *Australasian Journal of Gifted Education, 19*(1), 16-23.

Gross, M. U. M. (2002a). Social and emotional issues for exceptionally intellectually gifted students. In M. Neihart, S. M. Reis, N. M. Robinson & S. M. Moon (Eds.), *The social and emotional development of gifted children: What do we know?* (pp. 19-30). Waco, Texas: Prufrock Press, Inc.

Gross, M. U. M. (2002b). "Play Partner" or "Sure Shelter": What gifted children look for in friendship. *The SENG Newsletter* (2), 1-3.

Hattie, J. (2009). *Visible learning: A synthesis of over 800 meta-analyses relating to achievement.* London: Routledge.

Kervin, L., & Vialle, W. (2004). Aliens are coming tomorrow: The gifted student as peer tutor. *Australasian Journal of Gifted Education, 13* (1), 12-19.

Kulik, J. A., & Kulik, C-L. C. (1997). Ability grouping. In N. Colangelo & G. A. Davis (Eds.), *Handbook of gifted education.* (2nd ed., pp. 230-242). Boston, MA: Allyn and Bacon.

Levine, E. S., & Kitano, M. K. (1998). Helping young children reclaim their strengths. In J. F. Smutny (Ed.), *The young gifted child: Potential and promise. An anthology* (pp. 282-294). Cresskill, NJ: Hampton Press.

Meininger, L. (1998). Curriculum for the young gifted child. In J. F. Smutny (Ed.), *The young gifted child: Potential and promise. An anthology* (pp. 492-500). Cresskill, NJ: Hampton Press.

NAGC (2008). What is Giftedness? Retrieved from http://www.nagc.org/index.aspx?id=574

NSW Department of Education and Training. (2004). Policy and implementation strategies for the education of gifted and talented students.

Piechowski, M. M. (1991). Emotional development and emotional giftedness. In N. Colangelo & G. A. Davis (Eds.), *Handbook of gifted education* (pp. 285–306). Needham Heights, MA: Allyn & Bacon.

Porath, M. (2012). Understanding the Social Context of Learning: Gifted Students' Perspectives. In H. Stoeger, A. Aljughaiman, & B. Harder (eds.), *Talent development and excellence* (pp. 98-115). Münster, Germany: LIT.

Rankin, F., & Vialle, W. (1996). Early entry: A policy in search of practice. *Australian Journal of Early Childhood, 21*(1), 6-11.

Robinson, N. M. (2004). Effects of academic acceleration on the social-emotional status of gifted sudents. In N. Colangelo, S. G. Assouline, & M. U. M. Gross (Eds.), *A nation deceived: How schools hold back America's brightest students* (Vol. 2, pp. 59-67). Iowa City, IA: Connie Belin & Jacqueline N. Blank International Center for Gifted Education and Talent Development, University of Iowa.

Rogers, K. B. (1991). *The relationship of grouping practices to the education of the gifted and talented learner.* Storrs, CT: National Research Center on the Gifted and Talented, University of Connecticut.

Rogers, K. B. (2002). Effects of acceleration on gifted learners. In M. Neihart, S. M. Reis, N. M. Robinson & S. M. Moon (Eds.), *The social and emotional development of gifted children: What do we know?* (pp. 3-12). Waco, TX: Prufrock Press.

Silverman, L. (2002). Asynchronous development. In M. Neihart, S. M. Reis, N. M. Robinson & S. M. Moon (Eds.), *The social and emotional development of gifted children: What do we know?* (pp. 31–37). Waco, TX: Prufrock Press.

VanTassel-Baska, J. (1986). Acceleration. In C. J. Maker (Ed.), *Critical issues in gifted education* (pp. 179-196). Rockville, MD: Aspen Publishers.

Vialle, W., Ashton, T., Carlon, G., & Rankin, F. (2001). Acceleration: A coat of many colours. *Roeper Review,* 24(1), 14-19.

Vygotsky, L. S. (1978). *Mind in society: The development of higher psychological processes* (M. Cole, V. John-Steiner, S. Scribner & E. Souberman, trans.). Cambridge, MA: Harvard University Press.

Vygotsky, L. S. (1986). *Thought and language* (A. Kozulin, trans.). Cambridge, MA: MIT Press.

Wertsch, J. (1985). *Vygotsky and the social formation of mind.* Cambridge, MA: Harvard University Press.

Whan, L. (1993). Early entry to Kindergarten. In D. E. Farmer (Ed.), *Gifted children need help* (pp. 95-97). Strathfield, NSW: New South Wales Association for Gifted and Talented Children.

Wood, D., Bruner, J. S., & Ross, G. (1976). The role of tutoring in problem solving. *Journal of Child Psychology and Psychiatry, 17*(2), 89-100.

Philipp Martzog, Wei Chen, Heidrun Stoeger, Jiannong Shi, & Albert Ziegler

Specifying Relations Between Fine Motor Skills and Cognitive Abilities: A Cross-Cultural Study

Abstract

To investigate the relevance of preschool children`s fine motor skills for their cognitive development (Case-Smith, 1994), we examined three hypotheses. First, fine motor skills supporting environmental interactions (hand skill, eye-hand-coordination) should be more strongly related to cognitive abilities than those that do not support environmental interactions (fine-motor-speed). Second, fine motor skills and cognitive abilities should still be correlated after controlling for attention. Third, advanced fine motor skills should positively affect cognitive abilities. The first and second hypothesis was examined in a sample of 95 German preschool children. To examine the third hypothesis, the German sample was compared with a sample of 95 Chinese preschool children who were assumed to have advanced fine motor skills because of culturally-specific experiences in the fine motor domain (Chow, Henderson, & Barnett, 2001). Expectations concerning the first and second hypothesis were confirmed, the third hypothesis could not be examined as German and Chinese children's fine motor skills did not systematically differ. Results are discussed with regard to future research and educational implications.

1   Introduction

Fine motor skills in childhood are important for success in many daily routines. Fine motor skills support, for example, self-care activities such as dressing or eating (Henderson, 1995), which are essential for social independence from caregivers. Furthermore, fine motor skills represent the basis for competent play activities and manipulations of toys or objects (Eisert & Lamorey, 1996). In addition to and as a consequence of their supportive function with regard to successful environmental interactions, fine motor skills have been suggested to affect cognitive learning (e.g. Davis, Pitchford, & Limback, 2011). Specific and elaborated theoretical arguments leading to this assumption, however, have not yet been suggested. Therefore, in the first part of the chapter we will propose more elaborated reasons why fine motor skills could be an important factor within the development of cognitive abilities. From an empirical point of view positive correlations between fine motor skills and cognitive abilities have sometimes been interpreted as indicators for the causal role of fine motor skills with regard to the development of cognitive abilities (Dellatolas et al., 2003; Voelcker-Rehage, 2005). However, only few studies provide real support. The second part of the chapter therefore reports a study that investigated three issues which have not yet been addressed sufficiently by previous studies. The first is inferred from the assumption that fine motor skills affect cognitive abilities by facilitating environmental interactions (Davis et al., 2011). If this is true, specific dimensions of fine motor skills which support environmental interactions should be more strongly correlated with cognitive abilities than dimensions which are less involved in environmental interactions. The second issue addresses the question of whether the postulated link between fine motor skills and cognitive abilities remains substantial after a potentially confounding variable, namely attention, is controlled for. This seems of special importance considering the finding by Wassenberg and colleagues (2005) who reported a reduced link between a measure of motor and cognitive abilities once the influence of attention was controlled for. A final issue addresses the lack of evidence for the causal relevance of fine motor skills with respect to cognitive abilities. If fine motor skills indeed play a causal role in cognitive development, advanced fine motor skills should be associated with a corresponding advantage in cognitive abilities.

Before examining these questions we will report theoretical arguments for the link in the next section.

2   Theoretical Background

Several theoretical accounts have been suggested as explanations for the link between motor skills and cognitive abilities (Burrmann & Stucke, 2009; Everke & Woll, 2007; Exner & Henderson, 1995). Neurobiological explanations assume common cerebral mechanisms of motor and cognitive functions. In particular, it is assumed that motor-skill learning activates neural areas that also underlie cognitive functions and vice versa (Grissmer, Grimm, Aiyer, Murrah, & Steel, 2010).

Neurophysiological explanations, on the other hand, assume positive effects of physical exercise on cognitive functioning (e.g. Etnier, Nowell, Landers, & Sibley, 2006). Accordingly physical exercise and motor activity leads to enhanced blood flow and changes in the neurotransmitter constellations which in turn supports cognitive functioning (e.g. Etnier et al., 2006).

A third group of explanations stresses the importance of confounding variables. Factors that have been suggested as candidates are: Social background and parenting behavior (Luo, Jose, Huntsinger, & Pigott, 2007), focused attention (Wassenberg et al., 2005) and a common maturational mechanism (e.g. Diamond, 2000).

Developmental and learning theories (e.g. Piaget, 1952; Thelen, 1995) represent a fourth group of explanations. Theories from this fourth approach in our view explain best how fine motor skills might influence the development of cognitive abilities. In the next section we detail three variants of this approach. Each describes a different way in which children's motor skills could affect advances in cognitive abilities.

2.1   Developmental and Learning Theories

A first pathway of how children's fine motor skills might affect cognitive abilities derives from Piaget's work and more recently from the embodied cognition approach (e.g. Thelen, 2000). According to these approaches, children's knowledge about objects within their environment is identical with the actions that can be performed with these objects (Piaget, 1952). A tool, for example, would be represented by the specific actions that can be performed with the tool (e.g. a spoon can be used for eating). Accordingly skillful interactions with an object would support the acquisition of knowledge about the object. In order to acquire the concept of a spoon, the child would for example need certain prerequisite hand-eye-coordination skills. Support for this idea comes from studies finding stronger cognitive representations of objects which afford high amounts of manual experiences (book) vs. low amounts of manual experiences (bird) (Holt & Beilock, 2006; Siakaluk et al., 2008).

A second pathway through which fine motor skills could affect cognitive learning is inferred from an assumption of the information processing approach. Accordingly, the child's fine motor skills support cognitive learning in tasks which at the same time require fine motor manipulations (e.g. games such as memory, domino, three dimensional block play etc.). If children are able to skillfully manipulate play and learning materials, they will be free to focus attention on the cognitive demands of the task (Case, 1998; Kail & Park, 1990).

A third suggestion for how fine motor skills could affect advances in cognitive abilities refers to an indirect mechanism that assumes motivational and affective variables as mediators. As the number of fine motor tasks in children's everyday live is high (Marr, Cermak, Cohn, & Henderson, 2003), success should frequently depend on fine motor skills. Greater fine motor skills should in turn lead to more self-confidence, greater persistence in challenging tasks and reduced anxiety. These motivational and affective advantages should facilitate handling cognitively challenging tasks and therewith improve cognitive abilities.

All three of the above suggested mechanisms assume that advances in cognitive abilities are based on children's ability to interact successfully within the environment. However, considering the contribution of fine motor skills in terms of successful environmental interactions, it is unlikely that this applies for fine motor skills in a general sense. Instead it seems more likely that different dimensions of children's fine motor skills differ in their importance for environmental interactions.

In the following, we will elaborate this argument with regard to three central dimensions of children's fine motor skills: *(hand skill, eye-hand-coordination and fine-motor-speed)*. All three dimensions have been identified in factor analyses as separate dimensions (Baedke, 1980; Fleishman, 1972). Furthermore they were reported to correlate with cognitive abilities (e.g. Davis et al., 2011; Voelcker-Rehage, 2005).

Hand skill, as the first dimension, represents the ability to precisely control the finger of a hand in order to manipulate small objects in a skillful manner (Fleishman, 1954; Pehoski, 1995). The skill is involved in many daily routines (e.g. zip fastening), play behavior, management of toys (e.g. puzzles) and tasks that support incidental learning (e.g. calculation of objects). As this skill obviously supports environmental interactions it can be assumed to be directly related with cognitive abilities.

Eye-hand-coordination is a second dimension of children's fine motor skill repertoires. It represents the ability to perform visually guided motor movements with high precision (Baedke, 1980). Eye-hand-coordination is part of any action that requires precise reaching or control of small objects (e.g. transporting objects, reaching for objects in order to manipulate them, stabilizing objects in order to manipulate them, orienting of toys and objects etc). Compared to hand skill, eye-hand-coordination frequently precedes object manipulation rather than being directly involved in the manipulations themselves. Therefore, eye-hand-coordination should be more weakly related to cognitive learning than hand skill.

Fine-motor-speed is the third dimension. It represents the ability to act quickly on simple repetitive tasks requiring little or no eye-hand-coordination (Baedke, 1980). Because of both its simple structure and the speed orientation, this skill is of little relevance for typical object interactions such as exploring the physical properties of an object, tool use, building objects into a construction. Usually these object interactions requiring more sophisticated actions are of medium or slow speed and precision. Thus, although fine-motor-speed represents another dimension of preschool children's fine motor repertoire it should only weakly be related to cognitive abilities.

2.2 Empirical Evidence for the Link Between Fine Motor Skills and Cognitive Abilities

Although the above described theoretical explanations have not yet been examined explicitly some studies provide supportive hints. That is, consistent with the idea that fine motor skills support the cognitive development in preschool children, several authors have found positive correlations between both, fine motor skills and cognitive abilities. Recently Davis and colleagues (2011) reported high positive correlations between eye-hand-coordination and visual processing. Dickes (1978) identified a positive correlation between eye-hand-coordination and several factors of nonverbal and verbal cognitive abilities. The finding was replicated in other studies (e.g. Baedke, 1980; Roebers & Kauer, 2009). Solan and Mozlin (1986) found finger skill to be positively correlated with general intelligence. Smirni and Zappalà (1989) identified a moderate link between hand skill and both, speech comprehension, and visual spatial abilities. In addition to these cross-sectional findings a longitudinal study reports hand skill to positively predict aspects of executive functioning (Delatollas et al., 2003). Although experimental work is mainly lacking, Steward, Rule and Giordano (2007) found first evidence for the effect of a six month eye-hand-coordination training on aspects of attention. Besides this positive evidence other studies found no general link between fine motor skills and cognitive abilities (Piek, Dawson, Smith, & Gasson, 2008; Schewe, 1977). Overall, fine motor skills seem to be more frequently related than unrelated with cognitive abilities.

2.3 Shortcomings of Previous Research and Aims of the Present Study

The following section will outline three shortcomings of existing studies and the aims of our study. The first shortcoming of existing studies addresses a lack of knowledge about specific relations between different fine motor skills and different cognitive abilities. According to the second shortcoming, existing studies have not controlled for the influence of potential confounding variables, such as focused attention. The third shortcoming refers to the lack of studies with appropriate methodology to examine the causal role of fine motor skills in the development of cognitive abilities.

Shortcoming 1: A first shortcoming of existing studies with preschool children is the empirical status of specific relations between different fine motor skills and cognitive abilities, which has two aspects. First, no study has systematically examined different dimensions of fine motor skills and different dimensions of cognitive abilities at the same time. Hence it might be the case that different results between studies are due to variations in fine motor skills or to variations in cognitive abilities. Second, different studies have implemented different measures to assess the same dimension of fine motor skills and/or cognitive abilities (e.g. Davis et al., 2011; Dickes, 1978). It is thus not possible to judge whether differences in effect size in two studies result from different ability dimensions or whether they result from methodological variations (Davis et al., 2011; Smirni & Zappalà, 1989).

Aim 1: A first aim of the present study is therefore, the systematic examination of different dimensions of fine motor skills and different cognitive abilities, simultaneously, in the same study. Through this means, possible differences in the strength of correlations can be attributed to variations among dimensions of abilities rather than to differences in measures.

According to the idea that different dimensions of children's fine motor skills differ in their functional value for environmental interactions, we had specific expectations concerning their relation to cognitive abilities. It was assumed that the dimension of hand skill is more strongly related with cognitive abilities than eye-hand-coordination. Eye-hand-coordination should in turn be stronger related with cognitive abilities than fine-motor-speed.

First evidence for this particular pattern of relations comes from one of our own studies, which examined relations between the three fine motor skills and two cognitive abilities (knowledge and reasoning) in a sample of 77 five year old preschool children. Results confirmed strongest correlations between hand skill and both, reasoning and knowledge. Eye-hand-coordination and fine-motor-speed were found to be only weakly correlated with cognitive abilities (Martzog, Stöger, & Ziegler, 2009).

Shortcoming 2: A second shortcoming is that none of the existing studies has examined the influence of factors that have been suggested to confound the relation between motor skills and cognitive abilities (see section 2). Focused attention[1] is one factor which should particularly be considered as many fine motor and cognitive tasks demand, to some degree, attention. Thus, children who rank high in their ability to focus attention should demonstrate greater performance in both fine motor and cognitive tasks. Consistent with this argument Wassenberg and colleagues (2005) found reduced correlations between general motor skills and general cognitive abilities after attention was controlled.

Aim 2: Therefore the second aim of our study was to investigate the attention-controlled relations between fine motor skills and cognitive abilities. If the link between fine motor skills and cognitive abilities results from a causal effect of fine motor skills, attention should not completely explain the link. Specifically, it was assumed that attention confounds certain relations to a stronger degree than other relations. Relations between fine motor skills and cognitive abilities which are measured by tasks requiring a lot of attention should be particularly

---

[1] In the following the term attention is used for focused attention

confounded by attention. This should apply for eye-hand-coordination and hand skill as both skill dimensions depend on the precise execution of carefully visual guided movement and precision grasps (Cratty, 1986). Within the cognitive domain mainly reasoning should be affected. This is assumed because measures of reasoning usually demand close visual inspection of the figural test items[2] and thereby attention.

Shortcoming 3: A third shortcoming of previous research is the frequent use of cross-sectional designs which do not permit causal conclusions. Only few studies have examined the postulated causal role of fine motor skills with regard to the development of cognitive abilities. Dellatolas and colleagues (2003), for example, found in their longitudinal study with preschool children that finger skills were moderately predictive for some cognitive skills (semantic fluency) but not for others (digit span).

Aim 3: The third aim of the present study was to explore further indicators for a causal role of fine motor skills with regard to the development of cognitive abilities. Specifically, it was expected that children who have developed superior fine motor skills because of early learning experiences also demonstrate superior cognitive abilities. Children with no such learning experiences on the other hand should have both lower fine motor skills and cognitive abilities. To investigate this, the present study capitalizes on a finding from cross-cultural research. According to this research, Asian children possess superior fine motor skills compared to children from Western culture, perhaps because of unique socio-cultural influences. Specifically, it has been argued that Chinese children profit from the early use of chopsticks and drawing utensils as well as early parenting behavior (Huntsinger, Jose, Krieg, & Luo, 2011). Accordingly Chinese children are reported to show superior hand skill (Chow et al., 2001) and eye-hand-coordination (Huntsinger et al., 2011). Differences with respect to fine-motor-speed have not yet been investigated to our knowledge.

With regard to the reported findings of Chow and colleagues (2001) and Huntsinger and colleagues (2011) the present study will compare Chinese children's fine motor skills to German children's fine motor skills. If the advantage of Chinese children's fine motor skills can be replicated a corresponding advantage of their cognitive abilities is expected. By this means results are not only based on cross-sectional research but can carefully be interpreted as quasi-experimental.

3   Method

- *Sample*

The first and second questions were examined in a sample of 95 German preschool children aged 4 to 6 years (M = 60.1 months, SD = 9.6; 50 boys and 45

---

[2] Examples are subtests from: WPPS; K-ABC; Raven matrices; CFT 1

girls). To examine the third question, a sample of 95 Chinese children was selected and matched according to age and gender to the German sample (M = 59.8 months, SD = 9.6; 50 boys and 45 girls). All children had been selected from a population of normally developed (non-clinical) preschool children after informed parental consents were obtained for each child.

- *Procedure*

Children were examined individually in a quiet room of their kindergarten. Each child was assessed in the domains of fine motor skills, cognitive abilities and focused attention. The procedure was organized into three consecutive sessions which each lasted about 30 minutes. In each country, the highly standardized investigations were conducted by carefully trained native speakers.

- *Instruments*

Fine motor skills

Fine motor skills were assessed within the three domains of hand skill, eye-hand-coordination, and fine-motor-speed. The instrument consisted of items which either represented age adjusted adaptations from preexisting measures that had been used with older children (e.g. Baedke, 1980) or were directly adopted (Büttner, Frostig, Hammill, Pearson, & Voress, 2008). To maximize the reliability of the measures, all tasks were specifically prepared to be appropriate for young children. As each dimension was represented by three items the whole measure of fine motor abilities consisted of 9 standardized tasks. The tasks which had already been used in a pilot study with 77 preschool children (Martzog, Stöger, & Ziegler, 2009) were slightly improved for the present study. Results from confirmatory factor analysis verified that the 9 items could be assigned to the three expected skill dimensions (CMIN/DF = 2.19, SRMR = .042, CFI = .976, RMSEA = .08).

All of the fine motor tasks were performed with the preferred hand.

Hand skill: The measure of hand skill included a) *peg-placing*, b) *bead-threading* and c) *block-turning* (Chronbach`s Alpha = .87). In the *peg-moving* task the child had to quickly pick up 24 tiny pegs from a wooden board and place them in a row of holes in the same wooden board. The score resulted from a combination of two measures. The first represents the time that was needed to finish all 24 pegs. The second represents the errors (number of pegs dropped) during the trial. The task was performed in two similar trials.

In the *bead-threading* task the child had to quickly thread 20 small beads onto a vertical rod. The score is composed of the combination of two measures. The first represented the time which the child needed in order to put all 20 beads on the rod. The second represented the errors (beads dropped) during the trial. Two similar trials were conducted.

In the *block-turning* task, the child had to quickly flip 16 small wooden blocks that were inserted in slots in a board. In two similar trials the score resulted from a combination of two measures. The first represented the time which the child needed in order to flip the 16 blocks. The second represented the errors (number of blocks dropped) during a trial.

Eye-hand-coordination: The measure of eye-hand-coordination included a) *tracing* (subtest of the German version of DTVP-2, Büttner et al., 2008), b) *aiming 1* and c) *aiming 2,* (Chronbach's Alpha = .84). In the *tracing* task the child was asked to trace a line between two narrow lines without crossing them. Higher scores were received if the child only rarely crossed the border lines and/or the deviation from the centerline was small. Lower scores were obtained if the child frequently crossed the lines and/or the deviation from the center line was great. The two *aiming* tasks were quite similar and only differed in the arrangement of the targets stimuli. In both tasks the child had to aim with a pen at 20 small concentric circles (Ø = 0.7 cm) which were arranged on a sheet of paper (21x29cm). Higher scores were received if many circles were successfully hit in the center.

Fine-motor-speed: The measure of fine-motor-speed included three tasks which were all videotaped: a) *pen-tapping*, b) *bell-ringing* and c) *computer key-tapping* (Chronbach's Alpha = .75). In the *pen-tapping* task, the child quickly performed as many repeated taps as possible. Each tap was performed by a pen on a sheet of paper. In the *bell-task* the child quickly and repeatedly moved a device sideways in order to ring a bell. The child had to perform as many movements as possible. In the *computer-tapping* task the child quickly tapped the space bar of a computer-keyboard and, had to perform as many taps as possible. For each of the three tasks the number of movements in 10 seconds was recorded.

Cognitive abilities

Reasoning and knowledge were examined within the cognitive domain. The decision to select rather general cognitive abilities should help to identify differential effects of different fine motor skills that can be generalized across different cognitive dimensions. Reasoning and knowledge were assessed by subtests from an established intelligence test HAWIVA-III (Ricken, Fritz, Schuck, & Preuss, 2007). The Chinese version of the respective subtests was based on a translation of the German version and a corresponding back-translation.

Reasoning: Reasoning was assessed by the two subtests a) matrices and b) classifications. Both tasks required the child to visually inspect pictorial material and select the correct response by pointing at it.

Knowledge: Knowledge was assessed by the two subtests a) general knowledge and b) concepts. Both subtests were conducted in a face to face situation with the experimenter who verbally asked the child questions about various aspects of children's every-day knowledge.

Focused Attention

Focused Attention was measured by the German *„Konzentrations-Handlungsverfahren für Vorschulkinder"* [Concentration-Action-Test for pre-school children] (Ettrich & Ettrich, 2006). The child sorts 40 plastic cards according to predefined symbol combinations in four boxes. High scores of attention were obtained if many cards could be sorted in the correct boxes in short time.

4 Results

The first step of data-analyses refers to the results from the 95 German children. Table 1 presents descriptive statistics for all three dimensions of fine motor skills, the two cognitive abilities, and attention. Inspection of skew and kurtosis of the variables indicate that most variables approximate a normal distribution except for attention, which exhibited a negative skew.

For the subsequent correlation analyses the fine-motor-variables were z-standardized and combined to sum scores that constitute the three dimensions of hand skill, eye-hand-coordination and fine-motor-speed.

Table 1: Means and Standard Deviations for Fine Motor Skills, Cognitive Abilities and Attention

	Min	Max	M	SD
Hand skill				
Beads-threading	232[a]	78	74.42	20.02
Pegs-moving	212[a]	77	73.34	15.02
Blocks-turning	127[a]	41	74.84	18.27
Eye-Hand-Coordination				
Tracing	71	182	132.78	25.49
Aiming 1	23	58	46.14	6.43
Aiming 2	32	60	49.40	6.62
Fine-Motor-Speed				
Pen–tapping	24	56	40.34	6.93
Key-tapping	18	51	29.47	6.71
Bell-ringing	18	47	35.49	6.77
Cognitive Abilities				
Reasoning[b]	5	26	16.03	4.62
Knowledge[c]	7	40	27.20	7.82
Hypothesized Confounder				
Attention (AT)	14	40	31.01	6.25

Note. M = Mean; SD = Standard deviation; a = For beads, pegs and blocks higher values indicate lower performance, for all remaining variables higher values indicate better performance.; b = sum score of matrices and classifications; c = sum score of general knowledge and concepts.

To examine the first aim of the study bivariate correlations were calculated (Table 2). According to our expectations hand skill should be stronger associated with cognitive abilities than the other two fine-motor-dimensions (eye-hand-coordination and fine-motor-speed). Furthermore, eye-hand-coordination should correlate higher with cognitive abilities than fine-motor-speed.

With regard to the first aim of the study, results in table two show the expected relational pattern for the zero-order correlations (uc) between the three fine motor skills and reasoning. That is, hand skill correlated strongest with reasoning, eye-hand-coordination showed a weaker correlation and fine-motor-speed was not correlated with reasoning. As expected, hand skill also correlated with knowledge. It was, however, unexpected that knowledge was not related with eye-hand-coordination. Taken together, these findings however provide preliminary support for the assumption that those fine motor skills with high relevance for environmental interactions are stronger related with cognitive abilities than fine motor skills with lower relevance for environmental interactions.

Table 2: Zero-Order and Attention Controlled Correlations Between Fine Motor Skills and Cognitive Abilities in the German Sample (N = 95)

		Reasoning	Knowledge	Attention
Hand skill	uncorrected	$-.26_a^*$	$-.25_a^*$	$-.06_a$
	corrected	$-.25_a^*$	$-.24_a^*$	
Eye-hand-coordination	uncorrected	$.20^*$	.06	.17
	corrected	.17	.03	
Fine-motor-speed	uncorrected	.09	-.18	-.07
	corrected	.12	-.18	
Attention		$.22^*$	.19	

Note. corrected = controlled for attention; uncorrected = not controlled for attention; a = negative correlations indicate that shorter time to finish the Hand skill Task corresponds to higher values in Reasoning and Knowledge. $^*p < 0.5$

The second research aim examined the impact of attention which was assumed to partially confound specific relations between fine motor skills and cognitive abilities. To do so, attention controlled correlations were compared to zero-order-correlations (Table 2). Results indicate only a small explanatory contribution of attention in terms of the examined relations between fine motor skills and cognitive abilities. Regarding our specific expectations the link between hand skill and cognitive abilities remained almost unaffected after attention was partialed out. At the same time, the link between eye-hand-coordination and reasoning turned insignificant after attention was controlled for. A comparison of Fishers z-transformed coefficients yielded no significant difference between the original and the attention controlled correlations in neither case, $p > .10$.

The third research aim was to find out whether the link between fine motor skills and cognitive abilities results from a causal effect of fine motor skills on cognitive abilities. Specifically, it was intended to investigat whether advanced fine motor skills correspond to advanced cognitive abilities. In order to examine this question, a necessary condition had to be confirmed before. That is, it was investigated whether Chinese children demonstrate superior fine motor skills compared to German children, as has been reported in previous studies (e.g. Chui, Ng, Fong, Lin, & Ng (2007). Multivariate analysis of variance (MANOVA) was applied to analyze whether Chinese and German children differed on the three dimensions of fine motor skills. Results show that according to the omnibus test of multivariate analysis of variance, Chinese and German children differed significantly in terms of their fine motor skills, $F(3, 186) = 52.12$, $p < .000$; Wilk's $\lambda = 0.543$, partial $\varepsilon^2 = .45$. To decide if Chinese children differ from German children in the expected manner the mean performances on the three fine motor skill dimensions were inspected (Table 3).

Table 3: Means, Standard Deviations, and Effect Sizes for Differences Between Chinese and German Children

Variable	Germany n = 95		China n = 95		$F(1,188)$	p	Partial η^2
	M	SD	M	SD			
Beads	139.49[a]	31.99	160.05	45.40	13.01	.000	.065
Pegs	119,54[a]	24.14	132.98	28.32	12.39	.001	.062
Blocks	74.84[a]	18.27	82.64	18.31	8.64	.004	.044
Total Hand skill	**0.14[b]**	**0.77**	**-0.14**	**0.93**	**5.46**	**.02**	**.028**
Tracing	132.8	25.49	149.4	18.45	26.38	.000	.123
Aiming1	46.14	6.43	53.78	3.95	97.56	.000	.342
Aiming2	49.40	6.62	54.79	4.01	46.03	.000	.197
Total Eye-Hand-Coordination	**-0.46[b]**	**0.81**	**0.46**	**0.58**	**79.94**	**.000**	**.298**
Pen	40.34	6.93	33.47	10.57	28.02	.000	.130
Key	35.50	6.78	35.81	6.25	.11	.739	.001
Bell	29.47	6.72	29.47	6.72	1.28	.259	.007
Total Fine-Motor-Speed	**0.25[b]**	**2.36**	**-0.25**	**2.54**	**2.02**	**.157**	**.011**

Note. a = For beads, pegs and blocks greater values indicate lower performance, for all remaining variables higher values indicate greater performance; b = z-standardized variables.

The assumed superior fine motor skills of Chinese children were not confirmed generally. Contrary to our expectation, German children compared to Chinese children demonstrated advanced hand skill. At the same time Chinese children had better eye-hand-coordination which was consistent with the expectation. No differences were found between Chinese and German children with regard to the dimension of fine-motor-speed. The inconsistent finding of higher eye-hand-coordination but lower hand skill of Chinese children compared to German children indicated that the necessary condition for a quasi-experimental design was not realized in the present study. The subsequent comparison of Chinese and German children's cognitive abilities was therefore explorative. Results from t-tests for independent samples showed similar reasoning ability of Chinese ($M = 16.67$, $SD = 6.83$) and German children ($M = 16.03$, $SD = 4.63$). The small advantage for Chinese children was not significant, t (188) = .795, p = .449. Considering the difference between Chinese and German children's knowledge, a significant advantage of Chinese children was found (Chinese: $M = 29.74$, $SD = 5.62$; German: $M = 27.20$, $SD = 7.83$, t (188) = 2.56, p = .011).

5   Discussion

Previous research has assumed that fine motor skills are involved in competent environmental interactions during the preschool years and through these means support cognitive development (Davis et al., 2011, Thelen, 2000). In summing the main findings of the present study, the expected link between fine motor skills and cognitive abilities was demonstrated. This adds to the existing evidence reporting positive correlations between both ability domains (e.g. Davis et al., 2011; Dickes, 1978; Smirni & Zappalà, 1989). However, the current findings do extend previous research in several respects.

First, the present study provided evidence for a more differentiated rather than a global link between fine motor skills and cognitive abilities. The particular correlation pattern identified supports the idea that fine motor skills with high functional value for environmental interactions (hand skill) show higher correlations with cognitive abilities than fine motor skills with medium (eye-hand-coordination) or low (fine motor-speed) functional value for environmental interactions.

A closer look is necessary with regard to the weaker correlation between eye-hand-coordination and cognitive abilities compared to hand skill and cognitive abilities. On the one hand, the difference between eye-hand-coordination and hand skill was expected because it is consistent with the lesser significance of eye-hand-coordination for environmental interactions (Pehoski, 1995). On the other hand, a methodological feature of the current study provides a potential explanation. Namely, it is possible that the lower correlation between eye-hand-coordination and cognitive abilities resulted from restricted variance. This idea is supported by the comparison of the variances from the three fine motor dimensions which indicated the smallest variance for eye-hand-coordination. Moreover, the mean values in children's eye-hand-coordination suggested a ceiling-effect. Thus, it is likely that the measure of eye-hand-coordination did not differentiate enough between children. Despite this limitation, the general correlational pattern is still generally in line with the assumed differential relevance of the three fine motor skill dimensions. Thus it is can be argued that the correlation between eye-hand-coordination and cognitive abilities is lower than between hand skill and cognitive abilities, but higher than between fine-motor-speed and cognitive abilities.

Although the contribution focused on differences between fine motor skills, results also indicated a difference between the two cognitive abilities of reasoning and knowledge. In particular, this difference concerns the finding that eye-hand-coordination was more strongly related to reasoning than to knowledge. A possible explanation for this finding could be the common visual processing demands of eye-hand-coordination and reasoning tasks. Support for the idea comes from a study that found a tight link between eye-hand-coordination and visual processing ($r = .48$) during preschool (Davis et al., 2011). The same argument should apply for reasoning, which has been measured by tasks that required the child to visually search pictorial material. Knowledge retrieval, on the other hand, did not require any visual processing because it was measured by interview questions.

The second aim of the present study – that goes beyond previous research – was directed at the validity of the assumed causal mechanism. If the link between fine motor skills and cognitive abilities results from a causal effect of fine motor skills, relations between these two constructs should continue to exist after controlling the confounding influence of attention. In our study, the strong impact of attention regarding relations between general motor skills and general cognitive abilities reported by Wassenberg and colleagues (2005) was not confirmed. As attention had only a small but insignificant influence on the link between fine motor skills and cognitive abilities it be ruled out as a major explanation for the link.

The third aim of the study – that goes beyond previous research – was to explore further indicators for a causal role of fine motor skills within the development of cognitive abilities. The reported findings from the German sample are somewhat tentative in this regard because of the cross-sectional study design. To remedy this, we had indented to introduce an additional quasi-experimental condition, based on the assumption of better fine motor skills in Chinese children compared to German children. Unfortunately the assumed advantage of Chinese children's fine motor skills was not consistently found in the present study. Therefore the small advantage of Chinese children's cognitive abilities that was found could not be taken as an indicator for the causal relevance of fine motor skills.

At least two reasons might explain why the reported advantage in fine motor skills of Chinese children (Chow et al., 2001) was not found for hand skill. First, the present study did not control whether the Chinese children were actually exposed to conditions which have been reported to promote fine motor skills, such as early parent involvement (Huntsinger et al., 2011) or usage of chopsticks and drawing utensils (Chui et al., 2007). German children might, for example, have encountered conditions that specifically promoted their hand skill. Future cross-cultural studies should, therefore, control for differences between learning environments. A second explanation might be that German children were investigated by a male experimenter whereas Chinese children were investigated by a female experimenter. As preschool children in both countries are used to female caregivers, German children might have been more motivated during task completion than Chinese children. This should especially impact hand skill as the respective tasks demand both, high speed and accuracy and both task demands are affected by motivation (Schilling, 1974).

Limitations and Future Research
Although the present study incorporated several improvements compared to previous research, certain limitations have to be considered. A first limitation is associated with the cross-sectional design that was used and the failure to find between-group differences in the quasi-experimental condition. Because of these methodological limitations, no definitive inferences with respect to the postulated causal role of fine motor skills and the development of cognitive abilities can be made. Future research investigating the causal role of fine motor skills for cognitive abilities should, as a result, go beyond cross-sectional studies. (Quasi-) Experimental studies could serve as an economical and less intrusive first step to further explore the question of which fine motor skill is the most likely to be of causal relevance for cognitive abilities. Once specific fine motor skill dimensions have been identified, longitudinal studies should follow.
Experimental studies could then explore the mechanisms that have been postulated to underlie the assumed effect of fine motor skills on cognitive abilities.
A second limitation results from the specific focus of the present study. Specifically the focus was on differences between various dimensions of fine motor skills and not on differences between various dimensions of cognitive abilities. Accordingly it was suggested that the study provides information about how different effect sizes could be attributed to differences between fine motor skills. No information is provided about how the link between fine motor skills and cognitive abilities depends on different cognitive abilities. Considering the hypothesized relevance of certain fine motor skills for the exploration of objects, visual-spatial abilities might for example be linked to fine motor skills to a greater degree than reasoning and knowledge. It can, for example, be assumed that skillful manual object interactions would help the child to detect the relevant spatial attributes of the respective object. Support for this argument comes from results that found visual-manual activities of infants to be related to visual-spatial abilities (Soska, Adolph, & Johnson, 2010).

Practical Implications
Given the limitations of the present study only certain practical implications are now considered. Recommendations addressing fine-motor-skill interventions

are not possible as they require evidence for a causal role of fine motor skills with regard to cognitive abilities. For this reason recommendations focus on the issue of diagnosing cognitive abilities in children. Several published cognitive ability measures do not only assess cognitive abilities but to a certain degree fine motor skills which negatively affects the validity of these measures. Ziegler and Stöger (2010) showed that fine motor skill deficits interfered with the identification of elementary school students of high cognitive abilities. If tasks in cognitive ability tests require fine motor skills (e.g. PSB: Horn, Lukesch, Kormann, & Mayrhofer, 2002; K-ABC: Melchers, & Preuß, 2009) deficits in fine motor skill can lead to an underestimation of cognitive abilities.

Practitioners should thus consider at least two issues when using cognitive ability measures. A first aim should be the implementation of measures with low fine motor demands (Ruiter, Nakken, Meulen, & Luneborg, 2010). If measures with low fine motor demands are not available practitioners should try to estimate the impact of a child's fine motor skills when interpreting the results. To do so, it is suggested to additionally assess the specific fine motor skills that were required in the respective cognitive ability test (e.g. eye-hand-coordination). By this means cognitive ability measurement in early childhood can be optimized. Considering the low reliability of cognitive ability measures in early childhood (Stöger, Schirner, & Ziegler, 2008) this seems to be of particular importance.

Taken together the present study suggests a differentiated look on fine motor skills if relations with cognitive abilities are investigated. Further research is however necessary if the mechanisms behind the relations are to be understood. Only then it is possible to make informed educational decisions.

References

Baedke, D. (1980). *Dimensionen der Handgeschicklichkeit im Kindesalter [Dimensions of handskills in children]*. Dissertation, Philipps-Universität, Marburg.

Burrmann, U., & Stucke, C. (2009). Zusammenhänge zwischen motorischen und kognitiven Merkmalen in der Entwicklung [Relations between motor and cognitive characteristics during the development]. In J. Baur & D. Alfermann (Eds.), *Handbuch motorische Entwicklung [Handbook motor development]* (2nd ed., pp. 261–273). Schorndorf: Hofmann.

Büttner, G., Frostig, M., Hammill, D. D., Pearson, N. A., & Voress, J. K. (2008). *Frostigs Entwicklungstest der visuellen Wahrnehmung - 2: FEW-2; deutsche Fassung des Developmental test of visual perception, second edition (DTVP-2)*, D.D. Hamill, N.A. Pearson & J.K. Voress; Manual. Göttingen: Hogrefe.

Case, R. (1998). The development of central conceptual structures. In D. Kuhn & R. Siegler (Eds.), *Handbook of child psychology: cognition, perception, and language* (5th ed., Vol. 2, pp. 745–800). New York: Wiley.

Case-Smith, J. (1994). The Relationships Among Sensorimotor Components, Fine Motor Skill, and Functional Performance in Preschool Children. *The American Journal of Psychiatry, 49*(7), 645–652.

Chow, S. M. K., Henderson, S. E., & Barnett, A. (2001). The Movement Assessment Battery for Children: A Comparison of 4-Year-Old to 6-Year-Old Children From Hong Kong and the United States. *The American Journal of Occupational Therapy, 55,* 55–61.

Chui, M., Ng, A., Fong, A., Lin, L., & Ng, M. (2007). Differences in the Fine Motor Performance of Children in Hong Kong and the United States on the Bruininks-Oseretsky Test of Motor Proficiency. *Hong Kong Journal of Occupational Therapy, 17*(1), 1-9.

Cratty, B. J. (1986). *Perceptual and motor development in infants and children* (3. Aufl.). Englewood Cliffs: Prentice-Hall.

Davis, E. E., Pitchford, N. J., & Limback, E. (2011). The interrelation between cognitive and motor development in typically developing children aged 4-11 years is underpinned by visual processing and fine manual control. *British Journal of Psychology, 102*(3), 569–584.

Dellatolas, G., Agostini, M. de, Curt, F., Kremin, H., Letierce, A., Maccario, J., et al. (2003). Manual skill, hand skill asymmetry, and cognitive performances in young children. *Laterality, 8*(4), 317–338.

Diamond, A. (2000). Close Interrelation of Motor Development and Cognitive Development and of the Cerebellum and Prefrontal Cortex. *Child Development, 71*(1), 44–56.

Dickes, P. (1978). Zusammenhänge zwischen motorischen und kognitiven Variablen bei Kindern im Vorschulalter [Relations between motor and cognitive variables in preschool children]. In H.-J. Müller, R. Decker & F. Schilling (Eds.), *Motorik im Vorschulalter. Wissenschaftliche Grundlagen und Erfassungsmethoden* (2nd ed., pp. 119–132). Schorndorf: Hofmann.

Eisert, D., & Lamorey, S. (1996). Play as a window on child development: The relationships between play and other developmental domains. *Early Education and Development, 7,* 221-234.

Etnier, J. L., Nowell, M. P., Landers, D. M., & Sibley, B. A. (2006). A meta-regression to examine the relationship between aerobic fitness and cognitive performance. *Brain Research Reviews, 52,* 119-130.

Ettrich, K. U., & Ettrich, C. (2006). *Testmanual zum Konzentrations-Handlungsverfahren für Vorschulkinder [Manual of the Concentration-Action-Test for preschool children]*. Göttingen: Hogrefe

Everke, J., & Woll, A. (2007). Cognition and Motor Activity in Childhood – Correlation and Causation. *Sport Science and Physical Education (ICSSPE), Bulletin, 51*, 35–40.

Exner, C. E., & Henderson, A. (1995). Cognition and Motor Skill. In A. Henderson & C. Pehoski (Eds.), *Hand function in the child. Foundations for remediation* (2nd ed., pp. 93–110). St. Louis: Mosby/Elsevier.

Fleishman, E.A. (1954). Dimensional analysis of psychomotor abilities. *Journal of Experimental Psychology, 48,* 437-454.

Fleishman, E. (1972). Structure and measurement of psychomotor abilities. In R.N. Singer (Ed.), *The psychomotor domain* (pp. 78-196). Philadelphia: Lea & Febiger.

Grissmer, D., Grimm, K. j., Aiyer, S. M., Murrah, W. M., & Steel, J. S. (2010). Fine Motor Skills and Early Comprehension of the World: Two New School Readiness Indicators. *Developmental-Psychology, 46*(5), 1008–1017.

Henderson, A. (1995). Self-Care and Hand Skill. In A. Henderson & C. Pehoski (Eds.), *Hand function in the child. Foundations for remediation* (2nd ed., pp. 164–183). St. Louis: Mosby/Elsevier.

Holt, L. E., & Beilock, S. L. (2006). Expertise and its embodiment: Examining the impact of sensorimotor skill expertise on the representation of action-related text. *Psychonomic Bulletin & Review, 13*(4), 694–701.

Horn, W., Lukesch, H., Kornmann, A., & Mayrhofer, S. (2002). *PSB-R 4-6. Prüfsystem für Schul- und Bildungsberatung für 4. bis 6. Klassen. Revidierte Fassung [School and Educational Counseling Testing System for Grades 4 to 6. Revised version]*. Göttingen: Hogrefe.

Huntsinger, C. S., Jose, P. E., Krieg, D. B., & Luo, Z. (2011). Cultural differences in Chinese American and European American children's drawing skills over time. *Early Childhood Research Quarterly, 26*(1), 134–145.

Kail, R., & Park, Y. (1990). Impact of practice on speed of mental rotation. *Journal of Experimental Child Psychology, 49,* 227–244.

Luo, Z., Jose, P. E., Huntsinger, C. S., & Pigott, T. D. (2007). Fine motor skills and mathematics achievement in East Asian American and European American kindergartners and first graders. *British Journal of Developmental Psychology, 25,* 595–614.

Marr, D., Cermak, S., Cohn, E. S., & Henderson, A. (2003). Fine motor activities in Head Start and kindergarten classrooms. *American Journal of Occupational Therapy, 57,* 550–557.

Martzog, P., Stöger, H., & Ziegler, A. (2009, März). *Feinmotorische Fertigkeiten und kognitives Lernen im Vorschulalter[Fine motor skills and cognitive learning in preschool children]*. Vortrag auf der 51. Tagung empirisch arbeitender Psychologen (TeaP) in Jena.

Melchers, P., & Preuß, U. (2009). *Kaufman Assessment Battery for Children (deutsche Version) (8., unveränd. Aufl.)*. Frankfurt: Pearson Assessment.

Pehoski, C. (1995). Object Manipulation in Infants and Children. In A. Henderson & C. Pehoski (Eds.), *Hand function in the child. Foundations for remediation* (2nd ed., pp. 136–153). St. Louis: Mosby/Elsevier.

Piaget, J. (1952). *The origins of intelligence in children*. New York: International University Press.

Piek, J. P., Dawson, L., Smith, L. B., & Gasson, N. (2008). The role of early fine and gross motor development on later motor and cognitive ability. *Human Movement Science, 27*, 668–681.

Ricken, G., Fritz, A., Schuck, K. D., & Preuss, U. (2007). *HAWIVA-III. Hannover-Wechsler-Intelligenztest für das Vorschulalter; Wechsler Preschool and Primary Scale of Intelligence* (WPPSI; Wechsler, D., 1967*) - German version*. Bern: Huber.

Roebers, C., & Kauer, M. (2009). Motor and cognitive control in a normative sample of 7-year-olds. *Developmental Science, 12* (1), 175–181.

Ruiter, S. A. J., Nakken, H., Meulen, B. F., & Lunenborg, C. B. (2010). Low Motor Assessment: A Comparative Pilot Study with Young Children With and Without Motor Impairment. *Journal of Developmental and Physical Disabilities, 22*(1), 33–46.

Schewe, H. (1977). *Untersuchung zum Problem der Beziehung zwischen intellektueller und motorischer Leistungsfähigkeit bei Kindern [Examining the association of motor and cognitive performance in childhood]*. Dissertation, Technische Universität Carolo-Wilhelmina. Braunschweig.

Schilling, F. (1974). Neue Ansätze zur Untersuchung der Hand- und Fingergeschicklichkeit im Kindesalter [New approaches for the investigation of hand and fingerskill in childhood]. *Sportwissenschaft, 4*, 276–298.

Siakaluk, P., Pexman, P., Sears, C., Wilson, K., Locheed, K., & Owen, W. (2008). The Benefits of Sensorimotor Knowledge: Body-Object Interaction Facilitates Semantic Processing. *Cognitive Science: A Multidisciplinary Journal, 32*(3), 591–605.

Smirni, P., & Zappalà, G. (1989). Manual Behavior, Lateralization of Manual Skills and Cognitive Performance of Preschool Children. *Perceptual and Motor Skills, 68*, 267–272.

Solan, H. A., & Mozlin, R. (1986). The correlations of perceptual-motor maturation to readiness and reading in kindergarten and the primary grades. *Journal of the American Optometric Association, 57*, 28–35.

Soska, K. C., Adolph, K. E., & Johnson, S. P. (2010). Systems in development: Motor skill acquisition facilitates three-dimensional object completion. *Developmental Psychology, 46*(1), 129–138.

Stewart, R., Rule, A., & Giordano, D. (2007). The Effect of Fine Motor Skill Activities on Kindergarten Student Attention. *Early Childhood Education Journal, 35*(2), 103–109.

Stoeger, H., Schirner, S., & Ziegler, A. (2008). Ist die Identifikation Begabter schon im Vorschulalter möglich? Ein Literaturüberblick [Identification of giftedness, is it already possible at the age of pre-school? A Review of literature]. *Diskurs Kindheits- und Jugendforschung, 3*(1), 7-24.

Thelen, E. (1995). Time-scale dynamics and the development of an embodied cognition. In R. F. Port, & T. van Gelder (Eds.), *Mind as motion: Explorations in the dynamics of cognition.* (pp. 69–100). Cambridge, MA, USA: Massachusetts Institute of Technology.

Thelen, E. (2000). Grounded in the World: Developmental Origins of the Embodied Mind. *Infancy, 1*(1), 3–28.

Voelcker-Rehage, C. (2005). Der Zusammenhang zwischen motorischer und kognitiver Entwicklung im frühen Kindesalter – Ein Teilergebnis der MODALIS-Studie [Association of motor and cognitive development in young children – A partial result of the MODALIS-study]. *Deutsche Zeitschrift für Sportmedizin, 56*, 358–359.

Wassenberg, R., Kroes, M., Feron, J., Kessels, G. H., Hendriksen, G., Kalff, A., & et. al (2005). Relation Between Cognitive and Motor Performance in 5- to 6-Year-Old Children: Results From a Large-Scale Cross-Sectional Study. *Child Development, 76*, 1092–1103.

Ziegler, A., & Stoeger, H. (2010). How fine motor skills influence the assessment of high ability and underachievement in math. *Journal for the Education of the Gifted, 34*(2), 195-219.

Marianne Nolte

Mathematically Gifted Young Children – Questions About the Development of Mathematical Giftedness

Abstract

During the last years research about giftedness began to focus more and more on younger children. But still we hardly found any research results about the development of mathematical giftedness in kindergarteners. Due to this situation the article has to deal with two theoretical approaches. The first gives an impression about gifted education in mathematics. Based on the development of mathematical skills in very young children, the second part studies unusual mathematical abilities in kindergarteners.

In the primary and secondary grade mathematically gifted pupils increasingly use patterns of action in problem solving processes (Kießwetter, 1985). These, in the context of challenging problem areas, indicate a particular mathematical giftedness. The research about mathematical giftedness in kindergarteners is at the very beginning. So it is an open question what hints for giftedness we can find and whether even at this age we observe patterns of action. A first approach includes case studies as well as the results of a questionnaire we gave parents of mathematically gifted primary school children. These studies constitute the first steps towards a hypothesis for generating research findings for the development of mathematical abilities already from the kindergarten level.

1   Some remarks about giftedness at primary and secondary grade level

The university of Hamburg research about high mathematical giftedness started at the beginning of the eighties in 1983 as a William-Stern-Society project for fostering mathematical gifted pupils of the secondary level (between 12 and 19 years old)1. Since 1999 within the framework of the project called PriMa2 we have been working with mathematically gifted primary school pupils (8-10 years old).During the third grade and up to the end of the fourth grade the children visit the university and get started with a talent search process.. At this point the parents were given an extensive questionnaire about the development and interests of their children. Therefore we have got some data about the mathematical competencies children identified as mathematical gifted show as very young children. Together with interviews we made with three children the results can be regarded as a first approach towards research in the field of mathematical giftedness of kindergarteners.

One of the basic questions about giftedness in the field of mathematics is which characteristics does high mathematical abilities have. Especially in a developmental process this is a difficult question. Performance can be proved by knowledge and acceleration of knowledge acquisition often is interpreted as a sign for high abilities. But a certain amount of knowledge gives not sufficient information about abilities. At primary grade level a main content of mathematical knowledge is based on numerical knowledge. Children who are good in calculation do not necessarily show good performance in problem solving. Not until children are confronted with mathematical problems higher level thinking skills can be shown respectively developed. Krutetskii (1962, 1976) investigated mathematical giftedness and described special cognitive components of handling mathematical material, for example formalization of mathematical information, as characteristics of giftedness. Up to the present his findings have a great impact on research about mathematical giftedness. However, it should be analyzed whether characteristics, e.g. recognizing patterns and structures, can be described as characteristics which are specific for high mathematical abilities. Children with learning disabilities for example do display capabilities of recognizing patterns and structures (Scherer, 1995). Average children are able to solve problems via reversal processes.

Kießwetter (1985) changes the focus of characterizing giftedness to the question which kinds of capabilities successful problem solvers need and what kind of higher level thinking skills they show. Concerning research about pupils of the secondary level he specified special patterns of action, which are proved to be

---

[1] http://www.hbf-mathematik.de/ , headed by Prof. Dr. Karl Kießwetter

[2] PriMa is a cooperation project of the *Hamburger Behörde für Schule und Berufsbildung*, and the *William-Stern* Society (Hamburg), the University of Hamburg. (headed by Prof. Dr. Marianne Nolte, for further information please refer to the website http://blogs.epb.uni-hamburg.de/nolte/)

essential in the field of mathematical problem solving (Kießwetter, 1985). Some of these patterns of action are similar to those identified by Krutetskii (1962, 1976) for example the ability to generalize or of reversal thinking. Recognizing patterns and structures, building super signs (chunking), switching between levels of representation or finding connected problems are further patterns of action that are required in problem solving processes (Kießwetter, 1985, 2006).

Also at primary grade level investigations document that patterns of action are significantly more often shown by children who are capable of a deep understanding of mathematical contents (Nolte, 2004; Pamperien, 2004). Patterns of action are part of cognitive components of problem solving (Nolte, 2006). But can the use of cognitive components of problem solving - like reversal thinking - be seen as a characteristic of high mathematical capabilities? Whether patterns of action refer to special capabilities depends basically on how demanding a task is. In contrast to Krutetskii (1976) we do not define the appearance of cognitive components of problem solving as characteristics of mathematical giftedness. Nevertheless, it is reliable to say that given appropriate challenging problems of these components can be considered as signals of mathematical giftedness.

We define children as mathematically gifted when they are able to work on complex problems. In this learning environment they recognize patterns and structures. They are able to exploit these patterns and structures while working the problem. They can work on a high level of abstraction. They construct superordinate structures and gasp coherences. They are able to generalize their findings. So when children show special patterns of action in challenging and complex fields of problems we suppose high mathematical talent.

But do they occur even before children get a systematical education in school? And if they are essential for mathematical giftedness, can we find hints of them even in very young children? Because you need challenging problems to watch cognitive components of problem solving, rich experience about the construction of problems for a special age is necessary. At the moment we do not have enough knowledge about the question what kind of mathematical activities can be regarded as challenging for mathematical gifted kindergarteners.

The following considerations merely represent first steps towards a research related to giftedness among kindergarten children.

2   What do we know about special mathematical giftedness in younger children?

Very little research has been done on the development of special mathematical giftedness in this age set. Thus, I shall first outline the development of mathematical capacities in general while focusing on the development of the concept of number. On this process counting is central. Counting connects activities at a concrete level with the development of an abstract concept, the system of natural numbers. Also for parents this process is easier to describe. In everyday life knowledge about numbers attracts more attention than knowledge about unusual capabilities to categorize geometric objects or about patterns and structures. Additional the research about the development of mathematical knowledge focuses on the development of number sense (Krajewski, Grüßing et al., 2009).

In the recent years, there has been an increasing discussion on the development of mathematical capabilities since the first day, for example on the assumption that: "Children discriminate numerosities long before language acquisition and formal education, as early as at 3 hours after birth (Izard, Sann, Spelke, & Streri, 2009)." (Piazza, Facoetti et al., 2010) p. 33). The research about innate mathematical capabilities and the development of the concept of number also show a "sensitivity to large numbers in 4- to 6-month-old infants" (Dehaene, 2009).

The research about mathematical capabilities of infants prove that children are born with a core system of number (Dehaene, 1999), which gives them the capability to differentiate accurately between small numbers. Less than one year old, they can decide which amount of objects is bigger, if the difference between the numerosities is large enough (Xu & Spelke, 2000). First attempts to addition and subtraction has been described. "For instance, upon seeing five objects being hidden behind a screen, then another five objects being added, they appear to expect 10 objects and express a form of surprise through longer looking times when the screen collapses and only five objects are revealed (McCrink & Wynn 2004; Wynn, 1992; Dehaene, 2009)

Relying on an inherent number sense, children learn to compare quantities, they learn the number words, learn to count and to calculate. The first strategies combine many activities at a sensory level. Handling with objects teaches them to discover the meaning of concepts like more, less and equal, for example. These processes get along with the acquisition of language. The combination between number words and numbers of entities emerges. The knowledge that a certain number express a certain quantity develops at the age of about three or four years (Krajewski et al., 2009, p. 24). Between the age of four and six years thinking processes of children are bound to perception (Hasemann, 2003).

The Dutch TAL-project describes different domain-related levels of thinking. "…in the domain of working with numbers up to twenty, a different set of levels can be seen in counting than in calculation" (van den Heuvel-Panhuizen & TAL, 2001, p.14). The levels extend from context-bound counting, object-bound counting to pure counting and from calculation by counting and calculation by structuring to formal calculation.

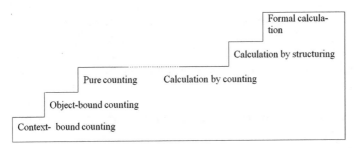

Figure 1: Levels of counting and calculation up to 20. (by van den Heuvel-Panhuizen, & TAL 2001, p.14)

(Caluori, 2004) investigated the development of numerical competences. His research showed that about 20% of the children between the age of four years, seven months and five years were able to count up to 20. The amount increases to 90% for the oldest children. (Caluori, 2004, p. 120) Caluori described that obviously counting without using objects is very hard during the first year of kindergarten. Some of the children refused to count beyond ten, some of them seemed not to be motivated at all. „The following fig. 61 depicts the percent increase of counting competence up to the number 20 in this study conducted in Switzerland. As a reminder: I (4;07 – 4;12), II (5;01 – 5;06), III (5;07 – 5;12), IV (6;01 – 6;06) and V (6;07 –6;12) and N = 70" (Caluori, 2004, p. 196).

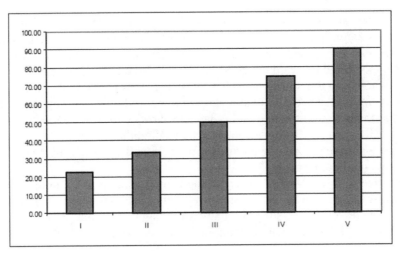

Figure 2: Increase of counting competence according to age starting with 4;07 year olds in I up to 6;12 year olds in V. (Caluori, 2004, p. 196)

According to (Kunze & Gisbert, 2007), most of the children of „age four can determine correctly an amount of eight to ten objects" (p. 61). By this age, they also can count properly when the number spaces are still limited. Shalev and

Gross-Tsur (2001) reported, that preschool toddlers correctly add and subtract numbers up to three. "By 3-4 years of age, they can count up to four items, and, about a year later, count up to 15, as well as comprehend the concept that numbers represent."(Shalev & Gross-Tsur, 2001, p. 337). Although these data are not exactly the same, they show a limited performance in counting concerning the number space as well as doing addition and subtraction. Dealing with numerosities also is bound on acting with concrete objects.

3   What do we observe in children who display exceptional capacities?

The results of this research show the normal spectrum of performance. But there are children who behave different. Until today we cannot categorize our observations, because unexpected behavior occurs by chance. Additional, what can be observed depends on the competencies of the observer. Also the question is whether impressive performances can be regarded as hints for later talent. During the process of development interests and activities in certain domains can change and by this also learning processes.

The following anecdotes were collected by a member of our research team. They illustrate quite well what kind of activities and thoughts of children are taken as indicating factors for mathematical giftedness. Later, both children - Marius and Sabine - were tested as high mathematically gifted.

3.1   Marius and Sabine

Marius, one and a half year old, and his father played with marbles. The father asked his son to put four marbles in a ball path. The boy counted four marbles and he was very proud that he could hold them in one hand. Two years and eleven month old he heard the question "How late is it?" and answered "a quarter past four". In this situation he also adjusted a clock to that time.

Marius' mother[3] wanted to read a story two month before the boy reached his third birthday. He was sitting on her lap and she said to herself: "where is page 48? " „Here, mama", the boy said. The stunned mother checked then if the boy had not only recognized the picture on page 48 and found out he could really read two-digit numbers.

At the age of three, Marius' sister Sabine could count up to 20. Four years old Sabine was asked "what is four and two?", the child answered six and after a short time of reflexion: "[…] and I always thought that 3 plus 3 equals always 6" . She loved doubling and dividing in halves, it was a game she developed by herself.[4]

---

[3] The mother is experienced in diagnostics of mathematical abilities.

[4] Further examples are on Carol Bainbridge's homepage („Advanced Math Abilities of Gifted Children"): "Shubhangi says : My grandson is could recite numbers up to 200 backwords, jumping and whatever way when he was 20 months old. He could recognise all shapes at 18 months, point out similarites in different and

In comparison with the results of research on the development of number sense, it becomes clear that this performance is far beyond of what can be observed normally. Still, do these examples really indicate a particular mathematical giftedness? In the first place, the described examples are anecdotes that encourage a further analysis.

We have tried to approach the issue in two different ways. Firstly, through half structured interviews and observations with children that we thought were outstanding and secondly, through a questionnaire in which the parents of children we had identified as gifted through tests would describe the development of their child from the retrospective point of view.

3.2   Interviews with Adelina, Johannes and Paul

Altogether three semi-standardized interviews were conducted with children, with Adelina, Johannes and Paul. The first conversation with Adelina describes a coincidental encounter in the subway. When Adelina was five years and three months old, she came to the university for further interviews. At the age of five Johannes learned to count up to 100 in Italian during his holidays in Italy and was introduced to us when he was six years old.[5] Paul was interviewed in his kindergarten when he was five years old. At the beginning, the interviews with Adelina and Johannes were oriented at an informal test of (Knappstein & Spiegel, 1995) for primary school beginners, but this text proved to be much too easy.

At the primary grade level mathematical giftedness can hardly be measured by a curriculum orientated performance test, because the most tests show a ceiling effect, they are insufficiently difficult to measure high mathematical abilities. This seems also to be the case in the pre-school area.

- *Adelina*

Adelina was 4 ½ old when I met her on the subway. We started our conversation:

A: Do you know what we will be doing next week?
N: No, what will you be doing?
A: We are going to Greece on holiday!
…
N: What will you do in Greece?
A: Swim, swim every day! Do you know how hot it is there?
N: 22 degrees?
A: No, that is cold, much too cold!

---

disparate objects. But hates learning by heart the times tables. He can, of course remember them easily."
http://giftedkids.about.com/b/2010/10/24/advanced-math-abilities-of-gifted-children.htm (original   spelling
and grammar, M. Nolte)
[5] The interviews were conducted in cooperation with Prof. Dr. F. Käpnick in 1996 at the University of Hamburg. A detailed article on this topic is planned tob e published in 2012 by Käpnick, & Nolte.

N: 24 degrees?
A: That is still too cold!
N: 60 degrees?
A: That is much too hot! (The father: We are not going to the sauna!)
N: 30 degrees?
A: I guess we will have around 30 degrees.
N: You are good with numbers.
A: And I can count already!
N: Do you know what 2 + 2 is?
A: 4, that is easy.
N: What is 4 + 4?
A: 8 (The father: she can also count up to more than 10!).
N: What is 8+4?
A: 12.
N: And 20 + 3?
A: 23.
N: 3 + 3?
A: 6.
N: And do you know what the double of 3 is?
A: 9.
N: Now, you made an error. The double of 3 is 6.
A: That is wrong. I know exactly that 3 times 3 equal 9.

This short episode shows that Adelina can arrange the temperature data in a relation: „is warmer than" and draws back on the succession of numbers up to 100. She can solve simple calculation tasks without support material. She does not know the term „the double", but she associates it correctly with multiplication.

During our interviews at the university Adelina was able to count up to 100, forward without any faults, backward only in parts. She calculated in the number space up to 20 using several strategies for addition. Sometimes she used her fingers, some tasks she knew by heart, some results she got by concluding the result from number facts she knew. When we gave her a 6x6 field and took away one row with six stones, she looked at the ceiling calculating 36-6 in her head. Besides her fingers she did not use materials to support calculation. Even some of her faults were based on considerations; she calculated 6+6 =12 and 7+7 = 13 and explained, „seven is one more than six". Although this is a fault it gives an insight into the connections between numbers, in this case almost doubling. She solved 60+70 as 67 and explained: 60+7 = 67. In this sense her solution is correct.

Johannes

His Mother told us, that at age two, Johannes discovered cars and car license plate numbers. He wanted to know what was written on the plates and what kind of car it was. At the age of three, he began to count.

Johannes was almost six, when he came to the university. At that time he could tell the preceding and succession number of any number up to 1,000,000. He was also able to read accurately large numbers (in digit writing).

His calculation ability was remarkable. According to himself, his favorite task was „98 + 98 = 196". Starting from here, he could without particular effort conclude that 99 + 99 = 198 and that 99 + 98 = must be197, since „99 is 1 number bigger than 98 and two times 99 must be 2 numbers bigger than two times 98, while 99 + 98 is only 1 number bigger than 98 + 98".

He was less good at multiplication and division.

However writing numbers in general was still difficult for him.

Figure 3: Johannes writes numbers

- *Paul*

With 5-year old Paul, I conducted an interview in his kindergarten. The interview was based on a schoolbook for preschoolers. Also for Paul the tasks were too easy. The question about his favorite task turned out to be a better access to his knowledge. Counting was his favorite task. Paul did it with and without material. He was able to count on from any number up to 100.

He said he could count up to 180 and counted correctly within the scope of 1-100 but not always. After 79 he counted 98, 99 hundred, one hundred, two hundred, four hundred…When asked how he came up with the number 180, he answers: "once you have counted up 100, you continue by counting 8 times up to 10".

Paul could calculate mentally for example, 5+9=16. He read many two-digit numbers. Sometimes he made inversion errors and read 78 as 87.

Like Adelina and Johannes, Paul possesses already a knowledge which goes far beyond the usual knowledge of that age. Although he does not know the procedure of counting up to 180, he understands the counting principle and the logical structures underlying counting. His reflections such as „counting up to 180

means counting up to 100 and then 8 times up to 10" demonstrate an insight into the cardinal counting principle. Even if we do not know if Paul knows the
numerals, he is able to explain that 8 times 10 also should be considered numerals. His mistakes are comparable to those other children also make during acquisition of the order of numerals.

3.3   What do these examples show us?

The interviews based on the motivation of the children to work with us. This is
far more difficult with younger children and depends on frame conditions.
Adelina did not solve tasks she was not in the mood to. Partly she modified
tasks the way she wanted. Also Paul behaved like this. He was curious at the
beginning, but was also very clear when he was no longer interested in working
with numbers.

Altogether we can conclude that in certain development areas of their mathematical skills, these children are miles ahead of the children their age. This does
not only apply to their knowledge but also to the way they use it. They do not
use any material for their calculations, i.e. they already got that knowledge on a
very abstract level. This knowledge is cross-linked; otherwise they would not be
able to draw conclusions to that extent.

These observations confirm that even young children show some of the described patterns of action. All children, including Marius and Sabine, showed
their knowledge without formal instruction. Using numbers as large as the children did, can be viewed as recognizing patterns and structures. The use of numbers in an exceptional number space shows their capability to generalize. These
findings support the results of Stapf and Stapf (1990), who assume that mathematical giftedness can already be determined at the age of three or four (p. 384).
In their studies, they noticed patterns of action similar to those described by
Kießwetter (1985).

The capacity to calculate context-free and without any material as well as the
capacity to count in a large number space can be considered as decisive variables as to the question of whether these children are mathematically gifted.
They calculated with abstract symbols. They have got remarkable counting
skills. Counting in a small space that corresponds to their daily world can be
generalized and be used for counting in a larger space. Their knowledge is not
bound to a specific level of action. They can execute operations context-free.
They developed an understanding of a complex system, the structure of our
numbers and their utilization. Thus, very early, they reach the level of "pure
counting" and that of "formal calculation" (by van den Heuvel-Panhuizen, &
TAL 2001, p. 14).

4   What do parents know about the abilities of their preschool children? Results of a Questionnaire

At the end of our project, parents were given a questionnaire related to the cognitive development of their children. We developed the questionnaire to collect broad information about different aspects of developmental processes of the children we tested as mathematically gifted. We also asked for evaluation of aspects of our fostering program. The goals were to collect data for later analyzing. The first part covers the parent's appraisal of their children's capabilities in reading and numbers at the point of their school enrollment. We questioned the appraisal of the actual intellectual abilities and their talents in sports and music. We also wanted to get information about possible developmental disturbances like ADHD. The second part focuses on environmental questions, the third part on questions about our fostering program.

The present interpretation is based on the answers to the questions about the calculation and counting skills. We posed the Questions: "To what extent was your child proficient in the cultural technique „calculating"at schooling stage? At ....years old, was he or she able to count up to ...., add up numbers up to..........., subtract numbers up to............, multiply numbers up to.............., and di-vide numbers up to.............. Some parents used an open question to tell us more about the knowledge of their children.

Due to the way of phrasing the question, the evaluation is not unequivocal. Some parents indicated the earliest point in time when their child displayed certain abilities, while others indicated the schooling time[6]. Beside this the retrospective view is only suitable to a limited extent to display the children's actual knowledge since in their early life, their handling of numbers and calculation operations are noticed rather by chance and unsystematically by their parents. Additional it is hard for parents to describe the counting skills of their children. Counting can be verbal or quantifying, it can show the capability of understanding aspects of numbers like cardinal or ordinal. These differentiations are hardly made by parents. Furthermore the recall of events can falsify what really happened. Nevertheless we expect to get an impression about the knowledge of mathematically gifted children in their kindergarten and prekindergarten years.

We analyzed 115 questionnaires, 16 could not be evaluated, because of missing information. Due to the fact that there were only two seven year's old children we did not use their data.

To make the scales easier to read concerning counting, addition and subtraction we differentiated between the age of two and three year's old children and four, five and six year's old. Due the number of children we changed the grouping concerning multiplication scales and made no differences in division scales.

---

[6] One of our next steps includes a rephrasing of the questions in order to provide answers which are more exact.

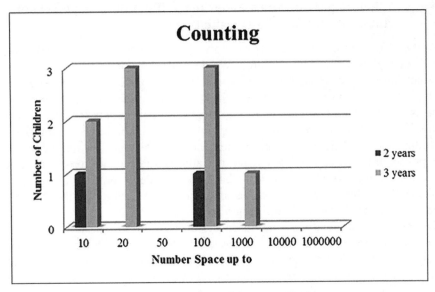

Figure 4: Counting of two and three years old children

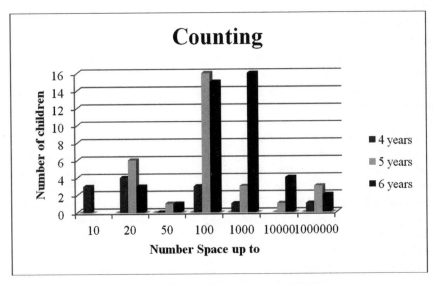

Figure 5: Counting four, five and six year's old children

Compared with the normal development of counting also in children with high mathematical abilities the number space in which they counted increased with growing age. Some children started counting already with two or three years. Five of the four years old counted not less than 100. The number increased for the five year old children up to 23 and the six years old up to 37. The number of children increases with larger numbers. But even between the four years old was one child who counts up to 1000.000. One can assume that children who started counting very early could count up to a high number at schooling stage as well.

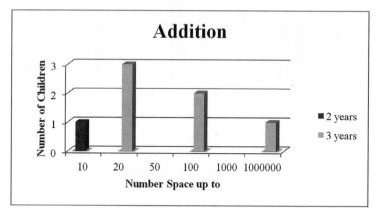

Figure 6: Addition two and three year's old children

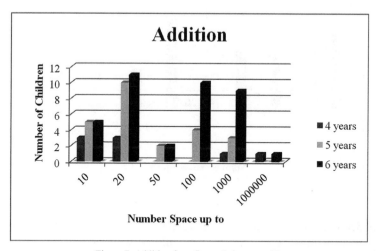

Figure 7: Addition four, five and six years old

That only one two year's old child adds and subtracts supports the observation, that counting comes before calculation. It is impressive to see, that even three years old children started with calculation. Even calculations up to 20 are far ahead compared with a normal development.

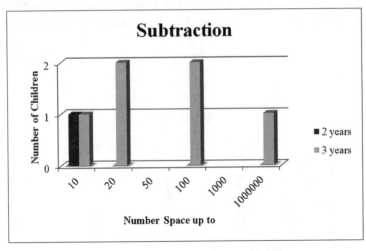

Figure 8: Subtraction two and three year's old children

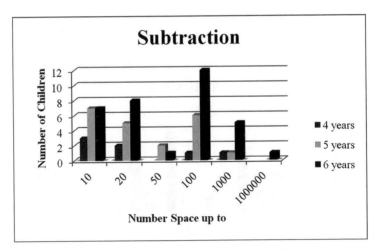

Figure 9: Subtraction four, five and six years old children

Expectedly the number space for subtracting is lower than for addition taking into account the age of the children. 17 children were able to do subtraction in the number space 100 and even five up to 1000. One of these children subtracted numbers up to 1.000.000. A quite lower number of the children can already multiply and divide.[7] But it is remarkable that even three and four year's old

---

[7] We do not know whether the parents mean numbers or number range.

children show knowledge about multiplication. Nevertheless it is not quite clear what is meant by multiplication up to ten, hundred or thousand; are these results or factors?

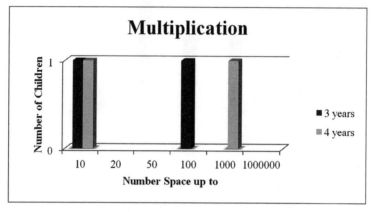

Figure 10: Multiplication: three and four years old children

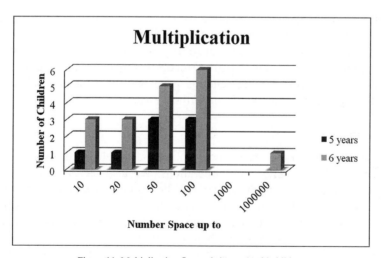

Figure 11: Multiplication five and six year's old children

No longer had we found two years old who know how to multiply. But even some of the three and four year's old children did multiplication tasks. It can be assumed that most of the children acquired first knowledge about multiplication before they go to school.

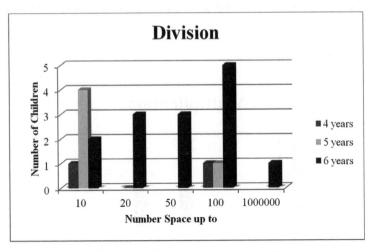

Figure 12: Division four, five and six years old

The knowledge about division is developed the lowest. Not even one two or three year old child was observed by doing division and only two of the four year's old. Anyway, 22 of the children did some divisions before formal schooling.

The parents' description indicates that the children display exceptional interests and competences in different areas. This however does not apply for every child. It is also interesting to note that some parents do not notice any distinctive features in their children. These parents report that their children acquired mathematical competences at a tremendous pace once they started school. This seems to be a phenomenon worth for further research.

5   Discussion

Our findings confirm the observations in normal development that calculation skills develop before skills doing operations. We also see that the knowledge increases over the years. Addition seems to be easier to acquire than subtraction, multiplication easier than division. Many children with high mathematical abilities have availability to counting and the first rules of arithmetic before they enter school. The findings show that before starting school, the majority of these children acquire knowledge that is abstract and is ahead of their peers'. It is still unclear how these processes run. Paul's mistakes, for example, suggest that his development takes a similar course to that of average children, except that it happens earlier in time. But for some of the children the development seems to be so fast that the question of a different quality arises.

The concept of "subjective domains of experience" (Bauersfeld, 1985) describes the development of knowledge dependent on personal experiences. At the beginning children are not able to see analogies between concepts in different contexts. More and more experiences in several contexts lead them to see the underlying similarities. Gifted children seem to recognize analogies and structures very fast and with a lot less of personal experiences. Their development raises questions concerning the general theories of development concerning the necessity of dealing with sensory inputs.

Motivation seems to play in important role. The children acquire the knowledge because they are interested in it. Therefore, it does not always correspond to a norm, as described in curricula of specific school years. This is a reason why conventional tests for one group or the older age group will not seize properly the children's capacities. In some areas, the children display a performance that can correlate with a certain grade, in others their performance is clearly lower than the grade would require. Johannes capabilities to add and subtract are at the level of third grade. His knowledge about the system of the natural numbers is as far developed as the curriculum of the fourth grade describes. But he is only at the beginning to multiply, contents of the second grade.

Even though most children who at a later point were identified as mathematically gifted attract attention through a special interest in numbers and abstract symbols, this does not apply for every child. Besides, the level of interest fluctuates. Children undergo phases in which they are interested in numbers and at other times show no interest in numbers. Therefore, statements on the mathematical giftedness of a child should be taken with caution. If a child displays an exceptional performance and shows no particular interest in numbers, his capacities obviously can stagnate in this field. If a child displays no particular performance, a special giftedness can be made visible through specific stimulation in school.

The following hypotheses can be deduced from the results of this study:
Before their formal schooling, mathematically gifted children

- display mostly very early interest in mathematical content such as numbers
- acquire the knowledge because they are interested
- can calculate context-free
- can relate the calculation to a given context
- calculate on a symbolic level
- achieve very early the capacity to count
- are able to generalize their insights at an early age
- recognize mathematical structures

It can be regarded as a problem to acquire the first rules of arithmetic as well as the knowledge about the system of the natural numbers. Even if children ask for information, they themselves use prior knowledge to adopt it to new numbers and new situations. Thus with caution we can say, that the children use cognitive components of problem solving in a very early age. In general, all these

demonstrate ways to patterns of action like the ability to think at an abstract level, the ability to find patterns and structures and the ability to generalize.
Even though a child does not display any of the mentioned capacities before schooling, he or she still can be mathematically gifted. Especially the fact that some of the children do not display any of these abilities indicates the necessity to provide for opportunities to carry out mathematical activities.
The question remains open as to whether the children undergo phases in the development of mathematical abilities at a faster pace or if the knowledge acquisition is of better quality. In a conversation in 2011 von Aster[8] referred to initial analyses using imaging techniques, which show that in mathematically weak children, the cross-linkage of knowledge is less pronounced. This confirms own observations in the work with children with learning disabilities. Our experiences in the field of giftedness lead us to the conclusion that mathematically gifted children cross-link their mathematical knowledge extensively. The children start doing so very early, some only after schooling. The fact that when offered the appropriate activities, the gifted children learn very fast and outpace other children their age corroborates the hypothesis that their knowledge acquisition must be of a better quality.

References

Bauersfeld, H. (1985). Ergebnisse und Probleme von Mikroanalysen mathematischen Unterrichts; Empirische Untersuchungen zum Lehren und Lernen von Mathematik [Results and problems of mathematical education microanalyses; empirical research about teaching and learning mathematics.]. In W. Dörfler & R. Fischer (Eds.), *Beiträge zum 4. internationalen Symposium für Didaktik der Mathematik in Klagenfurt vom 24. bis 27. 9. 1984. [Contribution to the 4. International symposium for didactic of mathematics at Klagenfurt between the 24. and 27.9.1984.]* Wien: Hölder-Pichler-Tempsky.

Caluori, F. (2004). *Die numerische Kompetenz von Vorschulkindern – Theoretische Modelle und empirische Befunde.[The numerical expertise of preschool kids- theoretical models and empirical results.]* Hamburg: Kovac.

Dehaene, S. (1999). *Der Zahlensinn oder warum wir rechnen können.[The number sense or why we are able to calculate]* Basel, Boston, Berlin: Birkhäuser.

[8] M. von Aster works in the field of neuroscience about learning disabilities. See http://www.neuroscience.ethz.ch/research/neural_basis/vonaster

Dehaene, S. (2009). Origins of Mathematical Intuitions; The Case of Arithmetic. In M. B. Miller & A. Kingstone. *The Year in Cognitive Neuroscience; Annals of the New York Academy of Sciences (1224, pp.232-259).* New York.

Hasemann, K. (2003). *Anfangsunterricht Mathematik [Beginning teaching mathematics].* Heidelberg: Spektrum.

Izard, V., Sann, C., Spelke, E.S., & Steri, A. (2009). Newborn infants perceive abstract numbers. *Proceedings of the National Academy of Sciences, USA, 106*(25), 10382–10385.

Kießwetter, K. (1985). Die Förderung von mathematisch besonders begabten und interessierten Schülern - ein bislang vernachlässigtes sonderpädagogisches Problem [The delivery of mathematically high gifted and interested pupils - an unattended special pedagogical problem.]. *Mathematisch-naturwissenschaftlicher Unterricht,38/5,* 300-306.

Kießwetter, K. (2006). Können Grundschüler schon im eigentlichen Sinne mathematisch agieren - und was kann man von mathematisch besonders begabten Grundschülern erwarten, und was noch nicht? [Are primary schoolkids able to act mathematically in the actual sense - and what can one expect from mathematically high gifted primary schoolkids, and whar cannot be expected?] In H. Bauersfeld & K. Kießwetter, *Wie fördert man mathematisch besonders befähigte Kinder? - Ein Buch aus der Praxis für die Praxis [How can one assist mathematical high gifted kinds? - A book out of practical experience for exercise.],* (pp.128-153). Offenburg: Mildenberger Verlag.

Knappstein, H., & Spiegel, H. (1995). Textbuch: Textaufgaben zur Erhebung arithmetischer Kenntnisse zu Beginn des 1. Schuljahres [Textbook: Word problems for investigation arithmetical knowledfe at the beginning of the 1. class.]. In G. Müller & E. C. Wittmann (Eds.), *Mit Kindern rechnen [Calculating with kids.]* Frankfurt: Arbeitskreis Grundschule, 96.

Krajewski, K., Grüßing, M, et al. (2009). Die Entwicklung mathematischer Kompetenzen bis zum Beginn der Grundschulzeit [The developing of mathematically skills up to begin of primary school.]. In A. Heinze & M. Grüßing. *Mathematiklernen vom Kindergarten bis zum Studium. Kontinuität und Kohärenz als Herausforderung für den Mathematikunterricht [Learning mathematics from kindergarten up to studies. Continuity and coherence as challenge for mathematically education],* (pp. 17-34). Münster: Waxmann Verlag.

Krutetskii, V. A. (1962). An Experimental Analysis of Pupils Mathematical Abilities. In J. Kilpatrick, & I. Wirszup. *Soviet Studies in the Psychology of Learning and Teaching Mathematics.* Standford University, University of Chicago.

Krutetskii, V. A. (1976). An Investigation of Mathematical Abilities in School-children. In J. Kilpatrick & I. Wirszup. *Soviet Studies in the Psychology of Learning and Teaching Mathematics, 2.* Chicago, Stanford University, University of Chicago.

Kunze, H.-R., & Gisbert, K. (2007). Förderung lernmethodischer Kompetenzen in Kindertageseinrichtungen [Exploitation learn methodical skills in a child-day care center]. In B. f. B. u. F. B. R. Öffentlichkeitsarbeit (Ed.), *Auf den Anfang kommt es an: Perspektiven für eine Neuorientierung frühkindlicher Bildung [The start counts: Prospects for a reorientation eary infantile literacy.,* (pp. 15-11). Bonn, Berlin.

McCrink, K., & Wynn, K. (2004) Large-Number Addition and Subtraction by 9-Month-Old Infants. *Psychological Science, 15,* 776-781.

Nolte, M., Ed. (2004). *Der Mathe-Treff für Mathe-Fans. Fragen zur Talentsuche im Rahmen eines Forschungs- und Förderprojekts zu besonderen mathematischen Begabungen im Grundschulalter.[The math-club for math-fans. Questions for the ability search in border of a research- and advance project to special mathematical giftedness in primary school.]* Hildesheim: franzbecker.

Nolte, M. (2006). Waben, Sechsecke und Palindrome. Zur Erprobung eines Problemfelds in unterschiedlichen Aufgabenformaten. [Combs, hexagons and palindrome. For proving a problem area in different exercise sizes.] In H. Bauersfeld & K. Kießwetter (Eds.), *Wie fördert man mathematisch besonders begabte Kinder? - Ein Buch aus der Praxis für die Praxis [How can one assist mathematical high gifted kids?- A book out of practical experience for exercise.],* (pp. 93-112).Offenburg: Mildenberger Verlags GmbH.

Pamperien, K. (2004). Strukturerkennung am Dreiecksschema. [Pattern recognition at a triangle pattern.] In M. Nolte (Ed.), *Der Mathe-Treff für Mathe-Fans. Fragen zur Talentsuche im Rahmen eines Forschungs- und Förderprojekts zu besonderen mathematischen Begabungen im Grundschulalter. [The math-club for math-fans. Questions for the ability search in border of a research- and advance project to special mathematical giftedness in primary school.]* Hildesheim: Franzbecker.

Piazza, M., Facoetti, A., et al. (2010). Developmental trajectory of number acuity reveals a severe impairment in developmental dyscalculia. *Cognition, 116,* 33-41.

Scherer, P. (1995). *Entdeckendes Lernen in Mathematikunterricht der Schule für Lernbehinderte. Theoretische Grundlegung und evaluierte unterrichtspraktische Erprobung. [Discovering learning in mathematically education in schools for learning- disabled. Theoretical basics and evaluatet practical education proving.]* Heidelberg: Universitätsverlag C. Winter.

Shalev, R. S., & Gross-Tsur, V. (2001). Developmental Dyscalculia. *Pediatric Neurology, 24*(5), 338-342.

Stapf, A., & Stapf, K. H. (1990). Zur kognitiven und motivationalen Entwicklung hochbegabter Kinder im Säuglings-, Kleinkind- und Vorschulalter. [Cognitive and motivation developing from giftedness kids during baby-, infant- and pre school age.] In K. Grawe, R. Hänni, N. Semmer, & F. Tschan (Eds.), *Über die richtige Art Psychologie zu betreiben [About the correct form to carry psychology]*, (pp. 377-390). Göttingen: Hogrefe.

Sternberg, R.J. (2000). Giftedness as developing expertise. In K.A. Heller, F.J. Mönks, R.J. Sternberg & R.F. Subotnik (Eds.), *International handbook of giftedness and talent* (2nd ed., pp. 55-66). Oxford: Pergamon Press.

van den Heuvel-Panhuizen, M. H., & Tal, T. (2001). *Children learn mathematics. A learning-teaching trajectory with intermediate attainment targest for calculation with whole numbers in primary school.* Freudenthal Institute (FI): Utrecht University.

Wynn, K. (1992). Addition and subtraction by human infants. *Nature, 358,* 749–750.

Xu, F., & Spelke, E. S. (2000). Large number discrimination in 6-month-old infants. *Cognition, 74*(1), B1-B11.

Zimmerman, B.J., Bonner, S., & Kovach, R. (1996). *Developing self-regulated learners; Beyond achievement to self-efficacy.* Washington, DC: American Psychological Association.

Dagmar Bergs-Winkels, Doren Prinz, & Peter Winkels

Individualised Support for Young Children in Preschool

Abstract

Pre-school children need a specific learning climate to support and develop their learning skills. This paper will focus on political, scientific and working-place conditions of individual support and self-regulated learning in pre-school. We will look at the role of individual support in German state issued education agreements and – by giving special consideration to the situation of gifted children – lay out some conditions for a successful learning environment. A close look at learning settings in kindergarten and at scientific research on self-regulated learning will show outlines for qualification and attitudes of pre-school educators.

1   Education in early childhood and individual support

As a result of the poor ratings for Germany in the PISA studies the early diagnosis of abilities and competences of children and the appropriate supporting
mechanisms are understood as an important social task.

Comparative school studies as PISA (Baumert et al., 2003) and IGLU (Bos et
al., 2007) have repeatedly proved the connection between early-childhood education and success in school. IGLU has shown that there is a high co-variance
between the length of a pre-school education and the reading competence of
children at the end of their primary school years. Children, who visited pre-
school institutions for two years or longer got test results approximately half a
standard deviation above those who attended Pre-School less than two years.
This difference equals the average increase of reading competence measured
with children between 3rd and 4th grade (Bos et al., 2007). The studies of Tietze incorporate also the aspect of quality. A good quality in pre-school child
care has positive effects on the overall development and well-being of children
(Tietze, 1998). The German debate on quality is based on three dimensions,
structural quality, focussing on input, process quality and quality of outcome
(Viernickel & Schwarz, 2009). All we can say for now is that a complex setting
shapes the effects of education and development while attending a kindergarten
(cf. Bundesministerium für Familie, Senioren, Frauen und Jugend, 2005).

Only recently, studies by Fried and Voss (2010) showed that the quality and
quantity of pre-school education make an important impact on the education
and upbringing of children. This is supported by international studies on the effects of institutional pre-school education that show at least positive short-time
effects in some cases even low positive long-term effects on the cognitive development of children (Biedinger & Becker, 2006; Rossbach, Kluczniok, & Isenmann, 2008). The studies of Bos et al. (2007) show that the time spent in pre-
school institutions covary with the reading competence measured in IGLU studies at the end of elementary school.

So, with this strong scientific support the importance of early education and the
demand for qualified pre-school educators are no longer questioned. Political
action followed and in the last ten years, every German federal state developed
education agreements.[i] They were imposed to improve educational institutions
and programs, to describe educational fields and to define the contents of elementary education. In these agreements, the mandate of institutions of pre-
school education begins with the birth of the child. It ends in some states with
the beginning of schooling; in some states it also covers the elementary school
system. All agreements have in common that they prescribe certain educational
fields for the elementary period. This is in line with the 10th Children and
Youth report from 1999 which demanded that the elementary educational institutions should play a role in supporting the social, emotional, ethical and cognitive competences of children (Krappmann, 1999).

However, international comparative research, like the OECD studies Starting
strong I and II (2004), show that kindergarten teachers in Germany are not suf-

ficiently qualified for this mandate. The German educational policies made early childhood education a central issue. This results for example in the program for the expansion of day care for children less than three years of age. The goal is to have 750,000 places in 2013. The German Youth Institution said in 2009 that 36,000 full-time positions are required (Deutsches Jugendinstitut, 2009). As most employees in kindergarten are working part-time, the demand for a better qualified work-force is much higher. Therefore, the professional and academic training must be changed in a very short time.

The education agreements, plans and recommendations deal with the educational task of kindergartens and their notion of education as well as with their educational standards. The educational agreements are meant as blueprints for preschool education. Although, they differ regarding comprehensiveness, structure, target group and content, they come up with a common task: To create a supportive learning environment for education in early childhood. In all agreements the child is seen as a unique individual personality and as an active participant in its own education. As much as these agreements speak about "individual child support" under the headline of diagnosis, unfortunately, hardly any reference is made to the competences of pre-school educators in this regard.

2 Supporting children with special abilities in kindergarten

If we look at the situation of children with special or high abilities in the educational system, we can outline some of the challenges and chances of individual support in kindergarten.

First, there is no notion of high abilities in the education agreements. Kindergarten curricula – where they already exist - only speak of "children with special needs" and "individual child support" in the field of diagnosis. The situation in academic training is rather bleak. Only the bachelor degree course "Education in early childhood" at the University of Applied Science in Hamburg knows a compulsory module on support of children with special abilities (Index of early and childhood education courses in Germany, n.d.). There are courses of advanced vocational training under the auspices of the European Council of High Ability (ECHA) in Germany and Austria ("certificate of preschool gifted education"; ICBF, n.d.) and the Karg Foundation (n.d.).

Nevertheless, international studies show the importance of the issue of special or high ability. Fourteen percent of children in each age group show symptoms of special or high ability (Fischer, 2006; Oswald, 2002). Institutions dedicated to individual support have to offer tools to diagnose children's talents early and to sufficiently support them. As the abilities come in broad variations, one has to look at them with a multitude of methods and perspectives.

Individual support means support for handicapped as well as specially gifted children. Higher education and vocational training curricula as well as education agreements often lack this double perspective. The diversity of children's potentials open a variety of perspectives on individual support and on the development of competences that meet the abilities of the children. Weinert (1998;

2000) and Baumert (1998) support dynamic models of education. Education should aim at flexible and individually designed networks of knowledge and competences. The connection to the life and environment of the children should be the centre of learning environments for the achievement of learning goals. This concept of education fosters methods of project learning, team learning, self-regulated learning, experimenting and a positive approach to mistakes.

For pre-school educators a focused observation documented for every child is a major step on the way to the individual support of abilities and talents. The idea of documenting development of the individual child is a central issue in all educational agreements. The observations should be focused on the possibilities and varieties of children's actions, perceptions, ideas, works and problem solving strategies. Competence is the key perspective, here. These documentations have to be produced on a regular basis. To this moment, there is no standardised instrument in German kindergartens. The instruments already applied vary from the rather open learning stories (Leu et al., 2007) to the more standardised Beller-table (Beller & Beller, 2010).

Beside the competence of a focussed observation and documentation the cooperation with parents is defined as a major task of pre-school educators. As results in PISA (Klieme et al., 2010) showed, the most important factors of a successful learning biography, seems to be the family environment. Social class, status, income, living conditions and the parents' education levels are clearly related to the child's learning processes and later academic performance in schools. But the quality of the learning environment at home seems to be even more important. Even though parents may not have reached a high education level, they can enhance their child's progress and development with regular activities in a positive learning setting. Those children will be ahead in both social and intellectual development at the age of three. This advantage continues through to age seven, and the latest report concludes that the effect is maintained through to age 10 (Sylva et al., 2004; Sammons et al., 2007). Early learning programs like for example HIPPY (Home Instruction Program for Preschool Youngsters, n.d.) are based on this idea (Bergs-Winkels & Halves, 2009; Halves & Bergs-Winkels, 2010).

The impact is evident across all social classes and ethnic groups, and different levels of parental involvement have a greater impact on achievement in the primary age range than the variation in school quality. Children receive not just skills, knowledge and intellectual stimulation at home; they also absorb a positive attitude towards learning and a strong self-image as a suc-cessful learner (Desforges, 2003).

So, pre-school teachers should listen to what parents have to say about their own child's capabilities and interests. They should combine this knowledge with their own observations. They also support children's learning at home directly with suggested activities in line with what the child is interested in pre-school (Siraj-Blatchford et al., 2003; Sylva et al., 2004; Desforges, 2003).

Observation, documentation and communication with colleagues, children and parents are important competences of pre-school educators. But they have to be amended with a specific attitude towards children. This attitude is characterised by the interest in the child's development and ideas, the own curiosity to explore new things, an explorative notion of knowledge, a genuine respect for children and their abilities and ideas, and the wish to take the role as a mentor and supporter in line with the interests and abilities of the children.

After establishing basic competences and attitudes of pre-school educators the question remains whether there are certain tools that help fostering individual support in kindergarten. In the following we turn to methods of creating a supporting learning setting and to self-regulated learning.

3   Learning settings in kindergartens

Learning settings encompass all factors concerning the learning situation, including the child as centre of focus, the teachers and his or her attitudes and the environmental settings of learning such as room, material and social context.

Taking a closer look at educational programs we find a good focus on the environmental aspect in the Reggio Emilia - approach and in the works of Maria Montessori.

In Reggio the understanding of "room" is widened to the rooms of the institution plus the surrounding of the children in their everyday life. This encompasses, the streets they walk, the public buildings in their city, the gardens, playgrounds etc. This approach lets the children be a part of the community. From the very beginning they learn in social contexts (Dreier, 2006).

In the Montessori didactical program (n.d.) children find a thoughtfully arranged environment in their rooms which is based on the needs of children according to close observation. The idea is to make the children independent of adults in constructing their learning settings. The surrounding has to fulfil high standards in respect of aesthetics and physical abilities. Material has to be positioned attractively. Social aspects are of importance. On the one hand every material exists only once so children have to communicate and on the other hand they have to show respect for the works of others, as they can indicate their work in process by using a certain space that no one else is allowed to work on, indicated by a piece of rug.

Rooms should be arranged in a way that children have an opportunity to question their surroundings. To enable children to do this material must be reachable. The material itself should be designed in a way that children are able to control their success on their own, without interference of educators. Providing age norms is not as important as the possibility to differentiate and the variety of its learning possibilities.

Educational professionals should know that learning happens in a social environment, should have challenging designs, should be fun and should foster self-efficacy. The learning environment has to allow divergent thinking as a starting point for productive, critical and creative thinking (Huser, 2007).

Although it takes time to re-design existing kindergartens along the ideas of the Reggio Emilia approach or the Montessori pedagogy there is the possibility of first immediate steps. For example, research studios are a possible environment for these learning processes. Freinet (Klein, 1996) was one of the first educators allowing children to learn by experiments. Focusing on learning processes of small children Schäfer emphasizes the self-learning potential of children (Schäfer, 2006). He believes that if children are fascinated by their own questions and ideas, they will develop learning strategies by themselves. If this is true for single learning acts, education – understood as a binding structure of a varied experience and sequences of learning – has to be acquired autonomously: education is always self-education. Structures mainly imposed by adults will be deficient, as they cannot deal with the child's perception and the constructions that derived from them. The only way to deal with these structures is submission and the development of self-dependency and self-efficacy is curtailed.

Fthenakis and Oberhuemer (2010) emphasizes the social process in joint learning of adults and children. Close to concepts of self-regulated learning, he underlines the importance of instruction phases, self-organization and reflection in the sense of a co-constructive manner. While constructing learning settings with children one can reflect on what and how children learn, developing a meta-cognitive level of learning.

4   Deliberations on self-regulated learning in preschool education

Self-regulated learning as a tool for individual support has come to the foreground in the consequence of PISA and IGLU studies (Baumert et al., 2003). It is understood as a form of learning, in which learners choose along their motivation one or several cognitive, meta-cognitive or intentional tools, and supervise their own learning progress (Schiefele & Pekrun, 1996). Self-regulated learning enables children to develop knowledge, competences and attitudes that support their future learning processes. The transformation of this knowledge to other contexts is always a part of the self-regulated learning process.

Stoeger and Ziegler (2008; 2005) describe the circle of self-regulated learning as follows:

- Assessment of own state of knowledge and own learning
- Autonomous definition of learning goals
- Choice of learning strategies and techniques adequate to these goals
- Mastering of learning strategies
- Supervision of learning processes
- Correction and adjustment of learning strategies
- Assessment of target achievement

The circle ends with the assessment and can be restarted. In every circle there is not only an achievement of learning goals but also an optimizing of learning competence. The teaching person has to design learning environments that support such learning processes.

Weinert (2000) postulates that a learning process should follow these principles:
- Active and constructive, meaning the inner participation of children in the learning process
- Goal oriented, meaning that the children are aware of their goals and those of their environment
- Cumulative, meaning that learning builds upon knowledge acquired before
- Systematic, meaning that the building of knowledge is oriented at the system of the theme
- Situated, meaning that knowledge is practice oriented and life oriented
- Self-steered, meaning that children should plan and control their learning process
- Cooperative, meaning that learning should happen in teams

Certainly, this approach, focussing on school settings, has to be adapted for pre-school education and modified according to the state of children's development. Preliminary abilities are in the focus here. Children develop their goals along their own questions addressed at the world around them. For pre-school educators this means that they have to introduce learning strategies and to create contexts including the prerequisite knowledge of children. With that they will be able to make the learning experience persistent. Learning should take place in a social context, which is inspiring, joyful and allows the experience of self efficacy (Bergs-Winkels, 2007).

Project work using exploratory learning methods is one good method to structure processes and to follow up on long-term goals. Here, the child's questions are honed, already known facts are collected, hypotheses are built and ways to prove them are looked for. Circular processes are formulated already in exploratory learning designs. There has to be time for experiments and critical inquiry. It is important to count on the explanations of children as a basis for hypotheses, not on the knowledge of grown-ups.

As mentioned before, the room for stimulation and curiosity is essential here. Autonomous thinking and individual learning strategies need a room to make self-regulation possible. The educator is more a learning companion than a teacher of facts. He or she has to give positive and constructive feedback, provide adequate tools and foster self-critique. The attitude of such a person towards the child can be described as reliable, curious about every single child and attentiveness.

5   Conclusion

To be able to learn children need the capacity to develop concepts of self-efficacy, namely to visualise their own position in the world. They need motivation and a certain control of impulses, to plan and design their learning ways. And they need social and emotional competences to learn in groups and social settings.

An intensive study of developmental psychology is required for pre-school educators to help children develop these character features. Therefore, for academic and vocational training of pre-school educators this means a revision of curricula and in parts a change of training structures. Examples of individualised pre school learning along the idea of supporting gifted children, in the sense of Best Practice are documented in a practice paper at the (ICBF) International Center for research on giftedness in Münster (ICBF, 2007). Individual support is only possible on grounds of tolerance of diversity, individual documentation of development and enough time for every child. These are the ingredients for providing children with good chances for their future, based on individual abilities and competences instead of social background.

References

Baumert, J.(1998). Fachbezogenes-fachübergreifendes Lernen. Erweiterte Lern- und Denkstrategien. [Curricular and cross-curricular learning. Enhanced learning and thinking strategies.]. In Bayrisches Staatsministerium für Unterreicht, Kultus, Wissenschaft und Kunst (Ed.), *Wissen und Werte für die Welt von morgen [Knowledge and values for tomorrow's world]* (pp. 213-231). München: Dokumentation zum Bildungskongress.

Baumert, J., Artelt, C., Klieme, E., Neubrand, M., Prenzel, M., Schiefele, U., Schneider, W., Tillmann, K. & Weiß, M. (Deutsches PISA- Konsortium) (Eds.) (2003). *PISA 2000- Ein differenzierter Blick auf die Länder der Bundesrepublik Deutschland. [PISA 2000 – a differentiated view on the stated of the Federal Republic of Germany].* Opladen: Leske & Budrich.

Beller, E. K., & Beller, S. (2010). *Kuno Bellers Entwicklungstabelle [Kuno Beller's development tableau].* Berlin, Germany: FU Berlin.

Bergs-Winkels, D. (2007). Individuelle Förderung im Elementarbereich [Individual advancement in elementary education]. In K. Fröhlich-Gildhoff, I. Nentwig-Gesemann, & P. Schnadt (Eds.), *Neue Wege gehen – Entwicklungsfelder der Frühpädagogik [Breaking new grounds – fields of development in early childhood pedagogics]* (pp. 102-111). München: Reinhardt.

Bergs-Winkels, D., & Halves, E. (2009). *Evaluation des Programms HIPPY Hamburg. Unveröffentlichter Abschlussbericht [Evaluation report on HIPPY in Hamburg. Unpublished final report].*

Biedinger, N., & Becker, B. (2006). *Der Einfluss des Vorschulbesuchs auf die Entwicklung und den langfristigen Bildungserfolg von Kindern. Ein Überblick über internationale Studien im Vorschulbereich [The influence of pre-school attendance on the development and long-term educational success].* University of Mannheim, Germany: Mannheimer Zentrum für Europäische Sozialforschung, Arbeitspapier Nr. 97.

Bos, W., Hornberg, S., Arnold, K.-H., Faust, G., Fried, L., Lankes, E.-M., Schwippert, K., & Valtin, R. (Eds.) (2007). *IGLU 2006. Lesekompetenzen von Grundschulkindern in Deutschland im internationalen Vergleich [IGLU 2006. International comparison of reading competence of primary school children in Germany].* Münster: Waxmann.

Bundesministerium für Familie, Senioren, Frauen und Jugend (Ed.) (2005). *12. Kinder- und Jugendbericht [Children and youth report].* Berlin.

Desforges, C. (2003). *The Impact of Parental Involvement, Parental Support and Family Education on Pupil Achievements and Adjustment: A Literature Review, Research Report RR433.* London: DfES.

Deutsches Jugendinstitut (2009). *Quantität braucht Qualität. Agenda für den qualitativen Ausbau der Kindertagesbetreuung für unter Dreijährige [Quantity needs quality. An agenda for the qualitative expansion of child care for children under three years of age].* München: DJI.

Dreier, A. (2006). *Was tut der Wind wenn er nicht weht? Begegnung mit der Kleinkindpädagogik in Reggio Emilia [What does the wind do when it is not blowing? An encounter with the educational approaches in Reggio Emilia].* Weinheim: Beltz Verlag.

Fischer, C. (2006). Begabtenförderung als Aufgabe und Herausforderung für die Pädagogik [The advenbcement of children with high abilties as task and challenge of pedagogics]. In C. Fischer & H. Ludwig (Eds.), *Münstersche Gespräche zur Pädagogik [Muenster talks on pedagogigs]* (p. 17). Münster: Aschendorff.

Fried, L., & Voss, A. (2010): Der vorschulische Bereich im internationalen und nationalen Vergleich [Preschool in an international and national Comparison]. In: W. Bos, S. Hornberg, K.-H. Arnold, G. Faust, L. Fried, E.-M. Lankes, K. Schwippert, I. Tarelli, & R. Valtin (Eds.), *IGLU 2006 – die Grundschule auf dem Prüfstand. Vertiefende Analysen zu Rahmenbedingungen schulischen Lernens [IGLU 2006- elemenatry schools at focus. Analyses to environmental influences on learning in schools]* (pp. 165-195). Münster Waxmann

Fthenakis, W., & Oberhuemer, P. (Eds.) (2010). *Frühpädagogik International. Bildungsqualität im Blickpunkt [Early childhood pedagogics international. Focus on educational quality].* Wiesbaden: VS Verlag.

Halves, E., & Bergs-Winkels D. (2010). Evaluation und Steuerung – Zu einigen Aspekten am Beispiel der Evalaution HIPPY Hamburg [Evaluation and steering – on some aspects related to the evaluation of HIPPY Hamburg]. In E. Halves (Ed.), *Standpunkt Sozial. Evaluation in der Sozialen Arbeit – zwischen Forschung, Steuerung und Entwicklung [Standpoint social. Evaluation in social work between research, steering and development]*, (p. 61). Hamburger Forum für Soziale Arbeit und Gesundheit.

Home Instruction Program for Preschool Youngsters. (n.d.). Retrieved from www.hippy-deutschland.de

Huser J. (2007). *Lichtblick für helle Köpfe: Ein Wegweiser zur Erkennung und Förderung von hohen Fähigkeiten bei Kindern und Jugendlichen auf allen Schulstufen. [A bright sport for bright kids: a roadmap of diagnosis and advancement of children with high abilities in all levels of education].* Zürich: Lehrmittelverlag.

ICBF [International Centre for research on giftedness]. (n.d.). Retrieved from www.icbf.de

Index of early and childhood education courses in Germany. (n.d.). Retrieved from www.fruehpaedagogik-studieren.de

Internationales Centrum für Begabungsforschung ICBF (Ed.) (2007). *Individuelle Förderung – Begabtenförderung Beispiele aus der Praxis [Individual support and support for gifted children. Examples from practise].* Stiftung Bildung zur Förderung Hochbegabter.

Karg Foundation (n.d.). Retrieved from www.karg-stiftung.de

Klein, L. (1996). Célestin Freinet. Aus dem Leben - für das Leben [Célestin Freinet. Taken from real life for real life]. *Kindergarten heute Wissen kompak spezial. Pädagogische Handlungskonzepte von Fröbel bis Situationsansatz*, 22-29.

Klieme, E., Artelt, C., Hartig, J., Jude, N., Köller, O., Prenzel, M., Schneider, W., & Stanat, P. (Eds.) (2010). *PISA 2009: Bilanz nach einem Jahrzehnt [PISA 2009. Ten years after].* Münster: Waxmann.

Krappmann, L. (1999). Die Lebenssituation von Kindern [The life situation of children]. *Welt des Kindes, 77*(3), 29-31.

Leu, R., Flämig, K., Frankenstein,Y., Koch, S., Pack, I., Schneider, K., & Schweiger, M. (2007). *Bildungs- und Lerngeschichten. Bildungsprozesse in früher Kindheit beobachten, dokumentieren und unterstützen [Education and learning stories. The observation, documentation and support of early childhood educational processes].* Berlin: Verlag das Netz.

Montessori didactical program (n.d.). Retrieved from www.montessori-didaktik.de

OECD- Starting Strong I und II (Länderbericht Deutschland 2004) (2004). *Die Politik der frühkindlichen Betreuung, Bildung und Erziehung* [Policies of early childhood care, learning and education]. Retrieved from http://www.oecd.org/dataoecd/42/3/33979291.pdf

Oswald, F. (2002). *Begabtenförderung in der Schule. Entwicklung einer begabtenfreundlichen Schule [School programs for gifted students. The development of a gifted-oriented school]*. Wien: Facultas.

Roßbach, H.-G., Kluczniok, K., & Isenmann, D. (2008). Kompetenzmessungen im Vorschulalter: Erfahrungen aus internationalen Längsschnittuntersuchungen [Measuring competence in pre-school age. Learning from international longitudinal studies]. In Bundesministerium für Bildung und Forschung (BMBF) (Ed.), *Kindliche Kompetenzen im Elementarbereich: Förderbarkeit, Bedeutung und Messung [Competence of children in elementary education: chances of support, meaning and measuring]* (pp. 7-88). Berlin: Bundesministerium für Bildung und Forschung.

Sammons, P., Sylva, K., Melhuish, E., Siraj-Blatchford, I., Taggart, B., Grabbe, Y., & Barreau, S. (2007). (Eds.). *Summary Report: Influences on Children's Attainment and Progress in Key Stage 2: Cognitive Outcomes in Year 5: Effective Pre-school and Primary Education 3-11 Project (EPPE 3-11), Research Report RR828*. London: DfES.

Schäfer, G.-E. (Ed.) (2006). *Bildung beginnt mit der Geburt. Ein offener Bildungsplan für Kindertageseinrichtungen in Nordrhein-Westfalen [Education starts at birth. An open education plan for child care facilities in Northrhine Westphalia]*. Weinheim: Beltz.

Schiefele, U., & Pekrun, R. (1996). Psychologische Modelle des selbstgesteuerten und fremdgesteuerten Lernens [Psychological models of self-regulated and extern-regulated learning]. In: F.E. Weinert (Ed.) *Psychologie des Lernens und der Instruktion. Enzyklopädie der Psychologie, Serie Pädagogische Psychologie, Bd. 2 [Psychology of learning and instruction. Encyclopedia of psychology]* (pp. 249-278). Göttingen: Hogrefe.

Siraj-Blatchford, I., Sylva, K., Taggart, B., Sammons, P., Melhuish, E., & Elliot, K. (2003). *The Effective Provision of Pre-School Education (EPPE) Project: Technical Paper 10. Intensive Case Studies of Practice across the Foundation Stage*. London: Univ. of London, Institute of Education, DfES.

Stoeger, H., & Ziegler, A. (2008). *Trainingshandbuch selbstreguliertes Lernen II. Grundlegende Textverständnisstrategien für Schüler der 4. bis 8. Jahrgangsstufe [Training manual for self-regualted learning 2. Basic strategies for text comprehension for 4th to 8th grade students]*. Lengerich: PABST.

Stoeger, H., & Ziegler, A. (2005). *Trainingshandbuch selbstreguliertes Lernen I. Lernökologische Strategien für Schüler der vierten Jahrgangsstufe zur Verbesserung mathematischer Kompetenzen [Training manual for self-regualted learning 1. Ecological learning strategies for 4th grade students to improve mathematical competences].* Lengerich: PABST.

Sylva, K., Melhuish, E., Sammons, P., Siraj-Blatchford, I., & Taggart, B. (2004) *The Effective Provision of Pre-School Education (EPPE) Project: Final Report. A Longitudinal Study Funded by the DfES 1997-2004.* London: University of London, Institute of Education, DfES.

Tietze, W. (Ed.) (1998). *Wie gut sind unsere Kindergärten? Eine Untersuchung zur pädagogischen Qualität in deutschen Kindergärten [How good are our kindergartens? A study on the pedagogical quality in German kindergartens].* Neuwied: Luchterhand.

Viernickel, S., & Schwarz, S. (2009). *Schlüssel zu guter Bildung, Erziehung und Betreuung - Wissenschaftliche Parameter zur Bestimmung der pädagogischen Fachkraft-Kind-Relation [Keys to good education and child caring. Scientific parameters to determin the relation between pre-school expert and child].* Alice-Salomon-Hochschule. Berlin: GEW.

Weinert, F.E. (1998). Neue Unterrichtskonzepte zwischen gesellschaftlichen Notwendigkeiten, pädagogischen Visionen und psychologischen Möglichkeiten [New teaching concepts between social needs, pedagogical visions and psycological possibilities]. In: Bayrisches Staatsministerium für Unterricht, Kultur, Wissenschaft und Kunst (Ed.). *Wissen und Werte für die Welt von morgen. Dokumentation zum Bildungskongress [Knowledge and values for the world of tomorrow. Cngress documentation].* München.

Weinert, F.E. (2000). Lernen des Lernens [To learn learning]. In Arbeitsstab Forum Bildung (Ed.), *Erster Kongress des Forum Bildung in Berlin.* Bonn: Forum Bildung.

---

[i] A compilation of all 16 education agreements on early childhood education can be found at Deutscher Bildungsserver http://www.eduserver.de/zeigen_e.html?seite=2027. Unfortunately, there are no comprehensive English translations.

III. Students' Characteristics and Gifted Education at School

Christine Sontag, Bettina Harder, Heidrun Stoeger, & Albert Ziegler

The Smarter the More Self-Regulated? A Study on the Relationship Between Intelligence and Self-Regulated Learning

Abstract

Today's literature yields inconclusive findings on the relationship between intelligence and a preference for self-regulated learning. In our study we sought to avoid common methodological weaknesses of previous studies to clarify the relationship in question. 368 fourth-graders took an intelligence test at the beginning of the school year and responded to a questionnaire based on Ziegler and Stoeger's (2005) cyclical model of self-regulated learning at three different points in time. Highly intelligent students did not prefer self-regulated learning over other forms of learning, and they did not prefer self-regulated learning more than their peers in the same learning environment. Differences in the development of the preference for self-regulated learning in the course of the fourth grade were not associated with intelligence. HLM analyses showed, however, that students in different classrooms differed in their development of the preference for self-regulated learning. Practical implications are discussed.

1   Introduction

People are quick to assume that gifted individuals, usually meaning those identified as highly intelligent, will show a higher rate of self-regulated learning,
will be better at it, and will profit more from trainings of self-regulated learning.
However, the debate about the relationship between intelligence and learning
skills has been in progress for years and still yields astonishingly inconclusive
scientific findings. In our view this might be due to varying definitions and
thereby operationalizations of intelligence and self-regulated learning, different
experimental designs and also methodological shortcomings. With the present
study, we seek to shed more light upon the empirical relationship between intelligence and self-regulated learning. To this end, we conducted an empirical
study in which we avoided a number of the methodological weaknesses of earlier studies. Before we move on to describing the current state of research on the
relationship between intelligence and self-regulated learning and of the shortcomings of existing studies, we will first provide a clarification of the terms
central for discussing previous studies and for our own work.

1.1   Intelligence

Studies of the relationship between intelligence and self-regulated learning rely
on a broad variety of definitions of intelligence. Most authors fail, however, to
explicitly define intelligence for their own inquiries but rather imply their conception through their choice of operationalization. Some authors measure only
verbal intelligence (e.g., Kron-Sperl, Schneider, & Hasselhorn, 2008), others
measure only nonverbal intelligence (e.g., Dresel & Haugwitz, 2005; Spörer,
2003). Still others employ scales from a multidimensional test battery (e.g.,
Bouffard-Bouchard, Parent, & Larivée, 1993; Ewers & Wood, 1993; Van der
Stel & Veenman, 2010). For our study, intelligence is defined as general cognitive ability in the sense of Spearman's g-factor. Accordingly we used a well-
established, one-dimensional non-verbal test of intelligence (Heller, Kratzmeier,
& Lengfelder, 1998; explained in more detail in the Method section).

1.2   Self-Regulated Learning

Definitions of self-regulated learning to date are equally heterogeneous. A central characteristic commonly found in most definitions is that individuals accept
responsibility for their own learning. Self-regulated learning is an active process: Individuals set their own goals for their learning; they plan how they will
learn; and they monitor, regulate, and evaluate their cognitions, motivation, and
behavior (Zeidner, Boekaerts, & Pintrich, 2000). Yet, fundamentally different
views exist regarding the conceptualization of self-regulated learning. Some researchers describe components and prerequisites of self-regulated learning (e.g.,
Artelt, Demmrich, & Baumert, 2001; Boekaerts, 1999), while others focus on

the process of self-regulated learning (e.g., Ziegler & Stoeger, 2005; Zimmerman, 1998).

We base our study on the cyclical process model described by Ziegler and Stoeger (2005), which in turn is based on a social-cognitive approach (Bandura, 1986). Self-regulated learning is described as a repeating cyclical process consisting of seven phases (see Figure 1): After (1) a self-assessment regarding their current state of understanding in a given area of learning, (2) individuals set their own learning goals, (3) strategically plan their learning process, (4) implement the chosen learning strategy, (5) monitor the learning process, and, if necessary, (6) adapt the chosen strategy. Finally, (7) they evaluate the results of their learning process. These evaluations then serve as the basis for the self-assessment when the cycle is traversed anew.

Figure 1: The cycle of self-regulated learning as described by Ziegler and Stoeger (2005)

Following Ziegler, Stoeger, and Grassinger (2010), we assume that learners will prefer one of three possible global approaches to learning: self-regulated learning, externally regulated learning, or impulsive learning. Thus, in our study we used a questionnaire in which students indicated their preferred manner of learning. Learners are categorized as *self-regulated learners* if they accept responsibility for their own learning during a majority of the seven phases averaged across different situations. In a similar way, individuals are categorized as *externally regulated learners* if they leave the responsibility for their learning process to other people (e.g., parents or teachers) most of the time. *Impulsive learners* are those who are of the opinion that it is not necessary to thoroughly think about their own learning. We have chosen to work with this categorization of general learning-approach preferences because it is useful to certain ends; it should be kept in mind, however, that we view self-regulated learning as a complex and highly individual construct. It is possible and even quite likely that the preference for certain approaches to learning will differ from phase to phase (e.g., learners who reflect on the goals, strategic planning, and execution of their own learning, look to their parents or their teachers in the area of evaluation, and proceed in a spontaneous, impulsive manner in the areas of monitoring and adaptation). Furthermore, learning-approach preferences can vary for the same person according to the situation. A learner might, for instance, independently set goals when studying for a test but fail to do so in the context of doing homework. We thus have expanded our categorization to include *mixed-strategy learners.*(i.e., learners who show no clear dominant learning-approach preference and instead, demonstrate an equal reliance upon two or all three of the learning approaches described above).

1.3   Findings and Limitations of Empirical Studies to Date

As we mentioned above, the literature on the relationship between intelligence and self-regulated learning is inconclusive (cf. Sontag & Stoeger, 2010, for a detailed discussion). A wide array of possible relationships exists between intelligence and self-regulated learning as well as between intelligence and the aforementioned subprocesses involved in self-regulated learning. In some processes, highly intelligent individuals demonstrated or reported a higher frequency or greater quality of self-regulated learning compared to individuals of average intelligence while in other processes there was no difference between these groups (e.g., Bouffard-Bouchard et al., 1993; Spörer, 2003; Zimmerman & Martinez-Pons, 1990). In some studies highly intelligent students reported even lower levels of self-regulated learning (e.g., Dresel & Haugwitz, 2005; Neber & Schommer-Aikens, 2002, in reference to the results of Wolters & Pintrich, 1998).

There are several reasons that make an interpretation of these heterogeneous results difficult. For example, as noted earlier, the studies are based on different conceptualizations of intelligence and self-regulated learning; the concepts are also operationalized in very different ways. In addition, there are five further areas of limitation that have received special attention in the design of our study.

First, many researchers investigate selected samples where variables are confounded: Higher intelligence comes with a higher preference for self-regulated learning, but the more intelligent students undergo a more stimulating schooling (cf. Ewers & Wood, 1993; Zimmerman & Martinez-Pons, 1990). Second, to our knowledge no study on the topic accounts for school-, grade-, and classroom-related contexts in statistical analyses. This is important as students drawn from the same classroom share a common learning environment and hence are probably more similar to one another than students from a random sample – thus violating the assumption of independence underlying many procedures of statistical analysis. Third, only very few studies of self-regulated learning in giftedness research investigate the process of self-regulated learning as a whole. Most studies only shed light upon single aspects like metacognition (cf., Ewers & Wood, 1993) or cognitive learning strategies (cf., Chan, 1996), while neglecting to analyze these aspects in the context of the complete learning process (exceptions consist for example in Bouffard-Bouchard et al., 1993; Spörer, 2003; Zimmerman & Martinez-Pons, 1990). Fourth, the focus of most studies is placed on the relationship between self-regulated learning and intelligence in a cross-sectional design. Thus, they do not allow for statements on the role of intelligence in the development of self-regulated learning over time. Fifth, a majority of studies focuses on students who were eleven years or older. This omission of younger children in research may reflect the long-held assumption that younger children lacked the metacognitive capabilities necessary for self-regulated learning (cf., for example, Baumert et al., 2000; Lai, 2011). We now know, quite to the contrary, that younger children are capable of carrying out less complex forms of self-regulated learning (e.g., Alexander, Graham, & Harris, 1998; Kron-Sperl et al., 2008; Roebers, Schmid, & Roderer, 2009; summarized in Wigfield, Klauda, & Cambria, 2011). Thus, the study of the relationship between intelligence and self-regulated learning is particularly relevant in the case of younger schoolchildren.

1.4   Goals and Research Questions

The goal of our study is to describe the role played by intelligence for the preference for self-regulated learning (as opposed to a preference for externally regulated or impulsive learning) among fourth-graders, that is, nine- to ten-year-old students. The choice of participants addresses the fifth of the above mentioned limitations. Our study design includes four further unique characteristics that are intended to address the shortcomings of earlier studies described above. First, we examined an unselected sample of students. Since, in Germany, all students receive their lessons together within the same group of children through fourth grade, the students experience similar learning environments. Furthermore, elementary school brings together individuals with the broadest span of cognitive abilities due to the tracking system only starting after fourth grade. Hence, variance in intelligence is guaranteed. Second, in order to account for the fact that students learning in the same classroom are surrounded by a comparable environment and thus are more likely to share similar characteristics than students representing a random sample, we also used hierarchical linear models for our statistical analyses. Third, our measurements of self-regulated learning are model-based, and all subprocesses (as described in the cyclical model by Ziegler & Stoeger, 2005) were assessed in the same manner. Fourth, we did not only look at our question from a cross-sectional perspective but also examined it from a longitudinal perspective.

We examined the role played by intelligence in the development of preferences for self-regulated learning among students in their final year of elementary school before their transition into secondary education. In Germany, where the study was conducted, fourth grade is less playful than previous grades and the demands increase. We assumed that, at the beginning of fourth grade, students would not yet have adapted their learning behavior to the new demands placed upon them; furthermore, we assumed that their learning behavior would change in a manner that reflects these new demands over the course of the first half of fourth grade. Therefore, even if, at the beginning of fourth grade, intelligence were irrelevant for students' preference for self-regulated learning, more intelligent students might be able to adjust their learning behavior better when demands increase.

The aims of our study were twofold. In a first step, we wanted to take a look at the situation at the beginning of fourth grade. We were interested in finding out if there is a relationship between intelligence and a preference for self-regulated learning and if highly intelligent students differ from other students in their preferred approach to learning (self-regulated, externally regulated, and impulsive learner type). In a second step we wanted to investigate changes in self-regulated learning over the course of fourth grade. In this regard, we sought to find out if the preference for self-regulated learning changes during fourth grade, and if intelligence predicts these changes in preference. As self-regulated learning requires a certain amount of learning motivation (e.g., Ames & Archer, 1988; cf. Zimmerman, 2011, for an overview) it may be possible that only the combination of intelligence and learning motivation predicts an increase in students' preference for self-regulation. Therefore, we included learning goal orientation (cf. Midgley et al., 1998) in the analyses.

2   Method

2.1   Study Design and Participants

The data set used for the current investigation forms part of a larger training study of fourth-graders in self-regulated learning. We only used data from control classes with regular instruction to investigate the aforementioned relationships between intelligence and the preferred approach to learning as well as its development. Data collection took place at three different points in time (T1, T2, T3): at the beginning of the school year (T1), eleven weeks later (T2) and again ten weeks after that (T3). Preference for self-regulated learning was measured at T1, T2, and T3, cognitive ability level, learning goal orientation and grades in the three main subjects (German, mathematics and basic sciences) were measured at T1. The testing sessions were scheduled during regular classroom hours and were led by trained research assistants or by the classroom teachers themselves.

At T1, 368 fourth-grade elementary school students from 19 different classrooms in rural or suburban Bavaria (a federal state of Germany) participated in the study. The drop-out-rate was quite low with 2.7 % missing at T2 and 3.2 %

at T3. The mean age of the students (at T1) was 9 years, 9 months ($SD = 4.85$ month), gender distribution was balanced (184 girls and 184 boys).

2.2 Instruments

2.2.1 Self-regulated Learning

Preference for self-regulated learning was measured with the 28 items of the "Fragebogen Selbstreguliertes Lernen-7" (Questionnaire of Self-regulated Learning-7, Ziegler et al., 2010). The questionnaire is based on Ziegler and Stoeger's (2005) seven-phase cyclical model of self-regulated learning. In four school-relevant learning situations the students are asked to indicate their preferred approach to learning in each of the seven phases of self-regulated learning (see Figure 1) by choosing one of three alternatives: self-regulated, externally regulated, or impulsive learning. A sample item for the situation of "studying for school", phase "goal-setting" is: How do you study for school? *a) I set a fixed goal for myself describing what and how much I want to study* [self-regulated learning], *b) The teacher or my parents should tell me which goal I should set for myself* [externally regulated learning], *c) When studying, I don't set a specific goal for myself. I can rely on my intuition* [impulsive learning behavior].

To measure preference for self-regulated, externally regulated, and impulsive learning, we calculated scores for each phase as well as an overall score for the whole instrument by counting the frequency with which a child chose for example the self-regulated option and dividing it by the number of items answered. The scores are reported as percentages. Example: For phase 2, goal-setting, a student chose the self-regulated alternative in 3 of the 4 situations, resulting in a score of 75% for this phase in the cycle. Regarding the entire questionnaire, that same student chose the self-regulated alternative for 13 out of 28 items, resulting in an overall score of 46%. In the same way, we calculated how often (in %) the students chose the externally regulated or the impulsive alternative. In addition, each student was classified according to his or her preferred that is, most frequently chosen, approach to learning. Those with equal frequencies for two or three alternatives were classified as mixed types.

Reliabilities for the questionnaire were calculated by including all answers to one type of learning (self-regulated, externally regulated, impulsive) over the four situations. Cronbach's alphas varied between .82 and .96 for the scales at T1, T2 and T3, which is highly satisfactory.

2.2.2 Intelligence

At T1 students completed the German version of Raven's Standard Progressive Matrices (SPM) Test (Heller et al., 1998). This non-verbal multiple choice test consists of 60 tasks in which students are asked to select an item that completes a given pattern. As there are no up-to-date German norms for this test, we labeled the students with scores at or above the 95th percentile within our sample as the "highly intelligent students" and all remaining students as "students of average intelligence" for group comparisons. In all other analyses, intelligence was treated as a continuous variable. The SPM's internal consistency came to Cronbach's α = .80 in our sample.

2.2.3   Learning goal orientation

To measure general academic learning goal orientation at T1, we used an adaption of the six-item learning goal orientation scale developed by Midgley et al. (1998). The adequacy of this six-point Likert scale for fourth-grade elementary school students had been demonstrated in earlier studies (e.g., Ziegler & Stoeger, 2004). A sample item reads as follows: *In school, I want to learn a lot of new things*, with the answer options 1 = not at all true to 6 = very true. The internal consistency of this scale was satisfactory (Cronbach's α = .72).

2.2.4   Academic achievement

At T1 students reported their grades for the latest tests in the main subjects math, German and basic sciences. The students used the German grading system with 1 = very good and 6 = insufficient. As indicator of general academic achievement, we calculated the mean value of the self-reported grades. In this study, academic achievement was used only in an exploratory analysis (see the Discussion section).

2.3   Data Analysis

We used hierarchical linear models[1] to analyze the data thus taking into account that students are clustered in classes. Students within one class are more similar to one another than compared to students from different classes. This fact is considered by modeling linear regressions for each level – the individuals and the classes – and at the same time allowing for a differentiated investigation of predictors' effects on the criterion (for details see e.g., Hox, 1998, 2010; Raudenbush & Bryk, 2006). For the study of changes over time, measuring points are clustered within individuals who are themselves clustered within classes, resulting in three-level-analyses. All analyses were conducted with HLM 6.08. HLM allows for the estimation of missing data (e.g. caused by participant drop-out) by using full information maximum likelihood (FIML) estimations, which reduces a potential bias due to sample drop-out.

To answer the question regarding differences at the beginning of fourth grade, we first analyzed descriptive data and then the relationship between intelligence and the preference for self-regulated learning, taking into account the hierarchical data structure. This was realized by setting up a two-level hierarchical model with preference for self-regulated learning as criterion and intelligence as

---

[1] This chapter is based on an article published in Talent Development & Excellence (2012). For more detailed information on methods and the results of the hierarchical linear models please refer to the aforementioned paper.

predictor on the individual level (no predictors on the level of classes). A closer look at highly intelligent students compared to those below the 95th percentile in our sample is taken by means of t-tests and chi-square tests, thereby allowing for easy comparisons with existing studies.

To analyze change in the preference for self-regulated learning three-level regressions were modeled comprising the three measuring points on level 1, individuals on level 2 and classes on level 3. We examined whether the change in self-regulated learning varies between students and if differences between students in their development over time can be explained by intelligence or by a combination of intelligence and learning goal orientation. All regressions were calculated for the overall preference of self-regulated learning and for each of the seven phases assessed by the self-regulation questionnaire.

3   Results

In the following sections we will first present results of the situation at the beginning of fourth grade starting with a descriptive overview of preferences for learning and the other variables. After that, we will explore the relationship between the preference for self-regulated learning and intelligence in detail. The second section of results treats changes in the preference for self-regulated learning in the course of fourth grade. First, we examine the changes in self-regulated learning per se; then we include intelligence and the combination of intelligence and learning goal orientation to find out whether these individual characteristics influence the development of the preference for self-regulated learning.

3.1   Situation at the Beginning of Grade four (T1)

Table 1 presents descriptive statistics for all variables included in further analyses. The percentage of the self-regulated learning choice is provided for all phases of self-regulated learning. Overall, students reported acting in a self-regulated manner in one third of the items presented in the questionnaire. For the different phases of the learning cycle the degree of self-regulation varied slightly between 26.13 % for strategy monitoring and 41.80 % for the self-assessment phase with relatively high variation between individuals. The intelligence values and the mean grades (academic achievement) were in the range expected for students of this age, and also the seemingly high means for learning goal orientation are not unusual (cf. Nicholls, 1984; Stoeger & Ziegler, 2008). The variation between classrooms (intra-class correlations) was rather low for self-regulated learning; large classroom effects were observed for intelligence; classroom effects were medium for learning goal orientation and academic achievement.

Table 1: Descriptive statistics for all variables used in further analyses

Scale	Min; Max	M	SD
Self-regulated learning (overall)	0;100	33.02	19.17
Self-assessment (phase 1)	0;100	41.80	28.81
Goal-setting (phase 2)	0;100	30.28	30.84
Strategic planning (phase 3)	0;100	34.85	29.27
Strategy implantation (phase 4)	0;100	31.50	30.50
Strategy monitoring (phase 5)	0;100	26.13	27.50
Strategy adjustment (phase 6)	0;100	26.81	30.18
Outcome monitoring (phase 7)	0;100	39.81	33.51
Intelligence	2;60	36.67	7.60
Learning goal orientation	1;6	5.18	.67
Academic achievement (grades)	1;6	2.48	0.84

Note. N=368 student from 19 different classrooms. Grades are *not* recoded: small values correspond to better academic achievement.

Figure 2 shows how often (in %) the students chose the self-regulated, externally regulated, or impulsive approach to learning in the FSL-7. Overall, the students chose the self-regulated learning alternative with approximately the same frequency as externally regulated and impulsive learning options.

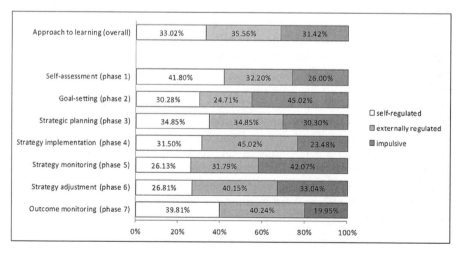

Figure 2: Students' preference for one of the three alternative approaches to learning (in %)

Table 2: Means (and SD) for the preference for self-regulated learning in highly intelligent and students of average intelligence

	High (n = 21)		Average (n = 347)	
	M	SD	M	SD
Self-regulated learning (overall)	30.44	24.32	33.18	18.84
Self-assessment (phase 1)	41.67	31.95	41.81	28.66
Goal-setting (phase 2)	30.95	33.45	30.24	30.73
Strategic planning (phase 3)	30.95	31.53	35.09	29.16
Strategy implementation (phase 4)	29.76	28.08	31.60	30.68
Strategy monitoring (phase 5)	17.86	29.73	26.63	27.32
Strategy adjustment (phase 6)	28.57	37.32	26.71	29.75
Outcome monitoring (phase 7)	33.33	35.65	40.20	33.39

Note. High = students at or above the 95th percentile in the SPM intelligence test. Average = students below the 95th percentile in the SPM intelligence test.

Analyzing the relationship between intelligence and the preference for self-regulated learning with hierarchical methods yielded the result that intelligence predicted the preference for self-regulated learning neither for the overall score nor for any of the phases of self-regulated learning. Intelligence did not serve to explain substantial variance between individuals or between classes (all Pseudo $R^2 \leq .03$). This suggests that intelligence and the preference for self-regulated learning are uncorrelated.

To take a closer look, we divided our sample into highly intelligent students (at or above the 95th percentile according to the result of the intelligence test) and those below the 95th percentile. To examine whether the two groups differed from each other in their preferred approach to learning, we first investigated whether one group chose self-regulated learning (overall or in single phases) more often than the other. The descriptive results are shown in Table 2. T-tests revealed no significant differences between the two groups of students.

Finally, we compared the distribution of the three learning types in highly intelligent and other students. The distribution of learning types (without mixed types) for highly intelligent students, students of average intelligence, and the total sample is listed in Table 3. A chi-square-test was used to test whether the learning type distribution differed between the two groups of students. While the choices of students of average intelligence are quite equally distributed among learning types with only slightly more students classified as externally regulated learners, highly intelligent students are clearly (52.4 %) overrepresented in the impulsive learner category. Overall, the distributions in the two groups are slightly different with $X^2(2, N = 355) = 4.281$, p < .10.

Table 3: Distribution of learning types in highly intelligent students, other students and the total sample

	High ($n = 21$)		Average ($n = 334$)		Total ($N = 355$)	
	n	$\%$	n	$\%$	n	$\%$
SRL	5	23.8	98	29.3	103	29.0
EXT	5	23.8	136	40.7	141	39.7
IMP	11	52.4	100	29.9	111	31.3

Note. High = students at or above the 95th percentile in the SPM intelligence test. Average = students below the 95th percentile in the SPM intelligence test. SRL = preference for self-regulated learning, EXT = preference for externally regulated learning, IMP = preference for impulsive learning.

3.2 Changes in the Preference for Self-Regulated Learning over Time

Figure 3 shows the preferences for self-regulated learning over time for the overall measure and for all phases. The development of the preference for self-regulated learning seems to be different for the different phases of self-regulated learning.

For each curve in Figure 3 we tested which model (a model containing only a constant, a linear model, a model with linear and quadratic components) fit the data best, again using HLM. Models with linear and quadratic components (increase followed by decrease) fit best for self-regulated learning (overall) and phases 1 through 3. Linear models (increase or decrease) fit best for phases 4 through 7. The coefficients (beta-weights in the regression) indicating the magnitude of linear and quadratic trends in the models only rarely differed significantly from 0. These results confirm the observation based on Figure 3 that there is relatively small change over time.

Hierarchical models can not only be used to describe the development of the whole sample, but also to analyze whether students and/or classrooms differ from each other in their development over time. Before we could examine whether intelligence influences the development of the preference for self-regulated learning alone or in combination with learning goal orientation, we had to test whether the students differed at all in their trajectories once classroom affiliation was controlled. Indeed, this was the case for the overall preference for self-regulated learning (marginally significant variance between individuals, chi-square test, $p = .083$), for self-assessment (phase 1, chi-square test, $p = .004$) and for strategy implementation (phase 4, chi-square test, $p = .003$).

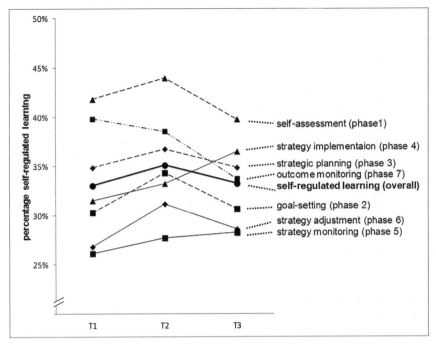

Figure 3: Percentage of the preference for self-regulated learning for different phases at different points in time

However, the student-level variable intelligence did not explain the variance in any of the three cases. This means, intelligence explained neither differences in students' overall self-regulated learning trajectories nor differences in their self-assessment or strategy implementation trajectories. The combination of intelligence and learning goal orientation did not explain variance in the trajectories either.

At the classroom-level we first looked for differences between classes in the development of the preference for self-regulated learning. We found significant variance in the development of the overall preference for self-regulated learning as well as in the development of all phases except for phase 6 (strategy adjustment). This is to say that classes differed in almost all aspects of self-regulated learning, whereas students only differed in three aspects (see above). As no specific classroom variables (classroom characteristics) were assessed in this study it was not possible to explain the variance between classrooms. Still, the results show that the preference for self-regulated learning changes in different ways for students in different classrooms.

4   Discussion

Today, traditional schooling cannot teach students everything they are going to need for their life and career. Knowledge has extended dramatically during the last decades and centuries, which implies that sooner or later one has to special-ize in a specific knowledge-domain in order to reach the performance levels ex-pected from a professional or even an expert. To reach high performance levels in a specific domain requires approximately 10'000 hours of intense training and learning ("deliberate practice", cf. Ericsson, Roring, & Nandagopal, 1997). This immense accumulation of knowledge and skills cannot be constantly moni-tored by teachers or mentors but must be supervised by the learners themselves. In the school context this changes the focus of the teachers' endeavors from teaching all relevant contents to teaching the skills to learn, thereby enabling students to follow a life-long path of learning. As learning skills are often not taught explicitly nor practiced systematically, students must acquire them more or less on their own when facing learning challenges. This is often expected es-pecially of highly intelligent students but only part of the literature supports the assumption that highly intelligent students are more likely to self-regulate their learning (e.g., in support: Zimmerman & Martinez-Pons, 1990; not in support: Dresel & Haugwitz, 2005).Therefore, if students do not acquire the necessary learning skills for independent knowledge acquisition on their own, the educa-tional system should take care of this essential task. Even if some students de-velop profound learning skills without additional help, they can still be support-ed to make their learning more effective or to further expand their strategy pool as studies on effective trainings of self-regulated learning indicate (Dignath, Buettner, & Langfeld, 2008).

The results of our study fit into this line of argumentation. They can be summed up in five statements. First, we can now reply to the question posed in the title – "The smarter, the more self-regulated?" – with "No, not always". High intelli-gence did not automatically come with a higher preference for self-regulated learning. This finding stands in line with the study by Dresel and Haugwitz (2005) finding that highly intelligent students used certain strategies even less, or the work of Neber and Schommer-Aikens (2002) that also showed no ad-vantages for gifted students. This means that highly intelligent students, too, should be instructed in self-regulated learning skills, they do not appear predis-posed to learning in a self-regulated way.

Second, highly intelligent students did not only fail to show a higher preference for self-regulated learning but, even worse, were significantly overrepresented among the impulsive learners. The causes for this result cannot be clearly delin-eated from our research. A possible explanation might be that the more intelli-gent students never learned how to study systematically and therefore have no other option than choosing the impulsive approach to learning. However, the fact that the impulsive learners in our sample had the best grades ($M = 2.28$, while self-regulated learners had grades of $M = 2.38$ and externally regulated learners $M = 2.71$) points to another explanation. It seems that impulsive learners do not need to take a conscious and self-regulated approach to learning as they easily fulfill the demands school poses.

A third important finding of our study concerns the variability in preferences for self-regulated learning. Individuals differed greatly within each phase as became evident in the high standard deviations displayed in Table 1. High interindividual variability could be due to the very different learning experiences of each student depending on his or her capabilities, previous successes and failures, the availability of effective feedback, and many other factors in the learning history.

The fourth finding we want to point out is the rather small-scale and unsystematic development of self-regulated learning over time. We observed small increases, decreases, and increases followed by decreases in the preference for self-regulated learning. The demands placed upon students in fourth grade increase compared to previous grades but still students do not make up for this by changing their approach to learning. It is conceivable that most students – irrespective of their intelligence – either do not notice the change in demands or do not feel the need to react to it by changing their approach to learning. In addition, students could be more aware of the importance of grades for their school career than we anticipated and therefore might feel it is safer not to experiment with new approaches to learning and/or think they will fare better if they learn exactly as parents or teachers tell them to learn. As for the more intelligent students, self-regulated learning might not be necessary yet as they manage the demands with an impulsive learning approach (see above). However, with regard to any student's future learning success a systematic improvement of learning skills should be the aim.

Finally, we found significant variability between classrooms regarding the preferences for self-regulated learning overall and in the different phases. This shows that learning skills developed differently under differing school environments' influences (e.g., teacher, classmates, interaction quality and content, challenges provided in class). Therefore, future research should focus on identifying relevant classroom factors and should investigate the interplay among these factors in real-world settings (cf. Perry & Rahim, 2011).

Taken together our results suggest that intelligence is no essential determining factor for the development of self-regulated learning among fourth-graders. Of much greater importance was the classroom a student attended. In consequence, this leads to a number of implications for education in elementary schools and for gifted education outlined in the following.

5   Practical Implications

The results of our study indicate that *all* students should be instructed in how to self-regulate their learning: The facts that (1) more intelligent students did not show higher preferences for self-regulated learning and (2) that these students were even more prone to impulsive learning draw special attention to highly intelligent students and implications for gifted education. The existence of (3) high interindividual variability and (4) only small-scale and unsystematic development of the preference for self-regulated learning point out the necessity of individually tailored and explicit training. Taken together with our findings that (5) classrooms make a significant difference regarding the development of students' approaches to learning, a next step towards the promotion of self-regulated learning may lie in including such individually tailored and explicit aspects into classroom instruction.

According to these results and to the literature (e.g., Dignath et al., 2008) self-regulated learning can be fostered in three steps. First, teachers should be informed of current findings on the topic to enable a sound promotion of students' self-regulation in learning. It is important for teachers to know that many students do not develop self-regulation skills on their own. Especially in gifted education teaching of learning skills is often neglected due to the assumption that intelligence is a main prerequisite for later outstanding achievements. But it must not be overlooked that excellent performance cannot develop without intense learning processes over years (e.g., Ericsson et al., 2007), which cannot always be supervised by a teacher or mentor. Thus self-regulated learning skills must be acquired to succeed in these long-lasting learning tasks. The sooner students begin to direct and monitor themselves while learning, the more they can optimize their advances in learning. Furthermore, teachers need to know about the processes that take place – as described by process models of self-regulated learning like the one presented in Figure 1 – to be able to intervene and assist in the phase in which the student's problems arise.

With the necessary knowledge teachers can take action. Thus, the second step should be an individual assessment of the students' preferred approach to learning. Ideally, this assessment should not only assign a label to students but build the basis for intervention. Questionnaires (like we used in this study), learning diaries, or talking about problems with certain tasks create an impression of the learners' strengths and weaknesses across their learning cycles. With this information at hand, teachers and learners can initialize systematic interventions to improve self-regulation. Improvements should become evident in subsequent diagnostic activities to motivate students to further work on their learning skills.

Finally, the third step involves systematic intervention. While research has already shown that teachers can successfully implement specific training programs over a distinct period of time (Dignath et al., 2008), it remains a challenge to find ways in which teachers can permanently create learning environments to foster self-regulated learning on a continuous basis. Drawing on our own results and on the literature (cf. Perry & Rahim, 2011) we believe these challenges can be met in the following way:

- Assigning tasks that are challenging and complex enough to necessitate self-regulated learning. This is especially relevant for highly intelligent learners who normally do not encounter the difficulty levels in regular instruction needed to develop self-regulated skills (Stoeger & Ziegler, 2010). At the same time tasks should not ask too much of the students to prevent experiences of inevitable failure.

- Supporting students in acquiring, coordinating, and practicing self-regulation skills such as self-assessment, goal-setting, strategic planning, strategy implementation, strategy monitoring, strategy adjustment, and outcome monitoring. To do this in a motivating and effective way, realistic tasks relevant to the respective curriculum should be used and embedded in regular instruction instead of practicing with specific learning-to-learn tasks, thereby avoiding transfer problems (cf. Dignath et al., 2008).
- Demonstrating the value of self-regulated learning by drawing attention to the connection between self-regulated learning and its advantage in form of better achievement.

As all students need to be taught how to learn effectively teachers should focus on the learning process and its optimization towards more effective self-regulation. This goes hand in hand with a more flexible perspective on students' gifts: Every student – highly intelligent or not – shows individual strengths and weaknesses in learning and thus in knowledge and its usefulness for new tasks. To foster students hence means to improve learning skills, which can best be done with individually tailored training. Self-regulated learning should therefore form a basic part of instruction at the elementary school level to prepare students for the higher demands they will have to master in secondary education and later on in life.

References

Alexander, P. A., Graham, S., & Harris, K. R. (1998). A perspective on strategy research: Progress and prospects. *Educational Psychology Review, 10,* 129-154. doi:10.1023/A:1022185502996

Ames, C., & Archer, J. (1988). Achievement goals in the classroom: Students' learning strategies and motivation processes. *Journal of Educational Psychology, 80,* 260-267. doi:10.1037/0022-0663.80.3.260

Artelt, C., Demmrich, A., & Baumert, J. (2001). Selbstreguliertes Lernen [Self-regulated learning.] In J. Baumert, E. Klieme, M. Neubrand, M. Prenzel, U. Schiefele, W. Schneider et al. (Eds.), *PISA 2000. Basiskompetenzen von Schülerinnen und Schülern im internationalen Vergleich [PISA 2000. Students' literacy on an international scale.]* (pp. 271-298). Opladen, Germany: Leske + Budrich.

Bandura, A. (1986). *Social foundations of thought and action: A social cognitive theory.* Englewood Cliffs, NJ: Prentice-Hall.

Baumert, J., Klieme, E., Neubrand, M., Prenzel, M., Schiefele, U., Schneider, W., … Weiß, M. (2000). *Fähigkeit zum selbstregulierten Lernen als fächerübergreifende Kompetenz [The ability to engage in self-regulated learning as an interdisciplinary competence].* Berlin, Germany: PISA Projekt Konsortium. Retrieved from

http://www.mpib-berlin.mpg.de/Pisa/CCCdt.pdf

Boekaerts, M. (1999). Self-regulated learning: Where we are today. *International Journal of Educational Research, 31,* 445-457. doi:10.1016/S0883-0355(99)00014-2

Bouffard-Bouchard, T., Parent, S., & Larivée, S. (1993). Self-regulation on a concept-formation task among average and gifted students. *Journal of Experimental Child Psychology, 56,* 115-134. doi:10.1006/jecp.1993.1028

Chan, L. K. S. (1996). Motivational orientations and metacognitive abilities of intellectually gifted students. *Gifted Child Quarterly, 40,* 184-193. doi:10.1177/001698629604000403

Dresel, M., & Haugwitz, M. (2005). The relationship between cognitive abilities and self-regulated learning: evidence for interactions with academic self-concept and gender. *High Ability Studies, 16,* 201-218. doi:10.1080/13598130600618066

Dignath, C., Buettner, G., & Langfeldt, H.-P. (2008). How can primary school students learn self-regulated learning strategies most effectively?: A meta-analysis on self-regulation training programs. *Educational Research Review, 3,* 101-129. doi:10.1016/j.edurev.2008.02.003

Ericsson, K. A., Roring, R. W., & Nandagopal, K. (2007). Giftedness and evidence for reproducibly superior performance: An account based on the expert performance framework. *High Ability Studies, 18,* 3-56. doi:10.1080/13598130701350593

Ewers, C. A., & Wood, N. L. (1993). Sex and ability differences in children's math self-efficacy and prediction accuracy. *Learning and Individual Differences, 5,* 259-267. doi:10.1016/1041-6080(93)90006-E

Heller, K. A., Kratzmeier, H., & Lengfelder, A. (1998). *Matrizen-Test Manual, Band 1* [accompanying manual for the ‚matrices-test', volume I]. Göttingen, Germany: Beltz-Test. [German version of Raven, J.C. (1976). *Standard Progressive Matrices.* Oxford: Oxford Psychologists Press.]

Hox, J. (1998). Multilevel Modeling: When and Why. In I. Balderjahn (Ed.), *Studies in classification, data analysis, and knowledge organization: Vol. 21. Classification, data analysis, and data highways* (pp. 147-154). Berlin: Springer.

Hox, J. J. (2010). *Multilevel analysis: Techniques and applications* (2nd ed.). New York: Routledge.

Kron-Sperl, V., Schneider, W., & Hasselhorn, M. (2008). The development and effectiveness of memory strategies in kindergarten and elementary school: Findings from the Würzburg and Göttingen longitudinal memory studies. *Cognitive Development, 23,* 79-104. doi:10.1016/j.cogdev.2007.08.011

Lai, E. R. (2011). *Metacognition: A literature review* (Research Report). Retrieved from http://www.pearsonassessments.com/hai/images/tmrs/Metacognition_Literature_Review_Final.pdf

Midgley, C., Kaplan, A., Middleton, M., Maehr, M. L., Urdan, T., Hicks-Anderman, L., ... Roeser, R. (1998). The Development and Validation of Scales Assessing Students' Achievement Goal Orientations. *Contemporary Educational Psychology, 23,* 113-131. doi:10.1006/ceps.1998.0965

Neber, H., & Schommer-Aikins, M. (2002). Self-regulated science learning with highly gifted students: The role of cognitive, motivational, epistemological, and environmental variables. *High Ability Studies, 13,* 59-74. doi:10.1080/13598130220132316

Nicholls, J. G. (Ed.). (1984). *The development of achievement motivation.* Greenwich, CT: JAI Press.

Perry, N. E., & Rahim, A. (2011). Studying self-regulated learning in classrooms. In B. J. Zimmerman & D. H. Schunk (Eds.), *Handbook of self-regulation of learning and performance* (pp. 122–136). New York: Routledge.

Raudenbush, S. W., & Bryk, A. S. (2006). *Hierarchical linear models: Applications and data analysis methods* (2. ed.). Thousand Oaks, CA: Sage Publications.

Roebers, C. M., Schmid, C., & Roderer, T. (2009). Metacognitive monitoring and control processes involved in primary school children's test performance. *British Journal of Educational Psychology, 79,* 749-767. doi:10.1348/978185409X429842

Sontag, C., & Stoeger, H. (2010). Selbstreguliertes Lernen und Hochbegabung [Self-regulated learning and giftedness]. *Journal für Begabtenförderung, 10* (1), 6-23.

Spörer, N. (2003). *Strategie und Lernerfolg: Validierung eines Interviews zum selbstgesteuerten Lernen* [Strategies and successful learning: Validation of an interview on self-regulated learning] (Doctoral dissertation, University of Potsdam, Germany). Retrieved from: http://opus.kobv.de/ubp/volltexte/2005/150/

Stoeger, H., & Ziegler, A. (2008). Evaluation of a classroom based training to improve self-regulation in time management tasks during homework activities with fourth graders. *Metacognition and Learning, 3,* 207-230. doi:10.1007/s11409-008-9027-z

Stoeger, H., & Ziegler, A. (2010). Do pupils with differing cognitive abilities benefit similarly from a self-regulated learning training program? *Gifted Education International, 26*, 110-123.

Van der Stel, M., & Veenman, M. V. (2010). Development of metacognitive skillfulness: A longitudinal study. *Learning and Individual Differences, 20*, 220-224. doi:10.1016/j.lindif.2009.11.005

Wigfield, A., Klauda, S. L., & Cambria, J. (2011). Influences on the development of academic self-regulatory processes. In B. J. Zimmerman & D. H. Schunk (Eds.), *Handbook of self-regulation of learning and performance* (pp. 33-48). New York: Routledge.

Wolters, C. A., & Pintrich, P. R. (1998). Contextual differences in student motivation and self-regulated learning in mathematics, Englisch, and social studies classrooms. *Instructional Science, 26*, 27-47. doi:10.1023/A:1003035929216

Zeidner, M., Boekaerts, M., & Pintrich, P. R. (2000). Self-regulation: Directions and challenges for future research. In M. Boekaerts, P. R. Pintrich, & M. Zeidner (Eds.), *Handbook of self-regulation* (pp. 749-768). San Diego, CA: Academic Press.

Ziegler, A., & Stoeger, H. (2004). Differential effect of motivational orientation on self-confidence and helplessness among high achievers and underachievers. *Gifted and Talented International, 19*(2), 61-68.

Ziegler, A., & Stoeger, H. (2005). *Trainingshandbuch selbstreguliertes Lernen I. Lernökologische Strategien für Schüler der 4. Jahrgangsstufe Grundschule zur Verbesserung mathematischer Kompetenzen [Accompanying manual for a training of self-regulated learning I: resource strategies for 4th grade elementary school students to improve math skills].* Lengerich, Germany: Pabst.

Ziegler, A., Stoeger, H., & Grassinger, R. (2010). Diagnostik selbstregulierten Lernens mit dem FSL-7 [Assessing self-regulated learning with the FSL-7.] *Journal für Begabtenförderung, 10*(1), 24-33.

Zimmerman, B. J. (1998). Developing self-fulfilling cycles of academic regulation: An analysis of exemplary instructional models. In D. H. Schunk & B. J. Zimmerman (Eds.), *Self-regulated learning: From teaching to self-reflective practice.* (pp. 1-19). New York: Guilford.

Zimmerman, B. J. (2011). Motivational sources and outcomes of self-regulated learning and performance. In B. J. Zimmerman & D. H. Schunk (Eds.), *Handbook of self-regulation of learning and performance* (pp. 49-64). New York: Routledge.

Zimmerman, B. J., & Martinez-Pons, M. (1990). Student differences in self-regulated learning: Relating grade, sex, and giftedness to self-efficacy and strategy use. *Journal of Educational Psychology, 82*, 51-59. doi:10.1037/0022-0663.82.1.51

Mei Tan, Catalina Mourgues, Abdullah Aljughaiman, Alaa Ayoub, Samuel D.
Mandelman, Dimitris Zbainos, & Elena L. Grigorenko

What the Shadow Knows: Assessing Aspects of Practical Intelligence with Aurora's *Toy Shadows*

Abstract

The proper identification and education of gifted children has become an increasingly powerful imperative as countries consider how best to meet new problems in a complex and fast-changing world. To address a dearth of innovative assessments for intelligence, the Aurora Battery was developed, based on Robert J. Sternberg's theory of successful intelligence. Containing subtests for the assessment of creative and practical abilities, along with analytical, Aurora has drawn international interest as a more wide-reaching measure of intelligence. In this chapter, we focus on one of Aurora's tests for practical intelligence in the figural domain, *Toy Shadows*, which was designed as a measure of individuals' implicit knowledge concerning the interpretation of shadows. Comparative analyses of *Toy Shadows'* performance in three countries with three distinct samples, looking at group performance, item analysis, and employing confirmatory factor analysis, show that this assessment draws upon a single latent factor across cultures. These results provide some measure of encouragement toward further validation of the assessment, and support Aurora's promise as a battery that may provide much needed new views on intelligence and the identification of gifted students.

1   Introduction

The search for new assessments for the identification of the gifted implies an active interest in just that—a look at something new, something that has not been looked at before, or something that has been overlooked or needs consideration in a new light. This may explain in part the international interest that has been expressed in the Aurora Project over the last five years, from countries such as Greece, India, Israel, the Netherlands, Mexico, Portugal, Saudi Arabia, Singapore, and Slovakia, among others. Aurora is the development of an assessment for intelligence (designed for ages 9-12) based on Robert J. Sternberg's theory of successful intelligence. As such, it introduces some unconventional types of assessments.

According to Sternberg's theory of successful intelligence (Sternberg, 1999; 2005), three types of abilities, selected and balanced as needed, contribute equally to the successful achievement of goals. These are: analytical intelligence, creative intelligence and practical intelligence. Analytical intelligence is exerted typically in situations that require evaluation, judgment, logic, comparing and contrasting. Creative intelligence comes into play when one is asked to generate new things or ideas—to imagine, invent, design. It also plays an important role, according to Sternberg, in an individual's ability to cope with relative novelty. And finally, practical intelligence is called to action when solving problems that come up in situations of everyday life, such as those encountered at home or at work or in non-academic aspects of school. The paper and pencil component of the battery contains subtests that address each of the three types of intelligence, within the domains of words, numbers and images.

In this chapter, we will focus on one of the subtests for practical intelligence in Aurora's paper and pencil group test battery, *Toy Shadows*, an assessment that comes at practical intelligence in a novel way. We will discuss its theoretical bases, compare its performance in the US, Greece, and Saudi Arabia, and consider what it can tell us about gifted individuals that may contribute to their further intellectual development. We propose that the *Toy Shadows* assessment is an appropriate and useful measure of a particular aspect of practical intelligence, and one that, moreover, behaves consistently across cultures.

2   The nature of practical intelligence and its assessment

As Sternberg and others have argued, practical abilities are as important to the full execution of one's intelligence as analytical and creative abilities. Whatever one's strengths, practical abilities help them come to fruition in the world. The scientific or mathematical genius has to come up with new ideas, then communicate his or her findings to the larger community. The creative genius has to evaluate his or her ideas, then know how to sell their creations (often unconventional) so that they can be appreciated and used by others. Our analytical, creative, and practical abilities are intertwined in our work and in our lives. Thus, recognizing and as-sessing for all three of these abilities, then addressing them in the classroom should be part of any educational program that strives to nurture children's full potential (Mandelman & Grigorenko, in press; Sternberg, 1999; 2010; Sternberg et al., 2000; Sternberg & Grigorenko, 2007).

Sternberg's view of practical intelligence may be decomposed into three basic aspects for the purposes of assessment: the ability to acquire knowledge and understanding without explicit instruction (tacit knowledge); the ability to appropriately and effectively apply knowledge (tacit knowledge, or knowledge that may have been learned explicitly in school or at home) to everyday or real life situa-tions; and the ability to successfully integrate oneself socially, by exercising social skills and, further, to exert one's social skills in a way that can effect change, such as by leading or persuading. The core factor here is the individual's successful interactions and operation within the external world, i.e. problem-solving or goal attainment in the context of life.

The defining feature of practical intelligence is that its execution is context-specific; that is, it is very difficult to separate practical problem-solving from the context in which it unfolds (Dixon, 1994; Sternberg et al., 2000; Wertsch & Kanner, 1994). Hence, the difficulty (almost contradictory nature) of developing assessments for practical intelligence is inherent, since its particular defining quality is that it is ostensibly practiced in the real world (and not only in test-taking contexts or environments, though certainly it is also practiced there, to some extent).

However, if we are convinced that practical intelligence is indeed a construct, then we must believe that it can be assessed in some way. Sternberg and colleagues and others have based much of their assessment of practical intelligence on tacit knowledge, its acquisition and implementation (Sternberg et al., 2000; Sternberg & Horvath, 1999; Sternberg, Wagner, Williams, & Horvath, 1995; Wagner & Sternberg, 1986).

Tacit knowledge, first named by Polyani (1962; 1966), refers to knowledge that is acquired through everyday experience with little or no environmental support (i.e., teaching) and is applied to solve problems toward the fulfillment of goals, particularly those that are personally valued (Sternberg et al., 2000). Both the acquisition of tacit knowledge and its application have an implicit quality; no explicit instruction has guided either process. Consequently, tacit knowledge may be relatively difficult to articulate (Wagner & Sternberg, 1985).

Assessments of tacit knowledge (i.e., practical intelligence) have been created in a number of spheres—for the work environment (e.g., occupational situational judgment tests, Berman, Down, & Hill, 2002; Elliott, Stemler, Sternberg, Grigorenko, & Hoffman, 2010; Sternberg, Wagner, & Okagaki, 1993; Wagner, 1987; Weekley & Ployhart, 2006); in the military (Hedlund, Antonakis, & Sternberg, 2002; Matthew, Cianciolo, & Sternberg, 2005); as well as in schools and universities (Cianciolo et al., 2006; Insch, McIntyre, & Dawley, 2008; Leonard & Insch, 2005; Somech & Bogler, 1999; Sternberg & Rainbow Project Collaborators, 2006). The target of these assessments is individuals' tacit knowl-edge of the most socially appropriate and effective solutions to everyday problem situations, which may be occupational, academic, domestic or personal. These situations may require different kinds of knowledge, such as technological, or-ganizational or social. Their common factor is that these areas of knowledge have been acquired tacitly, or solely through experience as opposed to explicit instruction.

A second aspect of practical intelligence that may be ostensibly tapped through assessment is the successful application of knowledge outside of the domain or context in which it was learned (e.g., school/academic setting), toward the solving of everyday problems. In these types of assessments, individuals may be asked to solve problems that occur in contexts such as shopping, cooking, common social situations or relationships, or local navigation, applying knowledge that they may have acquired in the academic setting, such as math skills, scientific knowledge, or geography facts. These tasks in themselves may seem mundane, but it is the underlying ability to apply one's knowledge efficiently and effectively within one's social and physical environment that is at the core of practical intelligence, and thus should not be overlooked in the development of gifted and talented individuals.

3   Assessing practical intelligence with Aurora

Aurora's practical subtests were designed to access different aspects of practical ability across the numerical, verbal, and figural domains, including the ability to work with money, mapping (numerical), decision-making, the interpretation of language for practical information (verbal), and the application of visual spatial skills that are learned implicitly. To give a sense of the range of Aurora's practical subtests, we describe each of Aurora's six practical subtests below, briefly.

3.1   Practical-verbal

Headlines presents newspaper-style headlines that have various interpretations; students must use their knowledge of both how the abbreviated style of newspaper headlines is used to convey meaning and of how they may be misconstrued. Responses are scored according to whether the student has captured the silly or serious meaning accurately; wording between students may differ.

Decisions presents scenarios in which a decision must be made. Students sort given information based on whether it constitutes an argument for or against the decision, leaving out irrelevant pieces of information. There is only one correct answer for each item.

3.2   Practical-numerical

Maps presents street routes on which students must draw a single line showing the shortest route to carpool between friends' homes and a movie theater, thereby applying their understanding of planning, distances, and map-reading to decide on a route that accomplishes their goal of efficiently. There is only one correct answer.

Money Math presents scenarios in which people make various purchases as a group (sometimes while owing each other money) and must divide "bills" appropriately so that all parties have paid in full for their items, and are not owed money. There is only one correct answer for each item.

3.3   Practical-figural

Paper-cutting presents photographs of folded pieces of paper with shaded areas indicating intended cut-out areas. Students must imagine cutting this shaded area out while the paper remains folded. Four photographs of cut-out, unfolded pieces of paper are presented; students must use their knowledge of how the folding and cutting of paper works to determine which represents correctly the original folded, to-be-cut piece of paper. There is only one correct answer for each item.

Toy Shadows is a shadow identification exercise. Each item first shows photographs of a toy from various angles. Next, another photograph depicts the toy po-sitioned on a table with a light shining on it. Students then choose from four more photographs the one which shows the exact shadow that would be projected using their understanding of how to "read" shadows for information, including consideration of the blurred edges and skewed proportions of some shadows. There is only one correct answer for each item.

Toy Shadows, thus, was designed to access a component of practical intelligence in the visual domain that involves knowledge that has been acquired tacitly or implicitly, that is, without explicit instruction or training. Unlike both the verbal and numerical subtests, which have often required substantial cultural adaptations, *Toy Shadows* generally remains unaltered (only needing direct translation of instructions) across cultures. To understand better the nature of the subtest and how it may contribute to our understanding of gifted students, we consider the information that shadows contain, the history of the study and uses of shadows, how individuals may acquire the skill of "reading" shadows, and how the *Toy Shadows* subtest is related to these.

4   The informative nature of shadows

The study of shadows within the domain of human visual perception has generated a wealth of empirically supported theories and conclusions about the nature of shadows, the information they provide, how they are used by the visual perception system, and for what purposes, although debates still remain (Dee & Santos, 2011).

First, shadows provide visual information on three aspects of the environment: the shape, size, slant and location and material nature (i.e., opaque or translucent) of the thing that is casting the shadow, generally referred to as the "caster"; the nature of the light source, including its orientation to and distance from the caster, and this source's width and intensity; and the surface upon which the shadow is being cast, including its texture or physical configuration (Casati, 2004; Dee & Santos, 2011). Leonardo da Vinci distinguished between two types of shadows: the attached shadow and the cast shadow. Attached shadows being those that an object casts upon itself, the sources of shading that help the viewer detect the texture and contours of an object. Cast shadows being those that an object casts upon a separate surface, such as the ground or a wall behind it. Inquiries concerning whether and how each piece of information yielded by shadows is used, in what combinations, at what level of complexity and for what purposes, have shaped the studies on shadows from the beginnings of science to today.

5   Three approaches to studying shadows

Human consideration of the shadow is age-old, starting with the use of shadows by early astronomers to study the relative motions of the earth, sun and moon, and their distances from each other; to confirm that the moon and other planets were of a similar nature to earth (via eclipses, particularly); and to measure time (Casati, 2007; Dee & Santos, 2011). The formal study of shadows themselves as mathematically consistent projections, however, began only in the early Renaissance, when painters began to struggle with the depiction of cast shadows in their work (which actually took about a century to satisfactorily achieve). Mathematicians of the time used painters' theories and practices for the depiction of shadows and systematized their measures (Casati, 2004; Da Costa Kauffman, 1993). Yet, how humans perceive shadows and cognitive aspects of shadow perception did not become the focus of scientific attention until the 20th century, with Piaget's account of children's explanations of how shadows are formed being among the first of such cognitive studies (Piaget, 1927).

Since Piaget, a few distinct scientific approaches to the use of shadows have become clear. First, there have been the formal, mathematically-centered scientific studies using shadows to discover or create related inventions, such as those studies conducted by early astronomers and by artists such as Leonardo da Vinci, who aimed to use shadows systematically to represent the third dimensional on a two dimensional canvas. Second, studies involving shadows have been used to explore the development of children's reasoning skills, as well as their understanding of the multidimensional nature of how shadows are created. And third, there have been many studies conducted in the field of visual perception that investigate how shadows are perceived and used every day by viewers to inform their understanding of the environment—the physical landscape and the shape, orientation, and motion of the items in it. The first type of studies we mentioned briefly above to provide some historical background. It is this third class of   studies that we will discuss primarily in this chapter, as it pertains to the informative nature of shadows, how the human visual system perceives shadows, accesses or not their information, and acts upon that information, all of which encompass the body of implicit knowledge we all acquire about shadows. Yet we include now a brief discussion of the second type of studies—concerning the development of children's reasoning—to recognize the import of these studies and to better distinguish them from the third, more naturalistic, approach to studying shadows.

Since at least the time of Piaget, psychologists have been interested in how and when children's understanding of shadows emerges in the course of their development. Piaget's initial inquiries concerned children's conceptions of the sources of shadows, and he subsequently proposed the stages of cognitive understanding that build toward the accurate knowledge of how shadows are formed: stage one (about age 5), children understand shadows as emanating from the object itself or from some external source, such as a location or other object; stage 2 (about 6-7 years old), shadows are understood to be emanating from the object alone; stage 3 (about age 8), children can predict the orientation of shadows, with and without an actual light source; and stage 4 (about 9 years old), the child understands how a shadow is made (Piaget, 1927).

Later on, Inhelder and Piaget used shadows to ascertain the development of children's complex reasoning, employing a "projection of shadows task" (Inhelder & Piaget, 1958). In this task, rings of different sizes were placed at varying distances from a light source, producing various shadows on a screen. (Shadow size is directly proportional to the diameters of the rings and inversely proportional to the distance between the rings and the light source.) Children were asked to produce shadows of the same size using different-sized objects by varying an object's distance from the light–source. The task was designed to explore children's capability to work with two parameters at one time (object size and distance from light source) to accomplish a task. A set of similar studies have followed, using this same task for deeper exploration of the same phenomenon—complex problem-solving. For example, Siegler (1978; 1981) tested his rule model of problem solving—that children develop from unidimensional to multidimensional problem-solving capabilities continuously, rather than in Piaget's stages—using the projection of shadows task. More recently, Ebersbach and Resing (2007) looked at the same developmental capacity using the same task but with slightly different methodology, while also investigating individuals' implicit and explicit beliefs about the non-linear relationship between shadow, object size, and distance from the light source. Among other findings, they ascertained that while 4-year olds' implicit and explicit beliefs about the relationship between shadow, object size, and light source distance did not correlate, older children's and adults' did. That is, the youngest children's verbalizations of their understanding of shadows did not match their performance on the task.

Other developmental studies concerning shadows have been carried out with similarly aged children, but these, more in line with the third type of shadow studies, are focused on simple shadow perception and the types of shadow information that children are able to use. For example, supporting Piaget's description of children in stage 1, Hagen (1976) found that kindergarten children

were unable to identify the correct direction of a light source based on the variations in shading and shadow in pictures. However, another developmental
study, focusing simply on the ability to use shadow information to recognize
certain physical details of objects, found that children as young as three years of
age can discriminate between convexity and concavity in a photograph based
solely on the orientation of the attached shadow (Benson & Yonas, 1973).
Yonas and colleagues (1978) further explored the developmental nature of sensitivity to shadow information in children ages three and four years old. These
preschool children's sensitivity to cast-shadow information was investigated using pictures in which the presence and shape of the shadow cast by an object
was varied. Results showed that three and four year olds can interpret shadows
in drawings to ascertain the shape and implied three-dimensionality of an object. In a second experiment, three year olds, five year olds and adults similarly
used   shadow information to judge the distance and height of spheres in a picture. The older children and adults were further able to judge the relative sizes
of the spheres using the shadows. Thus, while pre-school aged children may not
yet be able to assess all aspects of a shadow situation (e.g., characteristics of the
caster, the nature of the casting surface, and the distance, direction and intensity
of the light source), á la the Hagen study (1976), young children can and do use
shadow information to ascertain basic facts, such as the shape and location of an
object in a two-dimensional representation. The next question we will explore,
then, is what information from shadows is the human perceptual system naturally tuned to acquire, and for what purposes?

6   The peculiarities of the human perception of shadows

In their review of the literature concerning the perception and information content of cast shadows, Dee and Santos (2011) are particularly interested in contrasting the information that may be extracted from shadows by computer methods and what is generally perceived (i.e., deemed important by the visual
system) by the human perception system when using shadow information to
construct spatial representation from a visual scene. This comparison has
brought up some interesting points about the peculiarities of human shadow
perception, when considering the use of shadow information in naturalistic rather than academic settings.
First, the act of shadow perception itself would seem to be problematic, as shadows range in quality from having hard, clear outlines which make them appear
"solid," to having vague, fuzzy borders. And yet, people do not tend to mistake
shadows for solid object, nor do they appear to have any difficulty identifying
perceiving shadows that have vague borders (Dee & Santos, 2011). That is, the
human perceptive system seems to be attuned to identifying shadows in their
vari-ous forms.
Yet, while shadows may provide a great deal of information about a visual scene (Casati, 2000), in particular on the respective locations of objects within a
given scene (Mamassian, Knill, & Kersten, 1998), the visual system would first

need to sort out to some extent which shadows match which objects. This matching process, the so-called "shadow correspondence problem" (Mamassian, 2004), can be computationally complex. Studies have found, however, that for practical purposes, the human visual system instead uses a heuristic to find a quick solution to shadow correspondence, that is, a coarse matching between objects and shadows. Mamassian (2004) asked subjects to determine the location of the light source in simple object/shadow wire model presentations, of which one third presented "impossible" or non-matching shadows. These "impossible" shadows could be read in three different ways, each indicating a different light source direction. Subjects appeared to read the shadow based on the correspondence of the object's center of mass to the shadow, ignoring the details represented by the object and shadow stem and cap.

Thus, over the last 40 years, while useful aspects of shadow information have been empirically explored, the ways in which shadows can be problematic or obscure understanding, have also been discovered. On the one hand, shadows can provide information about a three-dimensional object's shape (Cavanaugh & LeClerc, 1989). Shading can be used to differentiate convex from concave sur-faces (Erens, Kappers, & Koenderink, 1993). Shadows can be used to infer the shape of the caster and its distance above the ground (Yonas et al., 1978). They can influence the perception of depth of motion (Kersten, Knill, Mamassian, & Bulthoff, 1996), and aid in stereo depth perception (Puerta, 1989).

Yet at the same time, shadows can cause flat objects to appear three-dimensional (Bulthoff, Kersten, & Bulthoff, 1994), and non-rigid motion to appear rigid. Further, observers have been known to ignore shadow information when making judgments about convexity (Berbaum, Bever, & Chung, 1983); and shadows can impair judgments of illumination direction in situations involving slants and tilt (Mingolla & Todd, 1986). Some models of object recognition argue for the crucial importance of shadow to provide information on shape and depth, yet Moore and Cavanaugh (1998) demonstrated that identifying two-tone novel (computer-generated) objects that have cast shadows can be difficult, as the shadows introduce confusing edges. Tarr and colleagues (1998), meanwhile, showed that cast shadows can improve the recognition of novel geometric objects; changing the illumination condition (altering the shadow aspect of the object) or otherwise manipulating the shape of the shadow was observed to slow down object recognition (Castiello, 2001; Tarr et al., 1998). And in a study of object recognition using naturally-occurring objects (i.e., fruits and vegetables; Braje, Legge, & Kersten, 2000), shadow presence appeared to have no effect on whether the object was recognized or not—that is, they neither impaired nor improved recognition of these natural objects. Interestingly, a study of cast shadows in art by Jacobson and Werner (2004) first observed the surprising relative absence of cast shadow in art, whereas attached shadows—those which give depth and form to the objects themselves—are ubiquitous. They concluded that, in the static representations of paintings, cast shadows did not seem to be critical to viewers' understanding of the pictorial scene and, in computer-generated images created to generate inconsistent shadows, incongruities or in-accuracies of cast shadow depictions were often overlooked, even in simple scenes.

These studies, among others, suggest that the human perceptual system uses (or ignores) shadows in particular ways. For example, it seems that the human perceptual system prefers to use shadow information for the interpretation of 3D motion over the cue of object size (Mamassian et al., 1998). Yet, several studies have examined the way the human perceptual system deals with inconsistent shadows (Enns & Rensink, 1990; Farid & Bravo, 2010; Ostrovsky, Cavanaugh, & Sinha, 2005) and found that in general, inconsistencies between the position of the light source, the caster, and the shadow are overlooked. Bonfiglioni, Pavani and Castiello found that real objects with fake shadows did not affect verbal interpretation of the scene presented, although they did affect the way the object was reached for (2004). These results suggest that our perceptual system uses cast shadows as coarse cues for information, or as general indicators of coherence. The visual system may "read" a position estimation from cast shad-ows early on in processing, then filter shadows out as immaterial players in the physical space (Dee & Santos, 2011; Rensink & Cavanaugh, 2004). These stud-ies also imply that shadow processing is both implicit (i.e., without conscious awareness) and automatic (i.e., carried out without active attention). Studies of cast shadow perception in people with brain injuries—whose ability to identify objects is effected by the presence of shadows, even though they cannot articu-late explicitly the presence or absence of shadows—indicate that the ability to process and interpret cast shadows is not dependent upon conscious awareness of them, and is therefore implicit. We are usually unaware of the effect shadows have on our perception (Castiello, Lusher, Burton, & Disler, 2003). That is, people bring much more than they realize to their reading and understanding of shadows—from conscious observation to the unconscious habits and skills they have developed from "reading," for practical purposes, our three-dimensional world.

It is these implicitly learned skills that are the target of the Aurora subtest, *Toy Shadows*.

7   A description of the *Toy Shadows* assessment

Toy Shadows, described above, is a collection of 8 multiple-choice items. Each item shows the child four views of a toy, then shows the toy oriented on a sur-face and the light source shining on it; that is, they see the caster and its orienta-tion and distance from the light source. The child is then presented with four shadows, only one of which has been produced by the presented scenario. In es-sence, the child must match the information conveyed by one of the shadows to the given scene, or read the given landscape and correctly predict the shadow. The only varying element in each scene is the position of the caster (a uni-dimensional rather than multi-dimensional problem). What the child brings to the task is knowl-edge of how a shadow is produced and the implicit ability to read the rough cues of the shadow. What direction should the shadow be facing? What object-light orientation results in skinnier or fatter areas of shadow? Or longer or fore-shorten-ed areas of shadow?

None of these skills are formally taught in any culture, that we know of, so we expect *Toy Shadows*, which generally requires minimal translation and adaptation in different countries, to behave similarly across cultures. First, we will look at its performance as a test. Next, using confirmatory factory analyses (CFA), we will look at the test's factor structure within and across cultures for consistency to determine whether or not *Toy Shadows* travels well.

8 *Toy Shadows'* performance within and across countries

To evaluate the performance of the *Toy Shadows* test across cultures, the most recently collected samples from the US, Greece and Saudi Arabia were selected. Their details are provided in Table 1.

Table 1: Sample descriptions by country

Country	N	Females	Males	Mean Age (stdev)
Greece	171	92	79	11.13 (.84)
Saudi Arabia	542	248	294	11.29 (1.30)
US	130	61	69	10.90 (.91)

All of these data were collected in similar fashion, in schools in a group test setting, as part of the rest of Aurora's paper and pencil battery (an abbreviated sample from Saudi Arabia is used here, as the entire set has not yet been data entered). The US sample was collected from a generally culturally homogeneous suburban, private parochial school located in the middle of the country. The Greek sample came from diverse geographical ethnic and social backgrounds: half were drawn from a school at the center of Athens, and the rest from two rural schools in southern Greece. About 60 percent oft he children were Greek in origin, and the rest from immigrant families. The Saudi schools from which we drew our sample were all government (public) schools, located in urban settings, with very limited diversity, i.e. over 90% native Saudi Arabian children, with the majority of the rest from nearby Arab countries such as Egypt, Jordan, Yemen and Syria.

8.1 Group performance and item analysis

First, group performance within each country was examined and item analysis was carried out to determine the fitness of these items to the three cultures. Table 2 shows the descriptive data for the children's performance in each country.

To determine the effects of gender on the total score of the *Toy Shadows* test for each country, we carried out an ANCOVA for each sample, in which the total score was the dependent variable, gender the independent variable, and age a co-variable, since all samples contain children with a range of ages. For Greece, there were no differences in the total score due to gender ($F_{(1,170)}= .230$, $p=.632$), but we did find gender effects in both the US ($F_{(1,129)}=5.213, p < 0.05$) and Saudi Arabian data ($F_{(1,532)}=19.191, p<.001$) with the females performing lower than the males.

Table 2: Descriptive data by country

	N			Mean scores			SD		
Country	Total	Females	Males	Total	Females	Males	Total	Females	Males
Greece	171	92	79	3.26	3.35	3.16	1.75	1.73	1.79
Saudi Arabia	542	294	248	3.11	2.69	3.61	1.83	1.57	1.98
US	130	61	69	4.14	3.69	4.54	2.03	1.91	2.06

To estimate the differences in the total scores between countries, we regressed both gender and age from the total score to adjust for the effects described above. We found significant differences between the countries ($F_{(2,840)}=16.07$, $p<.001$): the contrast *post hoc* with Bonferroni corrections showed that the US sample had the highest score, and as a group performed significantly differently from the Greek and Saudi Arabian children, with these latter groups performing equally.

Table 3 presents the means (frequencies), standard deviations and the correlations for each item-test. In this case, the mean is equal to the index of difficulty because there is no missing data. The correlation item-test shows the strength of the association between each item and the test. Further details are provided below[1]

---

[1] The data shown in Table 3 are interesting because it reflects how the items have different degrees of difficulty across countries. The percentage of items 1, 3 and 5 are similar in the three samples, around 50% of the children solved them successfully. Yet other items differentiate the countries, e.g item 8 is more difficult for the US and Greek samples than the Saudi Arabian; the same occurred with items 4 and 6; and item 7 is difficult for all of the countries—only 15% to 32% answered it correctly.

Table 3: Item means, standard deviations and item-test correlations

	Means (frequencies)			SD			Corr. Item-test		
	GR	SA	US	GR	SA	US	GR	SA	US
Item1	.84	.70	.65	.37	.48	.47	.212	.204	.325
Item2	.36	.52	.35	.48	.48	.50	.359	.285	.267
Item3	.44	.45	.48	.50	.50	.50	.137	.128	.262
Item4	.44	.62	.34	.50	.47	.49	.392	.377	.462
Item5	.49	.46	.45	.50	.50	.50	.180	.135	.189
Item6	.30	.52	.39	.46	.49	.50	.251	.262	.285
Item7	.15	.32	.18	.36	.38	.47	.252	.276	.204
Item8	.24	.54	.27	.43	.45	.50	.241	.401	.498

The correlations for the total scores across the countries (Table 4) show that all three tests are related, with the Saudi Arabian and Greek test performance being somewhat more closely related to each other than to the US test performance.

Table 4: Correlations between total scores (including all eight items)

	GR	US	SA
GR	1		
US	0.733	1	
SA	0.937	0.632	1

When tested with the null hypothesis $r = 0$, the correlation between the total scores for Greece and the US was significant ($t_{(6)} = 2.64$, $p < 0.05$), as for between Greece and Saudi Arabia ($t_{(6)} = 6.57$, $p < .001$). However, the correlation between the US and Saudi Arabia total scores was not significant ($t_{(6)} = 1.998$, p $= 0.092$).

8.2   Confirmatory Factor Analysis

Confirmatory factor analysis (CFA) was carried out based on the hypothesis that all items of the test load on one factor, i.e., the ability to "read" shadow information, which we posit reflects an aspect of practical intelligence in the figural domain. Baseline models were first created for each country's sample using LISREL 8.54 (Phase I; Joreskog & Sorbom, 2003). After noting that item 3 demonstrated a very low loading across two of the three countries (see also the correlation item-test above), it was deleted for the subsequent analyses. After combining the samples and deleting item 3, the reliability (Cronbach's alpha) of the test was 0.577; previously, it had been 0.567). Thus, an altered subscale with only 7 items was considered in the rest of the analyses.

Next, configural invariance in a multi-group model was examined (Phase II); that is, each country's data was tested for fit to a one-factor model that was consistent across all countries by constraining the variance/ covariance matrices to be equal across countries. This constrained model fit the data well. Findings suggested that regardless of culture, children showed fairly invariant performance in *Toy Shadows* test correlation patterns. Since any factor structure is derived from these variance/covariance matrices, results revealed that the *Toy Shadows* measures the same constructs, the factor structure across these four cultures should be very similar. Measurement equivalence was then tested to see if factor loadings corresponded across the countries (Phase III), and the factor-loading equivalence suggested that the *Toy Shadows* measurement scale is indeed the same across the countries. In Phase IV, we tested the hypothesis that in our model, the factor structure, loading factors and error variance are equal across countries.

Finally we compared the models in pairs, computing the S-B$_{\chi}^2$, and the observed p-values were not significant in the comparison between the Phase II and III models ($X^2_{(12)}$=20.09, p = 0.065), and between the Phase II and IV models ($X^2_{(26)}$=38.46, p = 0.054), confirming their similarity. If we take the ΔCFI criteria—the more practical criteria, whose difference across the models is 0 (Cheung & Rensvold, 2002)—we can conclude that the *Toy Shadows* test is invariant in its factor structure, factor loadings and variance error across the three countries. These analyses are summarized in Table 5 below; details are presented in a footnote.[2]

---

[2] The multi-group comparisons were performed using LISREL 8.54. Due to the dichotomous nature of the data, we used the diagonally weighted least squares (DWLS) like estimation method with polychoric correlation, and asymptotic covariance matrices were applied. We used the RSMEA to evaluate the fit of the structure in the data to the model, with RMSEA below .05 indicating a reasonable fit when its upper confidence interval is below .08. The comparative fit index (CFI) was additionally used, with a value between .90 and .95 indicating an acceptable fit, and above .95 indicating a good fit (Kenny, 2008). The ratio between the X2 and df was considered as a fit index, and the values close to 2.0 or 3.0 were considered good fits for the v2 to df ratio (Bollen, 1989). The Standardized Root Mean Square Residual (SRMR) is an absolute measure of fit and is defined as the standardized difference between the observed correlation and the predicted correlation. It is a positively biased measure and an absolute measure of fit. A value less than .08 is generally considered a good fit (Hu & Bentler, 1999).

Table 5: Multi-group goodness-of-fit indices for 7 items

Model	S-BX2	df	X2/df	CFI	RMSEA	RMSEA 90% CI	SRMR	ΔS-BX2	Δdf	ΔCFI
Phase I: Baseline model										
US	12.01	14	.857	1.0	.000	.000 – .073	0.069	-	-	-
Greece	9.69	14	.691	.86	.000	.000 – .050	0.073	-	-	-
Saudi	22.86	14	1.63	.99	.034	.000 - .059	0.057	-	-	-
Phase II: Configural invariance										
	45.1	43		1.0	.013	.000 –.043	0.073	-	-	-
Phase III: Measurement Equivalence										
	67.54	56	1.20	1.0	.027	.000 –.048	0.063	20.09	12	.00
Phase IV: Scalar Invariance or structural model										
	85.91	70	1.22	1.0	.028	.000 -.047	0.063	38.46	26	.00

9   Measuring shadow perception: Practical or not?

In the search for new ways to identify gifted and talented individuals, Aurora's *Toy Shadows* makes an unconventional contribution, but a suggestive and important one in attempting to represent one aspect of an area of cognitive ability not usually considered in the search for gifted children. It must be noted that *Toy Shadows* does not constitute an argument for implementing the study of shadows in school, but points more importantly to the assessment of skills and abilities that are not explicitly taught, in this case those that are related to visual perception. But what makes *Toy Shadows* worthy of consideration?

In the analysis of group performance on *Toy Shadows*, we see that children in different cultures may perform differentially, as the Saudi Arabian and Greek samples perform much more similarly to each other than to the US sample. In addition, performance on *Toy Shadows* may be differentially influenced by age and gender, with the US and Saudi Arabian samples being affected by both age and gender, and the Greek by age only. These differences may be explained in part by the fact that the US sample was drawn from a single private school in the US, while both the Greek and Saudi Arabian samples included several schools each, both urban and suburban. They may also be explained by possible cultural and environmental differences that may be explored in future studies.

Yet, in spite of these differences, CFA analyses show that the *Toy Shadows* assessment behaves consistently, with the 7 items contributing to a single factor across all 3 cultures. Whatever *Toy Shadows* measures, it appears to focus on a single latent factor, and its items perform in similar patterns across 3 very different samples. In the future, studies with larger, more representative samples may be carried out to validate the assessment.

What is this latent factor? On the surface, it has been argued that *Toy Shadows* appears to target more analytical abilities, as children ostensibly match the produced shadow choices with the given toy-light orientation. Yet, according to a sample of over 2,000 children who have taken the entire Aurora paper and pencil battery, *Toy Shadows'* performance is not particularly related to any of Aurora's analytical subtests. In fact, across Aurora's 16 other triarchically-related subtests, *Toy Shadows'* correlations range from -0.028, with one of the creative subtests, to .361, with *Toy Shadows'* companion practical-figural subtest, *Paper-cutting*. *Toy Shadows'* highest correlations with Aurora's highly analytical IQ portion (Aurora-g; 9 subtests) are .263, .267, and .284; these are with the three figural subtests, which are analogy, series and classification multiple choice tests, respectively. Further studies with larger, more representative samples may be carried out to validate the assessment.

The ability tapped by *Toy Shadows*, then, would appear to be quite distinct from those tapped by analogical reasoning tasks, or computational tasks. It is essential-ly distinct, also, from Piaget's projection of shadows task. In fact, as we have tried to show above, the human perception of shadows is not straightforward. It is often not precise, not analytically executed but rather as a rough estimation that may get discarded once it has been registered—a practical practice of "simplified physics" (Cavanaugh, 2005, p.301) that gets us through the day. It also allows us to appreciate and be "fooled by" even the most unrealistic depictions of light and shadow in works of art. And it explains why, while easily generated through algorithms on a computer, shadows can be the painter's bane as one of the greatest challenges of the craft. That is, while perhaps consciously and analytically understood, shadow perception is generally learned and executed unconsciously (an explanation, also, for the inability to articulate the behavior of shadows even though one can predict it, at an early age). As such, this ability may stand as an aspect of practical intelligence that represents a form of visual practice and understanding that has developed over time, is exercised and strengthened generally without conscious effort, and that may constitute meaningful differences between individuals. In gifted and talented individuals who harbor these quiet strengths, recognition and conscious harnessing of these advantages may help these children grow their abilities, use them to compensate for the weaknesses, and thereby increase their potential for success in life.

References

Benson, C. A., & Yonas, A. (1973). Development of sensitivity to static pictorial depth information. *Perception and Psychophysics, 13*, 361-366.

Berbaum, K., Bever, T., & Chung, C. S. (1983). Light source position in the perception of object shape. *Perception, 12*, 1162-1182.

Berman, S. L., Down, J., & Hill, C. W. L. (2002). Tacit knowledge as a source of competetive advantage in the National Basketball Association. *Academy of Management Journal, 45*, 13-31.

Bollen, K. A. (1989). *Structural equation modeling*. New York: Wiley.

Bonfigioli, C., Pavani, F., & Castiello, U. (2004). Differential effects of cast shadows on perception and action. *Perception, 33*(11), 1291-1304.

Braje, W. L., Legge, G. E., & Kersten, D. (2000). Invariant recognition of natural objects in the presence of shadows. *Perception, 29*, 383-398.

Bulthoff, I., Kersten, D., & Bulthoff, H. H. (1994). General lighting can overcome accidental viewing. *Investigative Ophthalmology and Visual Science, 35*(4), 1741.

Casati, R. (2000). *La scoperta dell'ombra [The discovery of the shadow]*. Milan: Mondadori.

Casati, R. (2004). The shadow knows: A primer on the informational structure of cast shadows. *Perception, 33*, 1385-1396.

Casati, R. (2007). *Shadows: Unlocking their secrets, from Plato to our time*. New York: Vintage Books.

Castiello, U. (2001). Implicit processing of shadows. *Vision Research, 41,* 2305-2309.

Castiello, U., Lusher, D., Burton, C., & Disler, P. (2003). Shadows in the brain. *Journal of Cognitive Neuroscience, 15*(6), 862-872.

Cavanaugh, P. (2005). The artist as neuroscientist. *Nature, 434,* 301-307.

Cavanaugh, P., & LeClerc, Y. G. (1989). Shape from shadows. *Journal of Experimental Psychology: Human Perception and Performance, 15,* 3-27.

Cheung, G. W., & Rensvold, R. B. (2002). Evaluating goodness-of-fit indexes for testing measuring invariance. *Structural Equation Modeling, 9*(233-255).

Cianciolo, A. T., Grigorenko, E. L., Jarvin, L., Guillermo, G., Drebot, M., & Sternberg, R. J. (2006). Practical intelligence and tacit knowledge: Advancements in the measurement of developing expertise. *Learning and Individual Differences, 16,* 235-253.

Da Costa Kauffman, T. (1993). *The mastery of nature: aspects of art, science, and humanism in the Renaissance.* Princeton: Princeton University Press.

Dee, H. M., & Santos, P. E. (2011). The perception and content of cast shadows: An interdisciplinary review. *Spatial Cognition and Computation, 11*(3), 226-253.

Dixon, R. A. (1994). Contextual approaches to adult intellectual development. In R. J. Sternberg & C. A. Berg (Eds.), *Intellectual development* (pp. 203-235). New York: Cambridge University Press.

Ebersbach, M., & Resing, W. C. M. (2007). Shedding new light on an old problem: The estimation of shadow sizes in children and adults. *Journal of Experimental Child Psychology, 97,* 265-285.

Elliott, J. G., Stemler, S. E., Sternberg, R. J., Grigorenko, E. L., & Hoffman, N. (2010). The socially skilled teacher and the development of tacit knowledge. *British Education Research Journal, 1,* 1-21.

Enns, J. T., & Rensink, R. A. (1990). Influence of scene based properties on visual search. *Science, 247,* 721-723.

Erens, R. G. F., Kappers, A. M. L., & Koenderink, J. J. (1993). Perceptionof local shape from shading. *Perception and Psychphysics, 54,* 145-156.

Farid, H., & Bravo, M. (2010). *Image forensic analyses that elude the human visual system.* Paper presented at the SPIE symposium on electronic imaging, San Jose, CA.

Hagen, M. A. (1976). The development of sensitivity to static pictorial depth information. *Perception and Psychophysics, 20*(1), 25-28.

Hedlund, J., Antonakis, J., & Sternberg, R. J. (2002). Tacit knowledge and practical intelligence: Understanding lessons of experience: United States Army Research Institute for the Behavioral and Social Sciences.

Hu, L. T., & Bentler, P. M. (1999). Cutoff criteria for fit indexes in covariance structure analysis: Conventional criteria versus new alternatives. *Structural Equation Modeling, 6*, 1-55.

Inhelder, B., & Piaget, J. (1958). *The growth of logical thinking from childhood to adolescence*. New York: Basic Books.

Insch, G. S., McIntyre, N., & Dawley, D. (2008). Tacit Knowledge: A Refinement and Empirical Test of the Academic Tacit Knowledge Scale. *Journal of Psychology, 142*(6), 561-580.

Jacobson, J., & Werner, S. (2004). Why cast shadows are expendable: Insensitivity of human observers and the inherent ambiguity of cast shadows in pictorial art. *Perception, 33*, 1369-1383.

Joreskog, K. G., & Sorbom, D. (2003). LISREL 8.54 for Windows. Lincolnwood, IL: Scientific Software International, Inc.

Kenny, D. A. (2008). Measuring model fit Retrieved from http://davidakenny.net/cm/fit.htm

Kersten, D., Knill, D. C., Mamassian, P., & Bulthoff, I. (1996). Illusory motion from shadows. *Nature (London), 379*, 31.

Leonard, N., & Insch, G. S. (2005). Tacit knowledge in academia: A proposed model and measurement scale. *The Journal of Psychology, 139*(6), 495-512.

Mamassian, P. (2004). Impossible shadows and the shadow correspondence problem. *Perception, 33*, 1279-1290.

Mamassian, P., Knill, D. C., & Kersten, D. (1998). The perception of cast shadows. *Trends in Cognitive Sciences, 2*, 288-295.

Mandelman, S. D., & Grigorenko, E. L. (in press). Questioning the unquestionable: Reviewing the evidence for the efficacy of gifted education. *Talent Development and Excellence*.

Matthew, C. T., Cianciolo, A. T., & Sternberg, R. J. (2005). *Developing effective military leaders: Facilitating the acquisition of experience-based tacit knowledge*. Washington, D. C.: United States Army Research Institute for the Behavioral and Social Sciences.

Mingolla, E., & Todd, J. T. (1986). Perception of solid shape from shading. *Biological Cybernetics, 53*, 137-151.

Moore, C., & Cavanaugh, P. (1998). Recovery of 3D volume from 2-tone images of novel objects. *Cognition, 67*(45-71).

Ostrovsky, Y., Cavanaugh, P., & Sinha, P. (2005). Perceiving illumination inconsistencies in scenes. *Perception, 34*(11), 1301-1314.

Piaget, J. (1927). Le problème des ombres [The problem of the shadows]. In P. J. (Ed.), *La causalité physicque chez l'enfant [The child's conception of physical causality]* (pp. 203-218). Paris: Alcan.

Polanyi, M. (1962). *Personal knowledge*. London: Harper.

Polanyi, M. (1966). *The tacit dimension*. London: Routledge and Kegan Paul.

Puerta, A. M. (1989). The power of shadows: shadow stereopsis. *Journal of the Optical Society of America, 6*, 309-311.

Rensink, R. A., & Cavanaugh, P. (2004). The influence of cast shadows on visual search. *Perception, 33*(11), 1339-1358.

Siegler, R. S. (1978). (Ed.). *Children's thinking: What develops?* Hillsdale, NJ: Erlbaum.

Siegler, R. S. (1981). Developmental sequences within and between concepts. *Society for Research in Child Development Monographs, 46*(2), 1-84.

Somech, A., & Bogler, R. (1999). Tacit knowledge in academia: Its effect on student learning and achievement. *The Journal of Psychology, 133*, 605-616.

Sternberg, R. J. (1999). The theory of successful intelligence. *Review of General Psychology, 3*(4), 292-316.

Sternberg, R. J. (2005). The theory of successful intelligence. *Interamerican Journal of Psychology, 39*(2), 189-202.

Sternberg, R. J. (2010). Assessment of gifted students for identification purposes: New techniques for a new millennium. *Learning and Individual Differences, 20*(4), 327-336.

Sternberg, R. J., Forsythe, G. B., Hedlund, J., Horvath, J. A., Wagner, R. K., Williams, W. M., Snook, S. A., & Grigorenko, E. L. (2000). *Practical intelligence in everyday life*. New York: Cambridge University Press.

Sternberg, R. J., & Grigorenko, E. L. (2007). *Teaching for successful intelligence, 2nd ed.* Thousand Oaks, CA: Corwin Press.

Sternberg, R. J., & Horvath, J. A. (1999). *Tacit knowledge in professional practice: Researcher and practitioner perspectives*. Mahwah, NJ: Erlbaum.

Sternberg, R. J., & Rainbow Project Collaborators, T. (2006). The Rainbow Project: Enhancing the SAT through assessments of analytical, practical, and creative skills *Intelligence, 34*, 321-350.

Sternberg, R. J., Wagner, R. K., & Okagaki, L. (1993). Practical intelligence: The natuer and role of tacit knowledge in work and at school. In H. Reese & J. Puckett (Eds.), *Advances in lifespan development*. Hillsdale, NJ: Erlbaum.

Sternberg, R. J., Wagner, R. K., Williams, W. M., & Horvath, J. A. (1995). Testing common sense. *American Psychologist, 50*, 912-927.

Tarr, M. J., Kersten, D., & Bulthoff, H. H. (1998). Why the visual recognition system might encode the effects of illumination? *Vision Research, 38*, 2259-2275.

Wagner, R. K. (1987). Tacit knowledge in everyday intelligence behavior. *Journal of Personality and Social Psychology, 52,* 1236-1247.

Wagner, R. K., & Sternberg, R. J. (1985). Practical intelligence in real-world pursuits: The role of tacit knowledge. *Journal of Personality and Social Psychology, 4*(2), 436-458.

Wagner, R. K., & Sternberg, R. J. (1986). Tacit knowledge and intelligence in the everyday world. In R. J. Sternberg & R. K. Wagner (Eds.), *Practical intelligence: Nature and origins of competence in the everyday world* (pp. 51-83). New York: Cambridge University Press.

Weekley, J. A., & Ployhart, R. E. (Eds.). (2006). *Situational judgment tests.* Mahwah, NJ: Erlbaum.

Wertsch, J., & Kanner, B. G. (1994). A sociocultural approach to intellectual development. In R. J. Sternberg & C. A. Berg (Eds.), *Intellectual development* (pp. 328-349). New York: Cambridge University Press.

Yonas, A., Goldsmith, L. T., & Hallstrom, J. L. (1978). Development of sensitivity to information provided by cast shadows in pictures. *Perception, 7,* 333-341.

The authors wish to thank Karen Jensen Neff and Charlie Neff for their generous support of this project. Correspondence regarding this chapter should be sent to Elena L. Grigorenko at the Child Study Center, Yale University, 230 South Frontage Road, New Haven, CT 06519-1124 (elena.grigorenko@yale.edu).

IV. Teachers' Characteristics and Attitudes

Martina Endepohls-Ulpe

Attitudes of German Secondary School Teachers Towards Students' Early Placement at University

Abstract

Early placement at university ("Frühstudium") is an enrichment and acceleration measure at German universities for students from secondary schools. Students participate in selected university courses and thus save time in their future
courses of study and enrich their knowledge in several fields. Results of evaluation studies (e.g. Solzbacher, 2008) have shown that the measure is highly accepted by the students. However, problems are caused by schools, which obviously do not support their students sufficiently.

The presented study consists of a survey and an analysis of attitudes of German
secondary school teachers towards students' early placement at universities
aiming to find out about possible concerns teachers might have against the
measure.126 teachers filled in a questionnaire with two open ended questions
and 23 Likert-items on possible advantages and disadvantages of students' early
placement at university. Answers to the open ended questions were analysed by
content analysis. Answers to the Likert-items were subjected to a factor analysis which yielded four factors: 1. positive effects / measure enhances motivation and achievement 2. negative effects / denial of the need of the measure, 3.
Organisational and social problems, 4. additional work load for teachers.

Results show that teachers in general look upon the measure favourably but at
the same time they fear organisational and social problems and additional work.
Notably teachers without any personal experience with the measure anticipated
more problems. Possible detrimental effects were seen amongst others in excessive work and emotional demands for the students.

Teachers' answers reveal that there is not only a lack of information on the
measure but also a lack of information on the field of giftedness in general.

1   Introduction

In the last decades a lot of successful programs for the education of gifted children have been developed. Many of them combine elements of acceleration and enrichment – two basic principles of differentiation frequently applied in programs for gifted students as well as in measures for individualized differentiation (Olszewski-Kubilius, 2003).

Acceleration means passing the normal curriculum faster than other students. Individualized organizational forms of acceleration are grade skipping and/or early admission to certain levels of schooling e.g. primary school, college or university. A possible benefit of saving time in the educational system can be enrichment. Enrichment "extends, supplements, and sometimes replaces aspects of a school's structure. The general emphasis in enrichment is on keeping children with their peers and fostering the development of higher cognitive and affective processes" (Coleman & Cross, 2005, p.270). Enrichment may happen as a part of the school program in the regular class or in special courses in the afternoon. There are also a lot of enrichment measures for gifted children outside school as e.g. weekend courses or summer camps (see Endepohls-Ulpe, 2009).

"Early placement at university" in German "Frühstudium", is a combination of acceleration and enrichment, which was established at numerous German universities in the last decade.
The main principle of "Frühstudium" is that students of grammar schools, or in exceptional cases of modern secondary schools (in German "Realschule"), who are highly motivated and interested and performing very well, get the chance to participate in university courses. The programs or possibilities at different German universities vary with respect to selection processes and courses of study offered. As students might miss part of their regular lessons at school while attending university courses schools usually have to give their permission for the participation. One usual condition of this permission is outstanding achievement at school. Some universities provide mentoring by older students, a measure which obviously prevents the students from dropping out early (Halbritter, 2004). If they meet all criteria, students can already take exams in their course of study while still attending school.

Evaluation studies of German early placement measures (Solzbacher, 2008; Endepohls-Ulpe, 2011a, b) show that the measures are highly accepted by the students. Results of an evaluation of "Frühstudium" at the University of Koblenz (Endepohls-Ulpe, 2011a) reveal that for students the desired benefits of the measure can be predominantly allocated to the field of enrichment: escaping from boredom at school, getting a deeper insight into an interesting subject, and gaining information for the personal process of their choice of occupation. The possibility of acceleration clearly plays only a minor role for students' motivation to participate.

But even though the students' main objective in the program is apparently not acceleration, more than half of them acquire certificates. There was not a single student who stated not being able to understand a subject matter as a reason for dropping out during the four-year period of evaluation at the University of Koblenz (Endepohls-Ulpe, 2011a).

Whereas students seem to be very satisfied with the support of the university they mostly do not seem to be very content with the assistance they get by their schools. Unfortunately the data of the study at the University of Koblenz cited above as well as of Solzbacher's evaluation of approximately 50 measures at German universities (Solzbacher, 2008; 2009) reveal that a great number of schools and teachers do not seem to be very supportive to their students concerning the measure. Actually, the first problem is that many schools do not inform their students about the program. Most of the students who participated in the measure at the University of Koblenz got their first information from the radio, newspapers, friends or parents, or other sources of information (other university, flyer, former teacher; Endepohls-Ulpe, 2011a). If students all the same manage to get into a program only a minority of them get support from their teachers to manage the double work load. Some students even feel mobbed or experience obstructive behavior by teachers. These problems are both reported by the students (Endepohls-Ulpe, 2011a) and their parents (Endepohls-Ulpe, 2011b).

In addition to parents, teachers are very important for the process of promotion of gifted and talented students. They can be crucial both for the identification of gifted students and the search for and placement in appropriate measures of furtherance. Actually, schools and teachers do not frequently seem to take early placement at the university into consideration when looking for a measure of furtherance. Moreover, even if students manage to get into early placement measures and manage to organize their studies at the university and complete their courses there, they still need assistance in organizational matters concerning the coordination of timetable at school and university or catching up on their school work. At least this task should be undertaken by the school, but apparently this is not the case.
There is no information on the possible causes of this situation - one can only speculate that the teachers might have the same concerns with respect to the measure as it can be often found against other measures of acceleration (Heinbokel, 2008). Hence it seemed necessary to analyze teachers' attitudes towards students' early placement at university to get a starting point for a change.

Aiming to find out the reasons for the obstacles teachers and schools build up for their students concerning the program, the presented study wants to answer the following three main questions:

(1) Do teachers see any positive aspects or possible benefits of early placement at university and if they do so what are these benefits?

(2) What are the problems or disadvantages that teachers see regarding early placement at university?

(3) Are there any differences between the attitudes of teachers who have already had personal experience with the measure and teachers without any personal experience?

2   Method

2.1   Measuring instrument

To measure teachers' attitudes a questionnaire was used, which contained some questions concerning personal data, two open-ended questions concerning possible positive or negative consequences of students' early placement at university, and 23 4-step Likert-items concerning possible consequences of the measure (all items are shown in Table 5). These Likert-items were gathered and developed by teacher students and students of pedagogy, who have attended a university course on the topic of identification and promotion of gifted children.

To make sure that teachers, who were not informed about the possibility of students' early placement at the university, could answer the questions, the questionnaire started with the following description : "Since a couple of years the University of Koblenz as well as numerous other German universities, offers the possibility of "Frühstudium". Students of grammar schools, or in exceptional cases of modern secondary schools, who are highly motivated and interested and performing very well, get the chance to participate in university courses. Attainments in these courses can be taken into account for future studies. The amount of time spent at university is not determined or limited. As the students may miss part of their regular lessons at school, schools have to give their permission. Participation in the measure does not bear any costs for the students. At the University of Koblenz participants are mentored by older university students."

2.2   Data collection

The collection of the data turned out to be extremely difficult. Data were gathered by students who wrote their bachelor and diploma theses on the topic of giftedness (Geis, 2011; Kempken, 2010) and by students who attended a university course on giftedness. Schools were not very cooperative and some even explicitly expressed their negative attitudes towards giftedness and programs for gifted students in their refusal (Kempken, 2010). Thus the response rate was approximately 25% (Geis, 2011), which is rather low – a fact that has to be considered with respect to the interpretation and discussion of the results of the study.

2.3   Analysis of data

The open-ended questions were subjected to a content analysis (Früh, 1998; Lisch, 1978). First a set of categories was built on the basis of about 50 questionnaires (Geis, 2011). In a second step the answers of the total sample were classified in this grid by an independent rater. In cases of uncertainties or doubt, rater and author discussed until an agreement was reached.

Answers to Likert-items were subjected to a factor analysis (principal component analysis with subsequent Varimax rotation). A scree plot analysis as criterion for the number of extracted factors (see Bortz, 1999), suggested a five factor solution (explaining 61% of the total item variance, Eigenvalues > 1). After testing scale reliabilities a four factor solution was preferred. The two items which had constituted the eliminated factor did not fit together logically and both showed also substantial loadings on factor I or II. Cronbachs α values, as a measure of reliability of the four scales, were good resp. acceptable for the first three factors (factor I: α= .87; factor II: α= .79; .factor III: α=.73). For factor IV Cronbachs α was .49 which is at the threshold of being not acceptable any more (Bortz, 1999). As the scale consisted of two items which logically fitted together well, the scale mean was still used for further analyses. Names of the four factors as well as constituting items and item means can be found in section 3.3.

T-tests and ANOVAs were calculated to analyze differences on the scale means of the four factors between different groups of teachers.

3   Results

3.1   Sample

The sample consists of 126 teachers of randomly chosen German grammar schools, the type of secondary schools which provide the highest level of school graduation in the German school system. Mean age of the participants was 42 years, 63 female, 58 male (4 missing data). Thus, with respect to gender ratio and mean age the sample does not differ from the total population of secondary school teachers at German upper secondary schools (Statistisches Bundesamt, 2005/2006).

More than 60% of the teachers worked in schools which were situated rather close to the University of Koblenz (distance below 10 km), 20% worked in schools with a distance between 10 to 30 km and 20% in schools which were situated in a distance of 31 to 50 km or more.

Most of the teachers reported that they had taught older students who were in the last three years of schooling (82%, N=104), 93% (N=117) had taught students in grade 8 to 10, both groups of students which possibly might participate in early placement programs.

Most of the teachers (82%, N=103) stated that they had already heard about the possibility of early placement of students at the university. 64% (N=80) said that they were sure that they had already taught a student who would have been able to participate in such a measure and 21% of the teachers (N=27) had already taught a student who participated in the measure.

3.2 Anticipated positive and negative consequences – results of the content analysis

In total teachers mentioned more positive (285) than negative consequences (250) in their answers to the open-ended questions. The difference between totally named numbers of positive and negative consequences was significant ($p<.05$).

Table 1: Number of advantages or positive effects mentioned by teachers

Number of named advantages per teacher		N	%
	0	13	10.32
	1	30	23.81
	2	32	25.40
	3	25	19.84
	4	14	11.11
	5	8	6.35
	6	3	2.38
	7	1	0.80
Total		126	100.00

The number of positive consequences named varied between zero (N=13) and seven (N=1), 69.05% of the teachers named one to three positive consequences ($M = 2.40$, $SD = 1.54$; distribution of numbers of named positive effects in table 1).

With regards to content, teachers first and foremost recognized early placement in general as a good measure for individual furtherance, followed by the possibility to get information on career options, enhancement of motivation and also for saving time in the educational system. Personality development, providing challenging tasks/reduction of boredom and consolidation of interests were also frequently named (see Table 2). Gentle entrance into academic studies, socializing, advantages for the school or society, gathering knowledge and relevance for the curriculum vitae were also mentioned, but in total seemed to play a minor role in teachers anticipated advantages.

Table 2: Frequencies of positive consequences/advantages

Category (subcategories in order of frequency)	Total N of mentions in the category	% of teachers who named one or more items of this category
Individual furtherance (specific furtherance; reasonable use of talents; development of individual strengths; early furtherance)	42	31.74
Saving of time (shortening of time of study; early entrance into career; possibility of a second degree; no loss of time)	37	26.98
Information on career options (early information on career options; no negative consequences in case of reorientation)	33	24.60
Personality development (enhancement of competencies; autonomy; organizational skills; structured learning; self-confidence by contact with other age group; self-regulated learning; authenticity)	30	12.70
Challenges (broaden one's horizon; collect new experiences; get to know structures outside school; get to know requirements of university; get to know one's own limits)	30	20.63
Motivation (enhancement of motivation; honor talent; honor achievement at school; stimulation of development; motivation for other subjects)	28	22.22
Prevent from lack of challenge (reduce lack of challenge; better utilisation of capacity; prevent from boredom; reduce frustration by lack of challenge)	22	16.67
Consolidation of interests (promotion of special interests; consolidation of interests by occupation with a special subject; satisfaction of thirst for knowledge)	15	11.90

Gentle entrance into academic studies (early contact to university, easy entrance into difficult fields of study; better orientation at the actual start of studies; assistance by older students; reduce fear of university; arouse interest for studies; get used to university life)	11	8.73
Social contacts (socializing; socializing with like-minded people; career relevant contacts)	11	8.73
Advantages for the school community (contacts between university, schools and teachers; motivation for peers; motivation for teachers; reasonable participation of advanced students in instruction; compensation of heterogeneity)	10	7.94
Knowledge acquisition (get to know scientific work methods; introduction to science)	10	7.14
Advantages for society (less expenses for society and parents; promote young researchers in certain professions; more years in profession; science and society profit from early knowledge)	6	4.76
Relevance for curriculum vitae	1	0.80
Total	286	

Remarkably 20 of the teachers (16.67%) did not see any negative consequences of the measure. 71.43% named one to three possible disadvantages (M=1.98, SD=1.44; distribution of number of named items see table 3).

Table 3: Number of disadvantages or negative effects mentioned by teachers

Number of named disadvantages		N	%
	0	21	16.67
	1	27	21.43
	2	38	30.16
	3	25	19.84
	4	6	4.76
	5	7	5.55
	6	1	.80
	7	1	.80
	Total	126	100.0

Apparently the main concern teachers had with respect to the measure was the possibility of work overload or excessive demands for the students. More than 38% of the teachers named an item from this category and nearly 25% of the negative consequences named altogether, came from this field (see table 4). Teachers also feared that students would have to neglect their private lives (19.84%), could have social disadvantages in their relations to peers (23,86%) or experience to much emotional pressure by work overload or stress (16.67%). Missed time at school (15.07%), negative consequences for the development of the non-cognitive part of the personality (11.90%) and a narrowed focus of interest, concentration on university matters (10.35), were also issues of concern. Problems such as too early specialisation, social immaturity of the participants, organizational problems, problems for the schools as a community and difficulties to identify suitable participants for the measure were also mentioned, but seemed to play a minor role (< 10%). Interestingly there was not a single answer that expressed negative effects or any problems for teachers such as e.g. enhanced work load.

Table 4: Frequencies of negative effects/ disadvantages

Category (subcategories in order of frequency)	Total N of mentions in the category	% of teachers who named one or more items of this category
Excessive demands (excessive demands in general; time pressure; coordination of university and school demands; work load; excessive cognitive demands; costs; too much occupation with university)	62	38.09
Neglect of private life (weakening of social contacts/relations; neglect of hobbies and leisure time; loss of peers; neglect of other areas of life; neglect of honorary posts)	33	19.84
Social disadvantages (social marginalisation by peers; envy of peers and their parents, lack of comprehension by teachers)	32	23.86

Emotional pressure (excessive emotional demands; stress; too much responsibility in early age; frustration by excessive demands; abnormal ambition of students and parents; loss of motivation by excessive demands; inferiority complex as a consequence of failure)	23	16.67
Missed time at school (missed school lessons; missed teaching content; expenditure of time to catch up missed teaching content; deterioration of final certificate ("Abitur"); no possibility to participate in non-instructional activities)	19	15.07
Negative personality development (skipping developmental phases – shorter childhood; overestimation of own capabilities; feeling of supremacy; lack of life experience by early start of university studies; lack of social competencies)	17	11.90
Change of interests (change of focus of interest from school to university; lack of interest in instruction at school; alienation from school and peers; neglect of social contacts at school; deterioration of marks due to lack of interest)	14	10.32
Too early specialization (specialization on one single subject matter; lack of general education; one sided accumulation of knowledge; concentration on content of studies)	14	9.52
Lack of emotional requirements (lack of integration at university due to immaturity; immature personality)	12	8.73
Organizational problems (lack of integration/interaction of school and university; organizational problems at school; demotivation by lack of support; lack of information for schools)	10	7.94
Negative consequences for the school community (reduction of odds for normal students; elite formation; loss of sense of community in class; demotivation of peers; evading problems in instruction)	8	6.35

Identification of participants (lack of diagnosis of aptitude; unable students get the chance too often; students might try to prosecute a claim for a university place)	6	4.76
Total	250	

3.3   Anticipated positive and negative consequences – results of the closed- ended questions

The four factors of the closed-ended part of the questionnaire were named:
Factor I: Positive effects for students / measure enhances motivation and achievement.
Factor II: Negative effects for students/ denial of the need of the measure
Factor III: Organizational and social problems
Factor IV: Additional work for teachers

Constituting items and item means are shown in table 5.

Table 5: Items on the four 4 factors and item means

	M *	*SD*
Factor I : Positive effects for students		
Early placement at university is a good possibility for gifted students to expand their knowledge.	3.48	.61
I would recommend the measure to an able student.	3.08	.81
"Frühstudium" is basically a good possibility to promote a gifted student.	3.18	.82
"Früstudium" could enhance learning motivation of unchallenged students.	3.52	.64
Gifted and motivated students are able to catch up missed school lessons on their own.	3.25	.63
A student could add to instruction in the studied subject.	3.07	.84
A student could develop his/her social competences by "Frühstudium".	2.47	.85
Participating in the measure could have a positive effect on achievement at school.	3.03	.66
By "Frühstudium" a student can develop organizational competencies.	3.12	.78
"Frühstudium" is a chance to get information about the choice of occupation.	3.29	.69
Factor II: Negative effects for students		
Frühstudium bears the risk of deterioration of achievement at school by missing lessons.	2.29	.74
Early placement at university is too much work load for students.	2.49	.83

Early placement anticipates too much of the subject matter in the studied subject.	2.30	.82
Students participating in the measure may not take school seriously any longer.	2.20	.74
Participation in the measure could make a student arrogant.	1.88	.73
Schools offer enough challenges for gifted students despite of "Frühstudium".	2.17	.82
Students would be intellectually overchallenged by "Frühstudium".	1.93	.75
Factor III: Organizational and social problems		
A student participating in the measure would not have enough leisure time left.	3.01	.81
Students risk to get ostracized.	2.70	.83
Participating students are socially and emotionally over-strained.	2.57	.88
Early placement at university bears too many organizational problems.	2.69	.85
Factor IV: Additional work for teachers		
By teaching a participating student I would have to put more effort in preparing myself for instruction.	2.17	.92
Supporting a student's participation in the measure would mean too much additional time and effort for me.	2.33	.89

* Answer options on Likert-items varied from 4= totally agree to 1=totally disagree; High values stand for high agreement

Sample means on the four scales show that in general teachers anticipated effects of the measure definitely in a positive direction. Nevertheless, in total they seemed to fear some social and emotional problems for the participating students (factor III).

Table 6: Scale means on the four factors

	N	M *	SD	Min	Max	
	valid	missing				
"Positive effects for students"	120	6	3.16	.50	1.80	4.00
"Negative effects for students/ measure is not necessary"	124	2	2.18	.54	1.00	3.57
"Organizational and social problems"	120	6	2.74	.64	1.00	4.00
"Additional work for teachers"	119	7	2.26	.76	1.00	4.00

* Answer options on Likert-items varied from 4= totally agree to 1=totally disagree; High values stand for high agreement

Values on the scales "negative effects for students" and "additional work load for teachers" were slightly higher than the scale mean of 2, so there may be some concerns in this direction (scale means on the four factors can be seen in table 6.).

3.4 Attitudes of teachers with and without experiences towards the measure

To answer the question whether teachers who have already had information on or experiences with the measure differed in their attitudes from teachers who have never heard about the possibility of early placement or had no experiences, t-tests on the scale means of the four factors of these groups of teachers were calculated.

Table 7 shows that there were no differences between teachers with and without information with respect to anticipated positive effects, organizational and social problems or fears of additional work load. But teachers without information anticipated more general problems and were in doubt about the necessity of the measure.

Table 7: Differences between teachers with and without information on the four factors

	Have you already heard about the possibility of early placement at the university?	*N*	*M*	*SD*	*T*	*df*	*p (2-tailed)*
"Positive effects for students"	Yes	99	3.19	.51	1.62	117	.10
	No	20	2.99	.43		30.50	
"Negative effects for students/ measure is not necessary"	Yes	102	2.11	.49	-3.47	121	.00
	No	21	2.54	.57		26.49	
"Organizational and social problems"	Yes	99	2.76	.62	1.14	117	.25
	No	20	2.59	.69		25.41	
"Additional work for teachers"	Yes	98	2.27	.78	.50	116	.61
	No	20	2.17	.71		29.11	

Teachers who stated that they had already taught a student who would have been able to participate in the measure anticipated significantly more positive effects of early placement at the university and significantly less negative ef-

---

fects. They also saw significantly less organizational and social problems. There were no differences in anticipated additional work for teachers between the two groups (see table 8).

Table 8: Differences between teachers who had or did not have an eligible student in their classes on the four factors

	Have you ever taught a student who would have been able to participate in the measure?	N	M	S	T	df	p (2-tailded)
"Positive effects for students"	Yes	78	3.25	.47	2.58	116	.01
	No	40	3.00	.524		72.32	
"Negative effects for students/ measure is not necessary"	Yes	79	2.09	.527	-2.80	120	.00
	No	43	2.37	.51		88.83	
"Organizational and social problems"	Yes	78	2.64	.64	-2.27	116	.02
	No	40	2.91	.58		86.27	
"Additional work for teachers"	Yes	77	2.27	.821	.02	115	.98
	No	40	2.26	.64		97.58	

Teachers who had personal experience with early placement – who have already taught a student who participated in the measure – did not anticipate more positive and only slightly less (p=.09) negative consequences of early placement. Besides, they anticipated significantly less organizational and social problems and in contrast to their colleagues without personal experience they rejected the notion that there could be additional work for teachers (see table 9).

Table 9: Differences between teachers who had and had not taught a student who participated in the measure

	Have you already taught a student who participated in the measure?	N	M	SD	T	df	p (2-tailed)
"Positive effects for students"	Yes	27	3.28	.48	1.28	115	.20
	No	90	3.14	.50		43.90	
"Negative effects for students/ measure is not necessary"	Yes	27	2.03	.47	-1.70	119	.09
	No	94	2.22	.54		47.53	
"Organizational and social problems"	Yes	27	2.47	.58	-2.58	115	.01
	No	90	2.81	.62		45.51	
"Additional work for teachers"	Yes	26	1.85	.54	-3.26	114	.00
	No	90	2.38	.78		58.38	

To find out whether attitudes of teachers with longer work experience concerning the measure were different from those of their younger colleagues an Analysis of Variance was calculated with age groups (24 to 35 years, 36 to 41 years, 42 to 50 years, > 50 years) as main factors and mean scores on the four factors as dependent variables. There were no differences between age groups on factor I to III. But older teachers (42 to 50 and older than 50 years) anticipated significantly less additional work ($p<.01$, $F=3.72$ $df=4$) than their younger colleagues. One cause for this fact may be that older teachers more often stated that they already had taught a student who participated in the measure ($p<.05$).

4 Summary and Discussion

Both teachers' answers to the open-ended questions and their answers to the closed-ended part of the questionnaire show that in general teachers look upon the possibility of students' early placement favorably. Values on factor I "Positive effects for students" were high, values on factor II "negative effects for students" expressed only slight concerns and teachers named significantly more positive than negative aspects in their answers to the open-ended questions. Nevertheless, values on factors III and IV reveal that at the same time teachers fear social problems for students and they also fear some additional work for themselves.

A closer look at the positive and negative consequences teachers named, displays that with respect to positive outcomes – aside from judging early placement generally as a good possibility to promote gifted students – teachers most frequently see outcomes from the field of acceleration: saving time in the educational system and gathering information on career options. Aspects, which were the most important aspects for the students in evaluation studies such as escaping from boredom at school or deepening interests in certain subjects, were also mentioned but not as frequently. Nevertheless, teachers also strongly anticipated a motivating effect of the measure for students.

Corresponding to seeing positive outcomes in the field of acceleration teachers' main fears or anticipated disadvantages of the measure concerned excessive demands – both intellectual and emotional – as the greatest danger of early placement at university. Social disadvantages with respect to peers and school and negative consequences of missed school lessons, another aspect of acceleration, were also foreseen. Thus teachers seem to be seriously worried about the well-being of their students and fear that they could suffer from work overload, have no leisure time left, neglect their private lives and get worse marks at school. However, the results of evaluation studies of early placement measures show that these well-meant concerns are not realistic. These studies show that students are relieved to escape from boredom and lack of challenge at school and most of them manage the double work load gladly and easily (Endepohls-Ulpe, 2011a, b; Solzbacher 2008).

Teachers who have never heard of the possibility of early placement before filling in the questionnaire anticipated significantly more problems. Thus information on the measure seems to reduce concerns about negative outcomes. Teachers who said that they have already taught a student who would have been able to participate in the measure had rather positive attitudes towards possible outcomes compared to teachers who stated that they have never met a student in their classes whom they thought to be able to participate. Maybe the latter group – after all 40 teachers, which is 31% of the sample – has general reservations against the topic of promoting gifted students which may also correspond with overlooking gifted students in their classes or simply denying their existence. Teachers who have already had personal experience with the measure did not differ in their general positive attitudes from teachers without experience but saw slightly less general and significantly less social problems for participating students and anticipated no additional work for teachers at all. Thus personal experience seems to reduce concerns about the measure. But the fact that teachers with experience anticipated absolutely no additional work at all can be also seen as a mixed blessing. On the one hand this may reduce difficulties for students to get into the measure, because teachers do not fear getting bothered by additional work, but on the other hand this could mean that teachers do not actively support students who participate in a measure. Exactly this lack of support from teachers e.g. with respect to catch up missed lessons at school was one alarming result of evaluation studies of early placement measures (Endepohls-Ulpe, 2011a, b; Solzbacher 2008; 2009).

Finally, when interpreting the result of this questionnaire study one has to keep in mind, that the sample of teachers most likely was a very selective one. As it was very difficult to collect the data and there were so many reservations against the topic in schools teachers who filled in the questionnaire may be a positive selection with respect to their attitudes. The fact that 21% of the sample has already had personal experience with the measure also points in this direction. The number of participants in the measure at the University of Koblenz is approximately 10 students per year, so the number of teachers in the sample who have already taught a student who participated in the measure seems rather high. Thus all in all it can be supposed that for the total sample of teachers of upper secondary schools more concerns about problems and more reservations can be found and even more non-realistic fears of negative consequences for students.

5   Conclusion

The result that teachers in general judge the consequences of students' early placement at university favorably is pleasant but does not explain the lack of support students get by schools and teachers. Looking at the concerns or reservations expressed by teachers it can be stated, that teachers' concerns are well meant but not very realistic on the whole. The nature of the anticipated negative effects shows that teachers do not seem to be very well informed about giftedness and about the problems gifted or very able students face in their everyday school life. Attending university courses is experienced as a relief from boredom at school by students and as a challenging experience, enriching knowledge and widening interests (Endepohls-Ulpe 2011a; Solzbacher, 2009). Excessive demands are rarely claimed. Students usually manage the double work load very well or they decide to quit the university courses when noticing that achievement school, leisure time or their private lives are affected.

So what could be done to change teachers' attitudes towards the measure and their support for students?
Of course, as the results of the study show, more information for teachers on the measure would be helpful. This is easier said than done, because many school offices do not seem to pass on the materials on the measures to their teachers and students (Endepohls-Ulpe, 2011a). Thus public relation by press, radio and internet concerning early placement measures still seems to be essential.
But the study also reveals that teachers at German upper secondary schools are apparently not well informed about giftedness and the necessity of measures of differentiation. This circumstance may be due to the fact that the German school system is a tracking system with three types of secondary schools – and teachers may be convinced that being instructed in the superior track is enough differentiation for very able students. Hence in the long run more information about giftedness in teacher instruction for teachers in upper secondary schools seems to be crucial for solving the problem.

References

Bortz, J. (1999). *Statistik für Sozialwissenschaftler [Statistics for social scientists]*. Berlin: Springer.

Coleman, L. J.; & Cross, T. L. (2005). *Being gifted in school*. Waco, Texas: Prufrock Press.

Endepohls-Ulpe, M. (2009). Teaching gifted and talented children. In L.J. Saha & A.G. Dworkin (Eds.), *International Handbook of Research on Teachers and Teaching. Volume II* (pp. 861-875). New York: Springer.

Endepohls-Ulpe, M. (2011a). Frühstudium – Acceleration and Enrichment for Secondary-School Students at the University of Koblenz-Landau. In C. Froese Klassen & E. Polyzoi (Hrsg.), *Investing in Gifted and Talented Learners: An International Perspective. Selected papers from the 2009 WCGTC World Conference held in Vancouver, Canada* (pp. 101-109). Winnipeg: Polar Bear Productions.

Endepohls-Ulpe, M. (2011). Early Placement at the University – the Parents' Perspective. *ECHA-News, 25*(1). Retrieved from www.echa.info.

Früh, W. (1998). *Inhaltsanalyse – Theorie und Praxis [Content analysis – theory and praxis]*. Konstanz: UVK Medien.

Geis, S. (2011). *Maßnahmen der Begabtenförderung – Überblick und Analyse der Einstellung von Lehrkräften an Gymnasien am Beispiel des Frühstudiums an der Universität Koblenz [Measures for educating the gifted – survey and analysis of gymnasium teachers' attitudes using the example of Frühstudium]*. Unveröffentlichte Bachelorarbeit im Studiengang „Bachelor of Education" im Fach Bildungswissenschaften an der Universität Koblenz-Landau [Unpublished bachelor thesis in the program „Bachelor of Education" in the faculty of educational sciences at the University of Koblenz-Landau].

Halbritter, U. (2004). Schüler an Hochschulen – Ausweg aus der Langeweile [Pupils to university – overcoming boredom]. In Ch. Fischer, F. J. Mönks, & E. Grindel (Hrsg.), *Curriculum und Didaktik der Begabtenförderung [Curriculum and didactics of educating the gifted]*(pp. 284-292). Münster: LIT Verlag.

Heinbokel, A. (2008). Enrichment or Acceleration. In J. Raffan & J. Fôrtíkovâ, *From giftedness in childhood to successful intelligence in adulthood. Proceedings (Selected Research Papers) of the 11th Conference of European Council for High Ability*, (p.81-88). Prague:The Centre of Giftedness.

Kempken, S. (2010). *Maßnahmen der Begabtenförderung. Diskussion des aktuellen Forschungsstandes und Analyse von Problemen der Umsetzung am Beispiel des Frühstudiums an der Universität Koblenz [Measures for educationg the gifted. Discussion oft the status of current research and analysis of problems of implementation using the example of Frühstudium at the University of Koblenz].* Unveröffentlichte Diplomarbeit im Fach Erziehungswissenschaften [Unpublished diploma thesis in the faculty of educational sciences]. Universität Koblenz-Landau.

Lisch, R. (1978). Kategorien. In R. Lisch & J. Kriz (Hrsg.), *Grundlagen und Modelle der Inhaltsanalyse: Bestandsaufnahme und Kritik [Principles and models of content analysis: survey and crititque]*(pp. 69-83). Reinbek bei Hamburg: Rowohlt.

Olszewski-Kubilius, P. (2003). Gifted education programs and procedures. In W. M. Reynolds, & I. B. Weiner (Eds.), *Handbook of Psychology, Vol7, Educational Psychology* (pp. 487-510). Hoboken: John Wiley & Sons.

Solzbacher, C. (2008). *„Frühstudium – Schüler an die Universität" [Frühstudium – pupils to university].* Bonn: Deutsche Telekom Stiftung.

Solzbacher, C. (2009). Early placement at German universities. *ECHA NEWS, 23*(2), 14-18.

Statistisches Bundesamt (2005/2006): *Bildung und Kultur. Schuljahr 2005/06 [Education and culture. Academic year 2005/06].* Wiesbaden: Statistisches Bundesamt. Retrieved from: www.destatis.de/basis/d/biwiku/schultab20.php

Afonso Galvão & Catia Perfeito

Expert Primary School Teachers: Teaching Strategies, Attitudes and Commitment

Abstract

This research was aimed at investigating expert teachers' characteristics. Participants were 10 teachers considered as experts by their peers. They were interviewed at length by means of semi structured interviews. Results suggest that in this teaching segment expert teachers possess technical skills along with intra and extra class attitudes and involvement with their work that is of a differentiated standard when compared with that of their colleagues. This makes them references within their professional area. These characteristics considered together match expertise concepts as presented in the literature.

1   Introduction

Experts are individuals who throughout their career become highly specialized in a given field of knowledge. They are people who develop a high ability to perform at the highest level (Ericsson, 2006; Ericsson & Smith, 1994). They have developed *expertise*. Expertise can be defined as a capacity acquired by deliberate practice to perform exceedingly well in a particular domain of knowledge. This definition that represents a synthesis of the view of several authors (Ericsson, 2006; Ericsson & Smith, 1994; French & Sternberg, 1989; Galvão, 2000; Galvão, Perfeito, & Macedo, 2011) brings about some important implications for the systematic study of the area. These are: the notion of deliberate practice, performance quality, and the notion of specific domain.

Deliberate practice is considered one of the most important factors associated with expertise development. It is a type of activity that is highly focused, programmed, sustained in the long-term and guided by conscious monitoring aiming at the identification and correction of mistakes (Galvão, 2003; Weisberg, 2006). Performance quality, the second important aspect in the definition mentioned, refers to the social evaluation of the performance of an individual. The social acknowledgment of an expert ability will depend on the culture in which the expert is inserted and how this culture values the domain. It sometimes happens that experts are not accepted as such for being ahead of their time – James Joyce and his *Ulysses* is a suitable example here. The third factor in the definition relates to the notion of 'specific domain'. A person, normally, is an expert in just one area, such a physics, math, chess, music, or literature (Galvão, 2003). Expert performance is also viewed as a problem-solving activity that involves intense and long dedication, clarity on the aims to be achieved, complex learning processes and planning and evaluation of results (Galvão, 2006). Those factors interact with those more particular characteristics of a learner that encompass personality, cognitive style, emotional balance, anxiety trace, amongst others. Studies on expertise are not merely concerned with identifying and describing expert behavior, but also with understanding how knowledge is acquired (Ericsson & Smith, 1994), how it is organized (Bedard & Chi, 1992), and how it is sustained as a long-term activity (Galvão, 2003, 2006).

Investigations on expertise in a variety of domains started from the 1980's onwards to influence research on teaching. The literature about people who exhibited qualitatively differentiated performance seemed pertinent in investigating the educational area as every story of expert learning was also related to expert teaching (Siedentop & Eldar, 1989). Henceforth, findings from expertise research started to offer clues to investigate learning processes of teachers who were positively recognized for their practice: expert teachers (Berliner, 1986, 1988, 1994, 2001, 2004).

Despite its importance, studies on teachers' expertise in the international literature seem to be a rare phenomenon. The few existing investigations tend to be limited in scope and range. Thus, the field of teaching expertise is an area still embryonary in which research is oriented by quite basic questions that include the characterization and definition of what an expert teacher is - in the case of our main research concern - of primary education. In this context, this research was aimed at identifying characteristics of expert teachers and at exploring concepts of expertise in relation to teachers.

2   Method

In this qualitative and exploratory research, participants were ten Brazilian female teachers with work experience ranging from 11 to 41 years. They were chosen amongst the best professionals, as indicated by peers, from the top ten Brasília schools that achieved the best results in the Federal Government's school rank test 'Prova Brasil' – 2007. The reasoning for choosing peer indication was that this criterion was considered the more trustable one in pre-research conversations with the academic community of the schools involved and a tradition in expertise research (Ericsson, 2006; Galvão, 2000).

The process of participants' identification was undertaken following a number of procedures. Firstly, the researchers explained schools' staff about research purposes (actually, this is compulsory according to the Brazilian law on conducting research with human participants) and showed them an explanatory document in written form that they were asked to sign in case they agreed to take part in the research (there were no refusals). Then, participants were explained about expertise research, including the researchers' own questions about what would constitute an expert teacher. Next, in a rather circular process of meetings and debates, those considered the best teachers were chosen. This whole process took about four months.

The teachers chosen were the ones whose students showed best learning results (objective criteria checked by the researchers) and motivation to learn (subjective criteria, 'sensed' by the researchers in the schools' context). Participants' age varied between 31 and 60, (mean age 46.1; SD, 8.03), with 23.3 years of average time of professional experience (SD 8.42). The less experienced teacher possessed 11 years of professional experience, whilst the most experienced accumulated 41 years.

Participants were interviewed at length by means of semi-structured interview. The strategy was to ask them to reflect about the main features of their own professional practice, using as starting point one basic question that guided the whole interview process – 'what is your opinion about the professional performance of a teacher with a high level of performance?'. As usual with qualitative research, the process of data 'generation' is a complex one in which context information is of high value and was taken into account. The interviews, which were recorded, occurred in the institutions in which participants worked, with an average length of one hour.

Data was analyzed by means of discourse analysis (Brandão, 2004; Gill, 2002; Orlandi, 1999). The interviews were transcribed in their totality and grouped around the original research questions. Then, the material was allocated into more specific categories that corresponded to specific discourse contents. Next, speech contents were compared by associative criteria of contingency, contrast, or similarity. Finally, the data analysed became a grounded theory on teachers' expertise.

3   Results and discussion

From the results there emerged a variety of characteristics that when considered together compose the behavior of a teacher whose performance is positively recognized by colleagues, students' learning results and students motivation to learn. The best teachers' teaching characteristics may serve to design a fair notion of what constitutes a primary school expert teacher. In order to do that, those characteristics emphasized by the participants were grouped into two distinct, although associated, segments. These refer to (i) the more technical aspects of the profession, and (ii) to attitudes and commitment.

3.1   Technical aspects

Expertise in different domains involves a deep appropriation of a related area. Here, a fundamental dimension concerns knowledge of technical nature. The literature shows few consistent references on what would be the more technical skills related to the expertise of primary school teachers. Angell, Ryder and Scott (2005) suggest that the skills of physics teachers are closely connected to four types of knowledge related to (i) teaching contents, (ii) curriculum, (iii) how students reason, and (iv) on teaching strategies. These four types of knowledge considered together seem to form the basic knowledge for teachers' actions.

The participants of this research emphasized the importance of knowing the curriculum. For them, teachers should master the curriculum and be able to identify learning objectives.

> *He (sic) should, at least, know it properly. To study the curriculum and see which objectives are expected for the level, the school year. To know the curriculum (V., 54 years-old).*

The curricular programs are guides to which teachers dedicate themselves. Teaching involves following a curriculum. School learning programs are cognitive instruments that allow teachers to organize their actions taking into account objectives, learning expectations, and chronological aspects. Therefore, curriculum programs exert an important role in unifying teachers' actions collectively orienting them to common contents and aims (Tardiff & Lessard, 2007).

In this way, it is important to understand participants' emphasis on curriculum knowledge, followed in a lesser degree of importance by the knowledge of the content to be taught. The interviewees see in the teacher a mediating function that, in order to work properly, should take into account the underlying intentions of the curriculum. From this specific knowledge, a teacher may be able to know the amount of knowledge that a child already possesses to promote the advancement of knowledge.

> *The first thing we should appropriate is the curriculum, to appropriate of . . . that, what we are going to teach. When we have that knowledge, of what we have to teach, of what we have to pass on to the child, then we are going to research what a child already knows how to do and undertake this mediation for the child to advance (A., 46 years-old).*

Knowledge on the content to be taught also emerged as an important characteristic of the teacher with high performance. However, this is secondary in importance to the student itself who is considered a protagonist - the central dimension and concern of teachers' actions.

> *. . . that does not mean that I am going to elect contents as the most important dimension. I am saying that I am. . . I know first the content, what I have to teach, but, I. . . I elect the student as the most important in such a way that I can. . . This student can respond adequately to that content . . . I have my aim. But I elect the child as the starting point for my work (V., 54 years-old).*

This particularity, according to Tardiff and Lessard (2007), becomes evident due to the nature of teachers' work. The work of the teacher is a type of student-centered practice, that emphasizes students as protagonists. The expert teachers who took part in this research stress teachers' need to possess a deep knowledge of the learning characteristics of the age range of their students. They also need a researcher's ability to observe and listen to students in order to be able to identify the subtleties of one's underlying learning mechanisms. They consider every student as an individual with his or her own characteristics that make this person unique. Hence, the need to understand individual learning must be taken into account in order to set up learning strategies that are adequate to obtain good learning results.

> *Teaching ability is, above all, being able to understand the specific learning features of a student. If we don't know how the student learns, the mechanisms that she uses to learn, I won't be able to help her learn. She can develop this ability to perceive differences, can't she? By observing, watching how a child responds to a learning strategy (V. 54 years-old).*

The teachers interviewed, by means of reflective practice, built up knowledge about learning strategies and seem to be able to adequate it to the classroom context in which they work.

You should change strategies in order to adapt yourself to the child. It is not the child who has to adapt in order to learn the way you want to teach. It is the other way around (M., 60 years-old).

Echoing Berliner´s investigations, in this study participants also stressed the same four fundamental types of knowledge – curriculum, teaching contents, students' learning characteristics, and teaching strategies. However, for these to be effective, it is necessary to have the ability to develop a detailed plan of action. This, as Tardiff and Lessard (2007) argue, is the careful selection and setting up of priorities in relation to teaching objectives. This should take into account the nature of the content to be taught, level of difficulty, place, and importance in the curriculum. The planning process allows teachers to be prepared considering the different dimensions and problems related to their job.

Planning is a characteristic of expert performance that is present in the different phases of the performance process. Expert musicians carefully plan both their learning of the music and the performance (Galvão 2006; Sloboda, 1995). They set up strategies to achieve specific results. With expert teachers it is not different. They think of planning as the device that makes it possible to guarantee the coherence, continuity, and sequence of pedagogical actions in order to favor students' learning.

Planning involves seek for relevant information. It involves simulation. . . anticipation of what could be a question, facts that may occur in classroom (C., 37 years-old).

Associated to participants' view of planning, the concept of routine emerged. This is viewed as a means to help students to deal with school time in a responsible manner. It is also a tool that serves to organize time and space for the development of activities. However, the notion of pedagogical routine does not mean always acting in the same way. Monteiro´s (2006) investigation on knowledge and practice related to the life-history of four successful primary school teachers, showed an emphatic concern of teachers with establishing routines for the development of playing and learning activities. The flow observed in the behavior of expert teachers who took part in Berliner´s investigations (1988, 1994, 2001) is associated with the adoption of learning routines.

... But, the day-after-day classroom is. . . We have our routine. Every day there is reading. Shared reading. We do it, isn't it? Every day I read for the kids. Then, there is the routine of Math, Portuguese. . . Then, our routine is cool. It is not boring. We always look for different things (C., 48 years-old).

Emphasizing that expertise is directly related to performance quality (Ericsson, 2006; Galvão, 2003), the interviewees showed a concern with self- monitoring the quality of the performance, particularly in relation to the results achieved. Here, the main reference of performance quality was their students' learning results. Thus, in participants' view, expert teachers are particularly concerned with the quality of students' learning, which is the main goal to be achieved.

> *Teachers' aims are always directed towards students' learning . . . It is from the level of learning of my students that I know about my success as a teacher (M., 49 years-old).*

The learning response of every student is the feedback that allows for evaluating how efficient is the work being undertaken. This evaluation process can be thought of as a self-reflective analysis about a teacher's own practice. When students' performance indicates that the performance of the teacher is not occurring as expected, the evaluation process is able to guide the need for changing strategies or attitudes. According to Ericsson (2006), the ability to monitor one's own performance is a highly important aspect of deliberate practice for it offers the individual opportunities to gradually refine his or her performance by means of repeating it or concentrating on its more critical aspects.

3.2   Attitudes and commitment

> *Among the personal skills that characterize a high-performance teacher, the emotional involvement with the work carried out was highlighted by the participants. Similar data was found by Monteiro (2006) whilst investigating successful literacy teachers. It was claimed that the observed teachers, besides having support from specific scientific knowledge, were acting according to emotions, feelings, and tenderness. Similarly to Berliner's studies (2001, 2004), it was shown that the expert teachers demonstrated love for teaching and respect for students.*

According to Galvão (2003), the learning process in some domains may look influenced, among other aspects, by a type of emotional link with the product being learned. Studies carried out by Galvão (2000) and Lemos (2010) opened some paths towards the understanding of the relationship between the *expert* individual and the object of knowledge. Regarding this kind of bond, the authors argue that the process of *expert* development is influenced by answers that comprise an emotional commitment with the object of knowledge and with key people involved in the process. In the context of this research, speeches related to the emotional-affective bond regarding the learning process were often observed. It is an emotion so deep that the participants feel moved when referring to their object of expertise.

> *It is because I like it so much, right? Of what I do. I love it. I adore it. I like to teach. So ya know, why I think I'm a little weird [laughs] (A., 31 years-old).*

> *I like it! I love this job very much! [Felt moved by] (C., 48 years-old).*

With less strength than the emotional bond with the field, the calling to be a teacher arose in the speech of half of the participants as a characterizing feature of an outstanding teacher. Historically, due to a culturally constructed and constrained association between gender and social role, the profession of primary school teacher has been associated to features that are thought of as typical of women-mother (love, affection, and dedication (Brasil, 2008). Participants in this research stressed that calling, love, natural duty, and responsibility are terms connected in the construction of teachers' professional identity.

> *Not everyone should be in this profession, because it... it... it... is a choice. Like, it is not just a profession. It is not just have a diploma. "Ah, Now I can teach". No. It is a calling... There are... teacher, that is a feature of... of... humankind, there is culture (A., 31 years-old).*

Tardif and Lessard (2007) claim that the teaching profession is still associated with religious aspects like devotion, virtue, availability, gift, and calling. Participants of this research that are considered experts for their professionalism, rather surprisingly reinforced this view. It represents a type of anti-climax for this group. Therefore, it was not expected that the notion of gift/calling could be present in the discourse of teachers that are living a historical moment marked by the pursuit of professionalization and professional respect.

Investigations on expert behavior have accumulated a considerable amount of evidence that contradict notions such as calling, gift, or talent for explaining expert learning (Ericsson, 2006; Ericsson & Smith, 1994; Galvão, 2003). Expertise seems to be the consequence of early involvement with a field, and long-term sustained deliberate practice, preferences, opportunities, and emotional ties with expertise objects (Galvão, 2003, 2006; Galvão & Galvão, 2006). The participants of this study cited dedication, responsibility, commitment, enthusiasm, and reflective practice as the main features of an expert teacher. These are common features of experts of different domains. However, in the case of teachers, all these aspects are related to relational skills that seem to be in the very heart of teachers' effectiveness. Actually, investigation by Naiff, Soares, Azamor and Almeida (2008) emphasised that the key elements of the best primary school teachers were, besides the mastering of content knowledge, commitment, patience, and responsibility. Our research participants added willingness to help and creativity.

Dedication is stressed as one of the main features of expert behavior from the very first attempts to design a general theory of the area. Simon and Chase's (1973) general theory of the structure of superior performance suggested expert learning as resulting basically from intense dedication to a domain of interest. To this, should be added, according to Gomes (2008), intense personal involvement that becomes emotionally charged. Thus, words like 'passion', 'love', and 'mission' recurrent in experts' discourse seem to represent deeper connections between experts and expertise objects that appear to be of emotional nature.

It's because [dedication] is a propellant spring. I think dedication... it makes you run after things, search for different ways... But it is dedication, I think it is fundamental because it is a propellant spring. It makes you run after the... the... it is... (M., 45 years-old).

Commitment and responsibility were other defining features of expert teachers' behaviour. This means being able to anticipate problems both at individual and group level, deciding about the most suitable teaching approaches to particular situations as well as developing adequate learning environments and atmosphere. Furthermore, there is also the issue of assessing learning outcomes in order to correct teaching strategies and to identify weaknesses in the learning process.

Several investigations on expertise in different domains (Lemos, 2010; Galvão, 2006; 2000; Kemp, 1996) have emphasized commitment and responsibility as defining features of expert learning and performance. Long-term expert learning involves a gradual change in learning regulation. This tends to be more external in the first moments of learning and gradually changing to more internal forms of regulation as time elapses and the learning process matures (Ericsson, 2006; Galvão, 2000, 2003; Sosniak, 1990). In the case of our research participants, most of their learning process occurred when they were already professionals. They started their practice in a situation of dependence of more experienced colleagues and, echoing expert learning processes, gradually became self-regulated, with a more reflective practice and able to manage and conduct their own performance progress. Berliner (1988, 1994, 2004) stressed that responsibility was a defining feature of the expert teachers participants of his research. His findings suggest that teachers, as they become more experienced, tend to feel more responsible for classroom events and learning results.

... But also, like, I think the teacher has to play the role. The teacher has to be responsible for everything. If everything a teacher do is his or her own responsibility, so there is not a chance not to be, huh? Unless this person does not indentify him or herself with the profession (C., 48 years-old).

Another dimension that emerged from participants´ speech concerning expert teachers was enthusiasm. One important investigation focusing on this topic in the educational area was undertaken by Rodrigues Jr., Pasquali and Moura (2009). Their review of the literature on enthusiastic teachers identified that enthusiasm is not always something naturally born with a teacher, a characteristic of one´s personality. Actually, mostly, enthusiasm seems to be a learned feature that teachers, as they gain practice, assimilate and incorporate it to their behavior. However, the authors present another, contrary view, according to which, enthusiasm would be a major, inborn, feature of a teacher`s personality that is present both inside and outside the professional context. It is possible that both views are true, as they are not self-excluding. Following Kemp's (1996) reasoning on introverts-extraverts, it might be that in some people enthusiasm trace is stronger than in others who develop it out of professional need. The fact is that enthusiasm emerged in this research as an important feature of expert teachers and that they intentionally develop it as they get more experienced.

> *Enthusiastic because it comes... The enthusiasm, it takes you to... to be always renewing, always improving professionally, and... How can I say? Changing the issue of... Let's say, considering better aspects of... of education. Improving all these aspects, because the enthusiasm leads to growth, appreciation, teaching... a better teaching, being in the students' shoes, huh? Professionally (M., 45 years-old).*

All professionals, experts or not, make mistakes. It is something intrinsic to human performance. However, in the case of expert teachers, there was a type of anxiety which was related to both anticipating mistakes and trying to avoid or overcome them. Similarly to the heart surgeons interviewed by Lemos (2010), they considered that their mistakes were more serious than those of most professions. They were aware that they were nurturing human beings. Teachers' mistakes and misjudgments could have a perverse effect on children's development. Due to this, they were highly demanding of themselves concerning their professional performance. This, they explained, brings about costs in terms of mental suffering and somatic disorders. Due to this, it was not uncommon for most of them, from time to time, to seek counseling or psychotherapy.

One of the most important dimensions of expert learning involves the development of accurate forms of self-feedback. One dominant feature of expert learning behavior involves the capacity of performance monitoring which is related to well developed metacognitive skills (Galvão, 2006; Ericsson et al., 1993) Participants showed awareness about assessing and monitoring their performance and were at ease with identifying those major features of expert teaching. As usual with experts, they did not consider themselves as such and held the opinion that there was a long road ahead of them before they could consider themselves experts. This prevalent feeling of modesty and respect for the field – the notion that the area is much bigger than what one can master – is quite common amongst experts. Usually, experts do not think of themselves as experts (Galvão, 2003; Galvão et al., 2011). This might be due to their knowledge of the dimension of the domain and of their own limitations.

> *My performance? So, I ain't perfect. I ain't perfect. I keep on watching my moves. I always want the best for my students, for the relationships I have here (A., 31 years-old).*

4   Concluding remarks

The attributes that singularise the expert behavior of teachers derive from the social assessment of peers, students, students' family, researchers, society, and of the teacher him or herself. In other words, the assessment of teachers' expertise, like that of any other form of expertise, is historically and socially situated (Ericsson, 2006; Galvão, 2003). In those more technical areas, expertise assessment is undertaken mostly by peers. In the case of teachers, where psychosocial characteristics are as relevant as technical attributes, the opinion of the wider society is also important.

This investigation has shown a number of defining features of expert teachers. The results allow us to suggest that primary school expert teachers are professionals that have developed, during many years of intensive dedication to teaching, a consistent set of knowledge about the different dimensions of the domain. That includes technical and personal ones. This seems to be sustained by an underlying affective-emotional attachment with the teaching area.

Finally, it should be emphasised that this area of investigation is still embrionary. Thus, in order to further our understanding of the underlying mechanisms that develop and sustain teachers' expertise, it is necessary to undertake other investigations in other areas of teaching. There is also the need to use other methodological approaches that employ, for instance, observation, interviews and questionnaires.

References

Angell, C., Ryder, J., & Scott, P. (2005). *Becoming an expert teacher: Novice physics teachers' development of conceptual and pedagogical knowledge.* Paper presented at The European Science Education Research Association Conference, Barcelona, Spain. Retrieved 05/02/2010 from http://www.fys.uio.no./carla/ARS_2005.pdf.

Bedard, J., & Chi, M. T. H. (1992). Expertise. *Current Directions in Psychological Science*, 1, 135-139.

Berliner, D. C. (1986). In pursuit of the expert pedagogue. *Educational Research*, 15, 5-13.

Berliner, D. C. (1988). The development of expertise in pedagogy. *American Association of Colleges for Teacher Education*, Washington, DC, 1-35.

Berliner, D. C. (1994). Expertise: The Wonder of exemplary performances. Em J. N. Mangieri & C. C. Block (Eds.), *Creating a powerful thinking in teachers and students.* (pp. 141-186). Fort Worth, TX: Holt, Rinehart and Wiston.

Berliner, D. C. (2001). Learning about and learning from expert teachers. *International Journal of Educational Research*, 35, 463-482.

Berliner, D. C. (2004). Expert teachers: their characteristics, development and accomplishments. Em R. B. Obiols, A. E. G. Martínez, M. O. Freixa & J. P. Blanch (Eds.), *De la teoria... a l'aula: formación del professorat y ensenyament de las Ciências Sociales [From theory to class: teachers' education and teaching of Social Sciences]*, (pp. 13-28). Barcelona: Universidad Autonoma de Barcelona.

Brandão, H. H. N. (2004). *Introdução à análise do discurso [Introduction to discourse analysis]* (2ª ed.). São Paulo: UNICAMP.

Brasil, I. C. R. L. (2008). *Significações da educação infantil na perspectiva de professores que atuam neste segment [Meanings of early childhood education: perspectives of teachers]*. MsC Dissertation, Universidade Católica de Brasília, Brasília.

Ericsson, K. A. (2006). The influence of experience and deliberate practice on the development of superior expert performance. In K. A. Ericsson, N. Charness, P. J. Feltovich & Hoffman R. R. (Eds.), *The Cambridge handbook of expertise and expert performance* (pp. 683-703). New York: Cambridge University Press.

Ericsson, K. A., & Smith, J. (1994). Prospects and limits of the empirical study of expertise: an introduction. In K. A. Ericsson & J. Smith (Eds.). *Toward a general theory of expertise: prospects and limits* (pp. 1-38). New York: Cambridge University Press.

Ericsson, A., Tesch-Romer, C., & Kramp, R. (1993). The role of deliberate practice in the acquisition of expert performance. *Psychological review, 100*(3), 363-406.

French, P. A., & Sternberg, R. J. (1989). Expertise and intelligent thinking: when is it worse to know better? In J. R. Sternberg (Ed.), *Advances in the Psychology of Human Intelligence* (pp. 157-188). New Jersey: Lawrence Erlbaum Associates.

Galvão, A. C. T. (2000) *Practice in orchestral life: an exploratory study of string players learning processes*. PhD Thesis, Reading University, United Kingdom.

Galvão, A. C. T. (2003). Pesquisa sobre expertise: perspectivas e limitações [Expertise research: perspectives and limitations]. *Temas em Psicologia*, Ribeirão Preto, 9, 223-237.

Galvão, A. C. T. (2006). Cognição, emoção e expertise musical [Cognition, emotion and musical expertise]. *Psicologia: Teoria e Pesquisa*, 22, 169-174.

Galvão, A. C. T., Perfeito, C. D. F., & Macedo, R. (2011). Desenvolvimento de expertise: Um estudo de caso [Development of expertise: a case study]. *Diálogo Educacional*, 34 (11), 1015-1033.

Gill, R. (2002). Análise do discurso [Discourse analysis]. In M. W. Bauer & G. Gaskell (Eds.), *Pesquisa qualitativa com texto, imagem e som: um manual prático. [Qualitative researching with text, image and sound.]*, (pp. 244-279), Petrópolis: Vozes.

Gomes, A. C. A. (2008). *A relação entre sujeito expert e objeto de conhecimento de expertise. [The relationship between expert subjects and expertise objects].* MsC Dissertation, Universidade Católica de Brasília, Brasília.

Lemos, A. C. M. (2010). *A pulsão de saber do expert [Experts' knowledge drive.*] MsC Dissertation: Universidade Católica de Brasília, Brasília.

Kemp, A. (1996). The musical temperament: psychology and personality of musicians. Oxford: Oxford University Press.

Monteiro, M. I. (2006) *Histórias de vida: Saberes e práticas de alfabetizadoras bem sucedidas. [Life history: knowledge and practice of succesfull literace teachers.]* PhD Thesis, Universidade de São Paulo, São Paulo. Retrieved 28/12/2010 from http://www.teses.usp.br/teses/disponiveis/48/48134/tde-04122007-155302/pt-br.php.

Naiff, L. A. M., Soares, A. B., Azamor, C. R., & Almeida, S. A. (2008). Ensino Fundamental e Médio: aspectos psicossociais do bom desempenho profissional. [Primary and secondary school teaching psychosocial aspects of effective professional practice.] *Arquivos Brasileiros de Psicologia*, 60, 64-76. Retrieved 27/12/2010 from http://psicologia.ufrj/br/abp.

Orlandi, E. P. (1999). *Análise de discurso: princípios e procedimentos. [Discourse analysis: fundaments and procedures.]* São Paulo: Pontes.

Rodrigues J.R., J. F., Pasquali, L., & Moura, C. F. (2009). Dimensões do construto entusiasmo como percebido em professores universitários. [Dimensions of the construct 'enthusiasm' as perceived in university teachers.] *Avaliação Psicológica*, 8, 391-403.

Siedentop, D., & Eldar, E. (1989). Expertise, experience, and effectiveness. *Journal of Teaching in Physical*, 8, 254-260.

Simon, H. A., & Chase, W. G. A. (1973). Perception in chess. *American Scientist*, 61, 394-403.

Sloboda, J. (1995). The musical mind: The cognitive psychology of music: Oxford: Oxford University Press.

Sosniak, L. A. (1990). The tortoise, the rare, and the development of talent. In M. J. A. Howe (Eds.), *Encouraging the development of exceptional skills and talents* (pp. 149-164). Leicester: The Bristish Psychological Society.

Tardif, M., & Lessard, C. (2007). *O trabalho docente: Elementos para uma teoria da docência como profissão de interações humanas. [Teachers' work: elements for a theory of teaching as a profession based on human interactions].* (J. B. Kreuch, Trad.) (3ª ed.). Petrópolis: Vozes.

Weisberg, R. W. (2006). Modes of expertise in creative thinking: evidence from case studies. In K. A. Ericsson, N. Charness, P. J. Feltovich & Hoffman R. R. (Eds.), *The Cambridge handbook of expertise and expert performance* (pp. 761-787). New York: Cambridge University Press.

About the Authors

Abdullah Aljughaiman, PhD
Abdullah Aljughaiman is a professor in the Special Education Department of King Faisal University, Saudi Arabia. He is currently the President of The International Research Association for Talent Development and Excellence, a position he has held since 2008. The primary focus of his professional activities is the development and education of gifted and talented students. He has published books, book sections, and peer reviewed articles on the identification of and services for gifted children. He has received multiple awards for his professional and administrative work in Saudi Arabia, the United Arab Emirates, and the USA. His research and practice have been supported by funds from King Faisal University, the Ministry of Higher Education, the Ministry of Education, the Ministry of Planning of the Kingdom of Saudi Arabia, the Education Office of the Arabian Gulf Countries, Mawhibah, and KACST.

Anjulie Arora
Anjulie Arora completed her Master of Arts in Psychology of Excellence in Business and Education at the Ludwig Maximilian University in Munich, Germany, in 2011. For her Master thesis Ms. Arora investigated gender differences in Science, Technology, Engineering and Mathematics. During her Bachelor studies in the USA she was awarded the David A. Leach Memorial Prize in 2004 for excellence in the field of Experimental Neuropsychological Research. She is a member of the International Research Association for Talent Development and Excellence and currently works as a counselor in a project which attempts to integrate young people with epilepsy into society.

Alaa Eldin A. Ayoub, PhD
Alaa Eldin A. Ayoub is an associate professor of educational psychology at Aswan-South Valley University, Arab Academy for Science, Technology & Maritime Transport, Egypt, and The National Research Center for Giftedness and Creativity, Saudi Arabia. He has published many studies and articles in the field of educational psychology and the identification of gifted students. He has made many contributions in the preparation of scientific scales and tests. He is also the coauthor and the translator of some specialized books. He has received multiple awards from different countries. His research interests are in the identification of gifted students and statistical programs.

Dagmar Bergs-Winkels, PhD
Dagmar Bergs-Winkels, PhD is Full Professor of Educational Sciences at the Applied University of Hamburg. She is *Program Director* of the European certificate of pre-school gifted education for the European Council for High Ability

(ECHA) and the International Center for the Study of Giftedness, University of Muenster. She is University lecturer at the University of Muenster. Her main research interests are giftedness and early childhood education.

Wei Chen
Wei Chen is a PhD candidate in the research center for supernormal children, Institute of Psychology, Chinese Academy of Science. She plays an active and important role in the cross-culture study on German and Chinese children's fine motor skills and cognitive development. Her research interests include the development of cognition and socialization of gifted children.

Xiaoju Duan, PhD
Xiaoju Duan completed her PhD in developmental and educational psychology in 2009, and is currently an assistant professor in the Institute of Psychology, Chinese Academy of Sciences.Her research interests include talent devlopment, education of gifted children, gender difference, and cross-culture psychology. She has authored papers in the fields of neurocognitive psychology, gifted identification and education, children development.

Martina Endepohls-Ulpe, PhD
Martina Endepohls-Ulpe, PhD, is senior lecturer at the University of Koblenz-Landau, Campus Koblenz, Institute for Psychology. She has published several articles dealing with influences on teachers' abilities of identifying gifted children and the impact of children's gender and social behaviour on their identification as gifted. Other topics of research and publishing have been gender differences, consequences of divorce for parents and children, and technology education for girls.

Afonso Galvao, PhD
Afonso Galvao is Professor of learning sciences of the Post-Graduate Research Program in Education of the Catholic University of Brasilia-Brazil, where he is currently Head of Department. His research interests focus on long term motivation and expertise development from different perspectives. He is also interested in the relationship between emotional states and cognitive functioning. He is member of the editorial board of several research journals. He publishes mostly on expert learning in different areas including music, medicine, teaching, and law.

Elena L. Grigorenko, PhD
Dr. Elena L. Grigorenko received her Ph.D. in general psychology from Moscow State University, Russia and her Ph.D. in developmental psychology and genetics from Yale University, USA. Currently, Dr. Grigorenko is Emily Fraser Beede Associate Professor of Developmental Disabilities, Child Studies, Psychology, and Epidemiology and Public Health at

Yale, and Adjunct Professor of Psychology at Columbia University and Moscow State University (Russia). Dr. Grigorenko has published more than 300 peer-reviewed articles, book chapters, and books. She has received multiple professional awards for her work and received funding for her research from the NIH, NSF, DOE, USAID, Cure, Autism Now, the Foundation for Child Development, the American Psychological Foundation, and other federal and private sponsoring organizations in the USA and worldwide.

Bettina Harder, PhD
Bettina Harder is research assistant and lecturer at the Department for Educational Psychology at the University of Erlangen-Nuremberg, Germany. She is vice-director and research coordinator of the departments' counseling center for the gifted. Her research projects focus on giftedness and the development of achievement excellence from different perspectives. In her PhD thesis she drew a theoretical and empirical comparison of common models of giftedness in the context of a longitudinal study.

Magdalena Kist
Magdalena Kist holds a master's degree in research of giftedness from the University of Leipzig, Germany. After a position as research assistant and lecturer at the Department for Educational Psychology at the University of Hanover, Germany she is now a lecturer at the Tongji University Shanghai, China.

Samuel D. Mandelman
Samuel D. Mandelman, M.Phil, is a doctoral student at Teachers College, Columbia University, where he is pursuing his Ph.D. in cognitive studies. He is also a graduate research assistant in the EG Lab at Yale University's Child Study Center. His primary research interests are human intelligence and intellectual giftedness.

Philipp Martzog
Philipp Martzog holds a master's degree in psychology from the University of Konstanz, Germany. In his current position as research assistant and Ph.D. candidate at the Chair for School Research, School Development, and Evaluation at the University of Regensburg he conducts research on specific relations between fine motor skills and cognitive abilities in preschool and elementary students.

Catalina Mourgues
Catalina Mourgues is currently a graduate student at the Pontificia Universidad Catolica of Chile. In her doctorate work, she is researching the relationship between brain activity and creative processes. Specifically, she is studying the characteristics of insight, or the 'Aha!' phenomenon, in young adults with dyslexia.

Marianne Nolte, PhD

Marianne Nolte is professor for Math Education at the University of Hamburg, Germany. She is heading the scientific part of a fostering and research project about mathematical giftedness within the framework of the project PriMa. This is a cooperation project of the Hamburger Behörde für Schule und Berufsbildung, and the William-Stern Society (Hamburg), the University of Hamburg. She is second chairwoman of the William-Stern Society (Hamburg). Her research focuses on high mathematical abilities, on problem solving and different questions concerning dyscalculia. (for further information please refer to the website http://blogs.epb.uni-hamburg.de/nolte/)

Catia Perfeito

Catia Perfeito holds a master's degree in education from the Catholic University of Brasilia-Brazil She is research assistant on the Teachers' Expertise Research Group of The Catholic University of Brasilia and a Primary School Teacher.

Shane N. Phillipson, PhD

Shane N. Phillipson, PhD, is an associate professor in the Faculty of Education at Monash University and previously
at the Hong Kong Institute of Education. His research focuses on conceptions of giftedness and learning and teaching and his recent books include Learning and Teaching in the Chinese classroom: Responding to individual needs (Phillipson & Lam, 2011), Learning diversity in the Chinese classroom: Contexts and practice for students with special needs (Phillipson, 2007), and Conceptions of giftedness: Socio-cultural perspectives (Phillipson & McCann, 2007).

Marion Porath, PhD

Marion Porath, Ph.D. is a Professor in the Faculty of Education at The University of British Columbia, Vancouver, Canada. She coordinates the graduate program in high ability. Her research interests are different forms of giftedness, children's views of themselves as learners, young children's social development, instructional applications of developmental theory, and problem-based learning. She is the recipient of numerous research grants. She has authored articles and chapters on giftedness, social intelligence, and applications of developmental theory to giftedness and co-authored two books on problem-based learning.

Doren Prinz, PhD

Doren Prinz, PhD is Assistant Professor at the Department of General, Multicultural and International Comparative Education at the University of Hamburg. Her research interests focus on the evaluation of educational systems, giftedness and resilient children. She is addressing questions surrounding quantitative and qualitative methods in the social sciences and statistics.

Katharina Schurr

Katharina Schurr graduated from the University of Augsburg a master's degree in educational sciences, psychology and philosophy. After her studies she worked at the 'Landesweiten Beratungs- und Forschungsstelle für Hochbegabung' of the University of Ulm and she could win as a supervisor of her doctoral project Prof. Drs. Albert Ziegler. As part of her PhD project she runs a counseling center for gifted children in Ulm. Her research interest is directed towards the training of parents of gifted elementary school pupil as mentors.

Jiannong Shi, PhD

Prof. Jiannong Shi is the director of the research center for supernormal children, Institute of Psychology, Chinese Academy of Science. He is the president of the Asia-Pacific Federation on Giftedness. His research on giftedness and talent development includes neuropsychological as well as educational studies and embraces various age groups and domains.

Christine Sontag

Christine Sontag holds a master's degree in psychology from the University of Regensburg, Germany. In her current position as research assistant and Ph.D. candidate at the Chair for School Research, School Development, and Evaluation at the University of Regensburg she conducts research on self-regulated learning with elementary and secondary school students.

Heidrun Stoeger, PhD

Heidrun Stoeger, PhD is chair professor for Educational Sciences at the University of Regensburg, Germany. She holds the Chair for School Research, School Development, and Evaluation. She is Editor-in-Chief of the journal HighAbility Studies, vice president of The International Research Association for Talent Development and Excellence and member of the editorial board of the German journal of Talent Development. Her publications include articles and chapters on giftedness, self-regulated learning, motivation, fine motor skills and gender.

Mei Tan

Mei Tan is a researcher in the EG Lab of Yale University's Child Study Center. She directs two projects concerning intelligence: the Aurora Project, the development of a new assessment for intelligence; and a project based in Saudi Arabia on the biological and environmental etiologies of giftedness. Ms. Tan received her BA/BS in English and Biology from the College of William and Mary, and her MA in Literature from the University of California at Berkeley. She is currently working on her Masters Degree in Cognitive Studies in Education at Teachers College, Columbia University.

Wilma Vialle, PhD

Wilma Vialle is currently a Professor in Education in the Faculty of Education, University of Wollongong. She teaches subjects on gifted education and had published extensively in this field. She is currently the President of the Australian Association for the Education of the Gifted and Talented and the editor of the Australasian Journal of Gifted Education. Wilma is also on the Executive board of the International Research Association for Talent Development and Excellence. Wilma's research interests focus on maximising intellectual potential and she is particularly interested in issues of social justice.

Peter Winkels

Peter Winkels, is head of the agency NEXT Intercultural projects. Since 15 years he has been designing and producing programs on the borders between education and arts.

He works for cultural and educational institutions, both public and private, like the German Youth and Children Foundation, the EFMD or the House of World Cultures.

Dimitris Zbainos, PhD

Dimitris Zbainos graduated from the Pedagogic Department of the University of Thrace and did his postgraduate studies at the Institute of Education, University of London, (Diploma in Education, M.A. in Psychology of Education) where he earned his PhD. He is currently a lecturer at Harokopio University, Athens. He has taught in primary schools, in the Department of Psychology of the University of Crete, and in postgraduate courses in the School of Philosophy at the University of Athens. His research interests include themes in the Psychology of Education, Assessment and Curricula. In particular he is interested in assessment and teaching for the development of cognitive abilities, motivation and curricula for the gifted.

Albert Ziegler, PhD

Albert Ziegler, PhD, is Chair Professor of Educational Psychology at the University of Erlangen-Nuremberg, Germany. He is the Founding Director of the State-wide Counseling and Research Centre for the Gifted. He has published approx. 300 books, chapters and articles in the fields of talent development, excellence, educational psychology and cognitive psychology. Presently he serves as the Secretary-General of the International Research Association for Talent Development and Excellence (IRATDE) and as the Editor-in-Chief of Talent Development & Excellence. His main interests in the field of talent development and excellence are the development of exceptional performances, the Actiotope Model of Giftedness, Educational and Learning Capital, sociotopes, and motivational training programs.

Talentförderung – Expertiseentwicklung – Leistungsexzellenz
hrsg. von Prof. Dr. Kurt A. Heller, Prof. Dr. Albert Ziegler

Talentförderung – Expertiseentwicklung – Leistungsexzellenz 9

Markus Dresel, Lena Lämmle (Hg.)

**Motivation, Selbstregulation
und Leistungsexzellenz**

L<small>IT</small>

Markus Dresel; Lena Lämmle (Hg.)
Motivation, Selbstregulation und Leistungsexzellenz
Aktuelle theoretische Ansätze zur Erklärung und Förderung herausragender Leistungen von Individuen
messen der Qualität und Quantität von Lernprozessen großes Gewicht bei. Sie rücken die Motivation und
die Selbstregulation der Lernenden dabei stärker ins Blickfeld als bisher. Der vorliegende Band bündelt
Forschung, die diese Perspektive auf hervorragende Leistungen einnimmt. Insgesamt 14 Beiträge stellen
neuere konzeptuelle Entwicklungen vor, geben einen Überblick über den aktuellen Forschungsstand und
berichten bislang unveröffentlichte Forschungsergebnisse.
Bd. 9, 2011, 280 S., 24,90 €, br., ISBN 978-3-643-11346-7

L<small>IT</small> Verlag Berlin – Münster – Wien – Zürich – London
Auslieferung Deutschland / Österreich / Schweiz: siehe Impressumsseite

Talent – Expertise – Excellence   10

Albert Ziegler, Christoph Perleth (Eds.)

EXCELLENCE

Essays in Honour of Kurt A. Heller

LIT

Albert Ziegler; Christoph Perleth (Eds.)
Excellence
Essays in Honour of Kurt A. Heller
This book is dedicated to the scholar and academic teacher Kurt A. Heller, who is considered internatio-
nally to be one of the most brillant excellence researchers. The wide spectrum of his writings and acti-
vities is reflected in the number of renowned international writers and scholars who contributed to this
unique collection of essays on excellence.
Bd. 10, 2011, 352 S., 49,90 €, br., ISBN 978-3-643-90128-6

LIT Verlag Berlin – Münster – Wien – Zürich – London
Auslieferung Deutschland / Österreich / Schweiz: siehe Impressumsseite